Philippe Ariès

and the Politics of French
Cultural History

Philippe Ariès,
strolling at Sailly,
20 August 1980

Philippe Ariès

and the Politics of French Cultural History

Patrick H. Hutton

University of Massachusetts Press

Amherst and Boston

Copyright © 2004 by University of Massachusetts Press
All rights reserved
Printed in the United States of America

LC 2003022910
ISBN 1-55849-435-9

Designed by Dennis Anderson
Set in Minion by Binghamton Valley Composition
Printed and bound by The Maple-Vail Book Manufacturing Group

Library of Congress Cataloging-in-Publication Data

Hutton, Patrick H.
    Philippe Ariès and the politics of French cultural history / Patrick H. Hutton.
        p. cm.—(Critical perspectives on modern culture)
Includes bibliographical references and index.
    ISBN 1-55849-435-9 (cloth : alk. paper)—ISBN 1-55849-463-4 (pbk. :
alk. paper)
1. Ariès, Philippe. 2. Historians—France—Biography.
3. France—Intellectual life—20th century.
I. Title. II. Series.
DC36.98.A74H88 2004
944'.0072'02—dc22

                                                    2003022910

British Library Cataloguing in Publication data are available.

All photos not otherwise credited appear by courtesy of Marie-Rose Ariès.

A volume in the series
Critical Perspectives on Modern Culture
edited by David Gross

for Lee,

her insight and inspiration

CONTENTS

Illustrations follow pages 28 and 158.

Old France in the
New History

MY BOOK IS a study of the life, work, ideas, and legacy of the French cultural historian Philippe Ariès (1914–84), with particular attention to his place in the historiography of the Western world during the late twentieth century. He is famous for his *L'Enfant et la vie familiale sous l'Ancien Régime* (1960), but the scope and influence of his scholarly contribution to a new cultural history reaches far beyond. Highlights of my interpretation include his pioneering conceptualization of a history of mentalities, his intellectual formation and transformation as a historian over a long and productive scholarly life, his place within French historical scholarship in the late twentieth century, and his autobiographical writing as the prototype of *égo-histoire*.

Although my interest in Ariès is primarily historiographical, it does have a political side. Without wishing to overstate the case, I argue that he found a way for French royalism, so tarnished by its association with the Vichy regime during the Second World War, to recapture a more respectable and alluring identity in the late twentieth century in the guise of a new cultural history. Neither an authoritarian nationalist nor a conservative Gaullist, Ariès emerged on the threshold of the postmodern age as an apologist for a new history of old France—not that of its kings and their courtiers but rather of the folkways of regional traditions, the sagas of families, and the secret passions of ordinary people in their private lives. Such topics would transform French historical writing in the late twentieth century. In promoting this venture, no one played a more influential role than he. In his histories of childhood and family, of death and mourning, and of the history of French history itself, he recast the political imagination of old France in erudite and stimulating ways.

The interpretation I explore concerns the way in which Ariès's turn to the cultural history of traditional French society—the mores of the world as it was before the French Revolution—became a refuge for his political commitments after the Second World War. Royalism as a political cause, relentlessly if quixotically pursued by its sympathizers for the better part of the Third Republic, seemed certain to disappear in the war's aftermath. The Vichy regime to which many royalists had rallied in 1940 proved to be their ruin by war's end. The promise of the regime's leader, Marshal Philippe Pétain, to restore the venerable traditions of old France was vitiated by the shame of Vichy's scandals. Royalism as a political cause in the contemporary world seemed destined to share the fate of Vichy's collaborators and fascist sympathizers. But if royalism was no longer a viable force in parliamentary politics, something of its mystique survived in the French public memory into our own times, thanks in some measure to its most sympathetic historian.

Historians do not remember Ariès as a political campaigner. While his traditionalist sentiments are well known, they would seem to have served primarily as the stimulus for his inquiry into the attitudes of ordinary people in their everyday lives in historical times far removed from our own. Ariès argued that his living memory of his own family's royalist loyalties had first inspired him to reinterpret the lifestyles of a traditional society whose mores now seemed all the more exotic for having been displaced by those of the modern world. He is remembered, therefore, as a provocative and engaging scholar who pioneered a new kind of cultural history and encouraged others to follow his lead into this unexplored domain.

Unexamined are the countless ways in which Ariès personally wrestled with the legacy of Vichy France, whose shame he sought to overcome in his rehabilitation of the historical memory of old France. I examine his political preoccupations in some detail as they emerge in the public record of the right-wing newspapers and magazines of commentary for which he wrote from the 1930s to the 1980s, in the Vichy papers on education at the Archives Nationales, and in his family archives and personal papers, now housed at the Ecole des Hautes Etudes en Sciences Sociales, Paris, where he taught from 1977 to 1982. I have interviewed friends from his university days as well as colleagues who shared his late-life scholarly projects to understand more fully the relationship between his personal ideals and his work as a historian.

For much of his adult life, Ariès was openly identified with right-wing political causes. During the 1930s, he was a youthful militant in the Action Française. At university, he was a rebel against the curriculum of the Third Republic, challenging the convictions of his republican teachers (including no less formidable an antagonist than Georges Lefebvre) in ways that thwarted his ambition to become a professor of history himself. His youth-ful dissatisfaction with modern republican historiography, however, even-tually prompted him to write *Le Temps de l'Histoire* (1954), a highly original history of French historical writing that prefigured the deconstructionist tenor of the historiographical scholarship of the late twentieth century.

Vichy provided Ariès with difficult challenges and unanticipated oppor-tunities that would reset his course in life. At the outset, he interested himself in educational reform and taught briefly at the Ecole Nationale des Cadres Supérieurs at La Chapelle-en-Serval, a center for the inculcation of Vichyite values in French youth. His first publication, *Les Traditions sociales dans les pays de France* (1943), a study of regional identities as a program for political decentralization, might be regarded as an apology for a vision of France that he had hoped Marshal Pétain would want to instill. It was during the Vichy era, too, that he found the administrative position in a documentation center in overseas commerce in tropical fruit that he held almost until the end of his life. He remained loyal to Pétain to his sad and inglorious end. After the war, he continued to write political essays for right-wing journals of commentary. I investigate his political activities and reconstruct his network of political associations during these years.

Not that Ariès the historian was reluctant to admit this past and these connections. Indeed, he expressed enduring pride in his venerable royalist heritage and identified it boldly in his autobiographical writings. But dis-illusionment with Vichy, together with the professional maturity he ac-quired through his historical research, enabled him to evolve from the naïve royalism that drew him to the Action Française in his youth to his historically informed support for regionalism and the environmental move-ment in his more politically detached old age. Characterizing himself as an "anarchist of the right," he pointed to the personalism and sociability of traditional culture as an antidote to the anonymity and expanding bureau-cratization of the contemporary welfare state.

Ariès's work as a historian might seem far removed from present-day political causes. But the 1960s, the years in which he made his reputation as a historian, marked the triumph of the welfare state, the embodiment of the social republic for which the left had struggled since the French Revolution. At a time when royalist politics appeared on the point of van-ishing, Ariès popularized in an attractive guise the lost or fading traditions of old France and so contributed to their reinvigoration in public memory. Obviously he was an important contributor to the history of collective mentalities that dominated academic historiography during the 1970s. Yet in less conspicuous ways his work contributed to a politics of culture that directed public attention to social values derived from a royalist heritage buried beneath the modern cult of individual ambition.

As a historian of old France, Ariès evoked idealized images of those traits of traditional French society that seemed threatened by modern culture: its politics for the personal loyalties it promoted, its religious rituals for the psychical security they provided, its traditions for the social stability they encouraged, and possibly most important, its families for the social networks they fostered. His tableau of the family of Old Regime France as an extended kin network contrasts in a pointed way with the pervasive imagery of the nuclear family in crisis in our times. The issue in the late twentieth century in a postindustrial country such as France, he suggested, is no longer how to overcome the poverty wrought by industrialization but how to protect the quality of life in an affluent society whose cost has been an increasingly complex social discipline and whose bane is the meretricious appeal of a mass culture.

In this respect, Ariès took advantage of a more general tendency in the postmodern world to cast the vision of the good society in aesthetic terms. By the 1960s, even Marxist intellectuals had shifted to this emphasis upon culture. Consider Lucien Goldmann's study of the changing image of God in the Old Regime, Roger Garaudy's dialogue with Christian religious thinkers, Albert Soboul's idealization of the communitarian values of the sans-culottes, and Henri Lefebvre's critique of the dreariness of mass culture in the modern world. To the failed promise of the good life that modern ideologies proposed, Ariès contended, the Old Regime offered appealing alternatives—not as models to which we might wish to return, but rather as places in our memory that inspire us to imagine other ways to live. For those who felt themselves alienated from a present-day mass culture conspicuous for its glittering fantasies, Ariès's depiction of old France was a tendentious stimulus to the imagination of a more authentic, if sobering future.

In his contribution to the new cultural history, Ariès found in popular culture a basis for the rehabilitation of a royalist cause discredited by the shame of Vichy. The history of mentalities that he pioneered dealt in those very issues bypassed by the historians of an earlier generation, who devoted their energies assiduously to reconstructing the political trends of the modern world. Despite the best efforts of these historians to mold the French past to the framework of the revolutionary tradition, nostalgia for the culture they would discard lingered in public memory. Ariès's talent as a historian was to locate in that ancient culture just those social qualities that modern historians were wont to set aside: habit as opposed to improvisation; tradition to revolution; cultural inertia to the innovations of the avant-garde; sociability to social discipline. Not that Ariès chose between the old ways and the new. He tried to show their coexistence, especially in the balance between them achieved in the nineteenth century, a time that he tended to portray as a golden age of popular culture.

Ariès's historical approach to the culture of the traditionalist past may have encouraged others. Consider the revealing essay by Emmanuel Le Roy Ladurie, perhaps the most respected of the historians of mentalities. In *Paris/Montpellier* (1982), he repudiated the Communist militancy of his university days and as a historian reexamined the traditionalist values in which he had been raised as a child in provincial France. His *Montaillou* (1975), a study of the mores of a rural community in a remote corner of medieval France, was a best-seller, and his capacity to engage a wide readership contrasted conspicuously with the retreat of so many left-wing intellectuals into a recondite and often obscure fascination with rhetoric that distanced them even from the educated public. Historical studies of the French left may have reached their apogee during the 1960s. But they were increasingly specialized and given to peripheral explorations of the unrealized projects of the revolutionary tradition. Ironically, just as the left consolidated its political power during the early 1980s behind the leadership of a socialist president, François Mitterrand, the historical mystique of the revolutionary tradition dwindled into petty squabbles among the official planners of the bicentennial of the French Revolution. The reemergence of the traditionalist right as a resurgent presence in French historiography, therefore, may be juxtaposed to the declining influence of the historiography associated with the revolutionary tradition, heralded in François Furet's celebrated reduction of the legacy of the French Revolution to its imaginary discourses.

In the end, the deeper measure of Ariès's contribution as a historian is more likely to be found in the way he opened the eyes of his colleagues to the commemorative character of modern historical writing itself. Following the method he sketched in *Le Temps de l'Histoire* in the 1950s, French historians by the 1980s were disassembling the conceptual frameworks of French historiography, with a critical eye to their mnemonic underpinnings. Conspicuous among the landmarks of this venture is the study of the French national memory, *Les Lieux de mémoire* (1984–92), edited by Pierre Nora. Nora likened his project to an archaeology of the many layers of the French national memory. The surface layer was composed of republican traditions, but the bedrock of the French identity dated from earlier times. In this study, old France, more so than the new, received the attention of the nation's most respected historians.

There is also a loose Gaullist connection to Ariès's rehabilitation of traditional French culture. Ironically, Charles de Gaulle himself, the savior of the Republic in 1944 and again in 1958, preferred to identify himself with the larger French heritage, and today has become one of the most powerful icons of its public memory. I am thinking, of course, not only of de Gaulle the statesman, but also of de Gaulle the writer of memoirs dedicated to preserving France's historic heritage. Whatever his politics, de Gaulle became for France in the late twentieth century an avatar of the national identity as the French struggled to reconcile a deep national heritage with an uncertain European future. Herein lies the particular significance of de Gaulle's relationship with the novelist André Malraux. As de Gaulle's minister of culture, Malraux took up the project of refurbishing France's national monuments, notably its royal chateaux, old churches, and monasteries (many of which had been turned into prisons in the nineteenth century). The project furthered the promotion of a mass tourism dating from the 1950s through which the public memory of France was rededicated to its royalist heritage. Ariès had little use for de Gaulle. But he was drawn to the epic grandeur of Malraux's conception of history, which reflected his own awe before the collective power of History's existential tide.

One notes that Malraux's project for the preservation of the historic ruins of France had once been the cause of the novelist and essayist Maurice Barrès, in whose vision of France the Action Française had been conceived at the turn of the twentieth century. The analogy is useful less for its specific links than for the echoing resonance in which Ariès the traditionalist pursued a politics of culture. Barrès and Ariès shared in the vision in which the Action Française was formed. But Ariès's historical appeal to the living testimony of the past was at once more subtle and disarming than was Barrès's literary appeal to political action. Unlike Barrès, Ariès was more interested in adaptation than in preservation. His sensibilities as a historian were too keenly attuned to the ongoing, dynamic process of change to identify naïvely with the inspiration of his heritage. Swept up in the upheaval of the Second World War, he recognized that he must change with the times. To value tradition was to recognize its resilient capacity for reinvention to meet the needs of the postwar world. In this sense, Ariès sought to understand how the traditional was assimilated to the modern. His inquiry into the relationship between the old and the new led him to his discovery of the emerging historical divide between public and private life during the early modern era. It is here that Ariès's essential insights as a historian are revealed, more so than in his famous study of the history of childhood, which anticipates this larger project. His mature vision of a comprehensive, collaborative study of the history of private life from antiquity to the present was his bequest to his colleagues at the Ecole des Hautes Etudes, who brought to fruition this project he had sketched but whose realization he did not live to see.

One can see the themes toward which my study of Ariès radiates. On the one hand, I explore his pioneering role in providing a conceptual framework for a new cultural history from the 1960s to the 1980s. On the other, I document the crucial importance of his experiences as a teacher and demographer in Vichy France during the Second World War for the way in which he came to formulate a new approach to cultural history. One can never be certain at the outset of a project how far one may succeed in turning up evidence to sustain a hypothesis. But the evidence I have gathered has substantiated most of the hunches I pursued. The point of departure for Ariès's original foray into the history of mentalities may be located in his experiences during the Vichy era. From there, I explore the wider connections into which his life and work led, insofar as my time, resources, ingenuity as an investigator, and good fortune have permitted me.

While my book concerns Ariès's life and work, it is not a biography in the conventional sense, constructed around a chronological narrative of the events of a life. Though I follow his life history loosely in my narrative, I highlight particular themes in each chapter, and move about rather freely back and forth in time to show their application. My larger purpose is to place Ariès in the context of the historiographical renaissance of the 1960s, relating his life and his work to the new directions in historical scholarship and the theoretical issues of the day. In this respect, I do not treat him only as a professional historian. Ariès the man of letters is always the shadow side of Ariès the historian, and from that perspective he is better perceived as a leading public intellectual of the late twentieth century and worthy of consideration for his place in the intellectual life of France and even America in that era. Here is a brief sketch of the principal themes of each chapter:

I begin by following Ariès's path into history. Using his seminal historiographical study of the 1950s, *Le Temps de l'Histoire*, as a guide, I note in chapter 1 five historiographical encounters crucial to his formation as a historian: his early royalist intellectual life in the Action Française; his ongoing dialogue with Marxist historians; his discovery of the pioneers of the Annales movement in French historiography and his eventual integration into its ranks; his postwar journalism as a kind of contemporary history; and his groundwork in historical demography as the setting for his discovery of "mentalities."

In chapter 2, I sketch Ariès's life history in light of his autobiographical writings, with particular attention to signatures of personal commitments that reveal his interests as a historian: the sociability of the extended family in traditional French society; the sense of community within the intermediate societies of old France; the virtue of loyalty to friends; the high ideal of "indissoluble" marriage; the link between attitudes toward death and destiny; the consolation of religious faith; and the meaning of becoming a historian as a vocation in life.

Turning to specific issues in chapter 3, I describe Ariès's interests and attitudes as he came of age: as a student at the Sorbonne; as a journalist for the student newspaper of the Action Française, and subsequently as an instructor at a Vichy-sponsored college for the training and moral rehabilitation of French youth. Material for this last topic is drawn from one of my principal research finds—previously undiscovered records about the school and its curriculum (including the syllabus of the course taught by Ariès) in the Vichy state papers on education, housed in the Archives Nationales. I make much of the personal friendships he formed during these early years.

Chapter 4 traces Ariès's now forgotten contribution as a journalist from the late 1940s to the mid-1960s. In the prime of life, he played out his chosen role as a public intellectual in behalf of what he knew to be the dying political cause of royalism. His newspaper articles placed the events and issues of his day in broad historical perspective. In their ensemble, his articles constitute a kind of contemporary history, a reference point for his more serious historical scholarship on the transactions between traditional and modern French culture from the sixteenth through the nineteenth century.

With his maturation as a historian in mind in chapter 5, I examine Ariès's developing conception of a history of mentalities, from his formulation of its meaning through his early work in historical demography in the last days of the Vichy era, to its uses as a working concept in his studies of childhood and family, to his historiographical reflections on its political meaning in light of the youthful ecology movement of the 1970s, to his re-visioning of the concept as the point of departure for a broader history of private life. This last project, which he envisioned and planned, served as a culminating synthesis of twenty years of Annales scholarship in the new cultural history. As his scholarly legacy for his colleagues, it is the best measure of his stature as a historian.

His most famous work, *Centuries of Childhood* (*L'Enfant et la vie familiale sous l'Ancien Régime*), looked at from the vantage point of the afterlife it took on among its readers and critics over several decades in America and France, is the subject of chapter 6. Without discounting the book's importance, I argue that it is in many ways Ariès's least successful venture as a historian and that its meaning must be appreciated in light of the whole body of his work. I note, however, that the staying power of the controversy over this book's thesis tells us something about the appeal of his writings.

I devote chapter 7 to interpreting the significance of Ariès's last major project of historical research—his history of attitudes toward death and mourning across the ages—in light of his own unfinished mourning for a tradition he had cherished, drawn forth in his dialogue with the left-wing historian Michel Vovelle, who wrote on the same subject. Their friendly debate during the 1970s and early 1980s played out as an elegy for the rivalry between royalism and Marxism in France's once vital revolutionary tradition.

Ariès's lifelong commitments of faith are addressed in chapter 8. One commitment was sacred—his religious beliefs; the other profane—his loyalty to friends and family. As tacit understandings, they sustained his passion for history in his intellectual life and for small-scale communities in his political life. One cannot understand his life and work without taking these convictions into account.

In chapter 9, I consider Ariès's late-life reinterpretation of the cluster of issues that constituted his work on childhood and family: his interest in the crisis of adolescence in his own times, his turn to issues of love, marriage, and sexuality in his later years, and his formulation of the larger significance of an emerging distinction between public and private life coeval with the rise of the modern era. My purpose is to show the significance of his ongoing growth and evolution as a historian until his death in 1984.

Chapter 10 opens with Ariès's late-life reflection on his early historiographical work, which I use as a basis for drawing out his ideas about historical time. I place his work within the context of the major historiographical issues of the era from the 1960s to the 1980s—what I characterize as the golden age of French historiography—with particular attention to his contribution to the cultural turn in Annales scholarship, the French obsession with the Vichy syndrome, the declining appeal of Marxist historical writing, and the dissolution of the grand narrative of modern French history in the deconstruction of the French national memory. My purpose is to challenge the standard interpretation of the historiography of this era, which focuses too exclusively on internal developments within the Annales movement without taking into account the intellectual life of the time. Moreover, it ignores the ongoing, if wavering, attachment among historians to the revolutionary tradition in which modern French history was originally conceived or the political significance of a new cultural history with roots in a dying royalism. In this respect, Ariès the outsider stands as a counterpoint to the eminent Annales insider Fernand Braudel in my effort to explain the remarkable originality of French historical scholarship in the late twentieth century.

THE CATALOG of my intellectual debt in pursuing this project is in effect an itinerary of my journey in research and writing, which has proceeded over several years. I have been buoyed by the interest of students and scholars in my topic, together with their practical help, information, advice, and generosity.

I thank the Council for the International Exchange of Scholars and the Franco-American Commission for Educational Exchange for seeing the merits of the project, and funding my year (1995–96) as a Fulbright scholar at the Ecole des Hautes Etudes en Sciences Sociales (EHESS) in Paris, where Philippe Ariès taught during his last years. Roger Chartier, who has seen to the editing and posthumous publication of a number of Ariès's writings, paved the way with an invitation. I am also indebted to him for facilitating my contact with the Ariès family and for sharing with me his knowledge of the Ariès papers. During the year, I learned a great deal from François Hartog, Pierre Nora, and Jacques Revel, faculty members of the EHESS, in whose seminars on historiography I participated. These provided a stimulating setting for my research and a testing ground for my ideas as I began to conceptualize my project.

I spent much of my time that year in the public archives and libraries—at the annex of the Bibliothèque Nationale in Versailles, where I canvassed the corpus of Ariès's newspaper articles; and at the Archives Nationales, to whose directors I am grateful for their permission to examine the Vichy papers on education. The Bibliothèque de la Maison des Sciences de l'Homme proved to be a useful repository of the scattered journals in which Ariès published much of his work, and a pleasant place to work productively.

When I began my research, Ariès's personal and professional papers were scattered in various private collections. I am deeply indebted to Marie-Rose Ariès, Philippe's only surviving sibling, for opening an important cache of her brother's correspondence for my perusal and for providing me with a genealogy of the Ariès family. In addition, she helped me to make contact with some of her brother's old friends and permitted me to make copies of a number of her family photographs. I gained a personal perspective on her brother and her family from my several conversations with her. She also authorized my examination of an enormous valise containing drafts of Ariès's manuscripts and offprints of his articles held by the Seuil publishing house. There Ariès's former editor, Jean-Pie Lapierre, kindly provided me with space in his office to study the collection and then arranged for the reproduction of documents needed for ongoing reference.

I enjoyed the many formal interviews I arranged, for impressions formed as well as for information obtained. Most of Ariès's closest friends from his university days survived him, and I profited from their recollections of their associations with him. I thank especially Jean Bruel, Philippe Brissaud, Raoul Girardet, François Leger, and Gilbert Picard. Ariès's colleagues at the Ecole des Hautes Etudes and in the profession also shared their memories of the man and their perspectives on his work, among them Nicole Castan, Yves Castan, Pierre Chaunu, Arlette Farge, and Jean-Louis Flandrin. Jacqueline Hecht and Jeannine Verdès-Laroux, scholars who have worked on Ariès, also aided me in my research. I also express my appreciation to Marcos Veneu, a graduate student at the Ecole des Hautes Etudes, for the benefit of our many conversations about Ariès's ideas and historical interpretations.

My American colleagues in French history have been just as helpful. I am especially indebted to Orest Ranum, who was one of Ariès's closest personal friends during his later years. We talked at professional meetings over the years, and as I neared completion of my research, he shared with me some of his correspondence from Philippe and Primerose Ariès, as well as beautiful memoirs he had written of their last days. While he has not agreed with all of my interpretations, he has been continually generous and supportive of my work.

I have received letters of scholarly references, citations of relevant books and articles, editorial advice and important evidence from a large number of colleagues, many of them old friends from our shared experiences in the Society for French Historical Studies, including Edward Berenson, Stuart Campbell, Natalie Davis, Barbara Day-Hichman, Leslie Derfler, Elborg Forster, Robert Forster, James Friguglietti, John Hellman, Peter Homans,

Matthew Hutton, William Irvine, William Keylor, Paul Mazgaj, Karen Offen, Mark Phillips, Roderick Phillips, and Patricia Ranum. At the University of Vermont, Robert Gordon, Janet Whatley, Luther Martin, Robert V. Daniels, R. Thomas Simone, and Richard Sugarman have exchanged ideas with me on this and related historiographical topics.

Since my Fulbright year, I have returned to France frequently on shorter trips, and I am grateful to the Graduate College of the University of Vermont for an award that funded some of this research. Each time I turned up new finds. In the past few years, the Ariès papers have been drawn together in the public realm at the Archives de l'Ecole des Hautes Etudes en Sciences Sociales, thanks to Brigitte Mazon, the archivist, and Guillaume Gros, who has inventoried the collection. I have appreciated their help, which enabled me to consolidate my evidence on these all-too-short visits to Paris.

Earlier versions of some chapters of my text have appeared in learned journals: *French Historical Studies* 21 (1998), *Historical Reflections* 28 (2002), *The Journal of Contemporary History* 34 (1999), *The Journal of Family History* 26 (2001), and the anthology *Symbolic Loss,* ed. Peter Homans (University Press of Virginia, 2000). I am grateful to the editors of these publications for permission to publish that material here.

I thank my editors, Clark Dougan and David Gross, for recognizing the promise of this book and Kay Scheuer for her careful copyediting of the manuscript.

Lastly, I thank my wife Lee. It was her encouragement that prompted me to take up this project, which has inspired several journeys to France on which she happily accompanied me.

Chronology of the Life of Philippe Ariès

Heritage and Childhood

1884 birth of Emile Ariès, Philippe's father, at Haux (Gironde)

1886 birth of Yvonne Ariès, his mother, at Saint-Pierre (Martinique)

1910 5 April marriage of Emile and Yvonne Ariès, at Bordeaux (Gironde)

1914 21 July Philippe, born at Blois (Loir-et-Cher)

1920 Ariès family moves to Paris, 16e arrondissement

Troubled Adolescence

1920s studies with the Dominicans

attends the Collège St. Louis de Gonzague (Jesuit), rue Franklin (Paris, 16e)

attends the Lycée Janson de Sailly (Paris, 16e); joins the "Lycéens et collègiens d'Action Française"

1930s apprenticed as an accountant at Les Andelys (Eure)

earns a "certificat d'histoire du Moyen Age" at the University of Grenoble; attends the lectures of the philosopher Jacques Chevalier

College Years

1930s matriculates at the University of Paris (Sorbonne); earns *licence* in history and geography

1936 successfully defends his thesis "Les Commissaires-Examinateurs au Châtelet de Paris au XVIe siècle" for his diplôme d'études supérieures in history and geography at the Sorbonne

November   joins the "Cercle d'Etudes Politiques" of the Action Française, led by François Leger; builds a circle of close friends through its activities

1936–39 works as a journalist for *L'Etudiant français,* a student newspaper of the Action Française; supports the cause of Charles Maurras

1939 fails the agrégation in history for the first time

Trials of Coming of Age

1939 September   enters officer candidate training in the French army; demobilized the following August

1940 retreats to the Bibiliothèque Nationale to study for the agrégation in history

1941 fails the agrégation for a second time

invitation to the soirée of Daniel Halévy, the first of many and the setting for his acquaintance with Louis Chevalier, Joseph Czapski, Gabriel Marcel, André Sigfried, and Henri Boegner

1941–42 accepts a post as an instructor at the Ecole Nationale des Cadres Supérieurs at La Chapelle-en-Serval (Oise)

1943 accepts a position as director of the documentation center of the Institut des Fruits et Agrumes Coloniaux (IFAC), after the war renamed the Institut de Recherches sur les Fruits et Agrumes (IRFA). He would hold the position for 37 years.

publishes his first book, *Les Traditions sociales dans les pays de France* (Editions de la Nouvelle France)

1943–50 pursues research in historical demography

1945 23 April   death of his brother Jacques (age 26) in combat at Uttenweiller (Württemberg)

1946 completes draft of *Histoire des populations françaises;* begins work on a historiographical project concerning the historians' representation of time

The Habits of Young Adulthood

1945–46 joins the editorial staff of the newspaper *Les Paroles françaises* as co-director with Pierre Boutang; becomes a reader for the Plon publishing house

1947 10 April marries Marie-Rose (Primerose) Lascazas de Saint Martin in Toulouse (Haute-Garonne); they take up residence in Paris, 16e

1948 publishes *Histoire des Populations françaises* (Editions du Self)

1950–60 pursues research for a project on the history of the family

1950–75 serves as editorial director of the collection "Civilisation d'hier et d'aujourd-hui," and with Robert Mandrou of the collection "Civilisations et mentalités," for the Plon publishing house

1954 publishes *Le Temps de l'Histoire* (Editions du Rocher)

1955–65 journalist for *La Nation française*

1956–57 convalesces for ten months at the sanitorium Tressaly at Pau (Basses-Pyrenées) to cure tuberculosis

1950s the Ariès move to a new home in Maisons-Laffitte (Yvelines)

1960 publishes *L'Enfant et la vie familiale sous l'Ancien Régime* (Plon); 1962, translated into English as *Centuries of Childhood* (Random House)

The Sea Change of Middle Age

1963 begins research on his project on the history of attitudes toward death and mourning

1964 death of his mother Yvonne (age 78) (later immortalized in his tableau of the "death of Mélisande")

1965 first visit to the United States, in connection with his professional work as an archivist; visits New York City and also the University of California at Berkeley

Primerose and Philippe make a pilgrimage to Saint-Pierre, Martinique (birthplace of his mother)

1969–78 plays a leadership role in the expanding network of computerized information on agriculture among participating nations of the European Community and for UNESCO

1971 February   death of his brother Georges (age 47)

August   death of his father Emile (age 86)

invitation from Orest Ranum to give lectures at Johns Hopkins University

publishes a new edition of *Histoire des populations françaises* (Editions du Seuil)

1973 publishes a new edition of *L'Enfant et la vie familiale* (Editions du Seuil)

April   delivers four lectures on attitudes toward death at Johns Hopkins University; 1974, these lectures published as *Western Attitudes toward Death* (Johns Hopkins University Press); 1975, augmented edition in French as *Essais sur l'histoire de la mort en Occident* (Seuil)

1974 participates in conference at Strasbourg on attitudes toward death and mourning, the beginning of his running debate with Michel Vovelle, 1974–83

1975 invitation from James Billington for study at the Woodrow Wilson International Center in Washington, D.C.

beginning of professional friendship with Yves and Nicole Castan of Toulouse

1976 January–August   spends six months in Washington, D.C., as a scholar at the Woodrow Wilson Center; works on his project on the history of attitudes toward death; also gives guest lectures at Princeton, Ann Arbor, and Los Angeles

1977 publishes *L'Homme devant la mort* (Editions du Seuil)

1977 1 October   appointed visiting director of studies, Ecole des Hautes Etudes en Sciences Sociales

1978 1 October   elected to the faculty of the Ecole des Hautes Etudes en Sciences Sociales as a director of studies; retires 1 October 1982

1979 30 September   retires from his position as director of documentation at the Institut de Recherches sur les Fruits et Agrumes

1980 4 January   interview with Michel Winock, published as *Un Historien du dimanche* (Seuil, 1980)

1981 14 October   fête on the bateau mouche honoring the Ariès

22–24 October   delivers keynote address, "Indissoluble Marriage," to the Western Society for French History at the University of Kansas, Lawrence

1982 publishes *Sexualités occidentales* (Editions du Seuil), proceedings of his seminar at the Ecoles des Hautes Etudes

Reckoning with Dying

1981 conference at St. Maximin (Var), culminating his debate with Michel Vovelle

1983 the Ariès move to Toulouse (Haute-Garonne)

spring sojourn in Berlin, Federal Republic of Germany, in connection with his project on the history of private life

11 May   directs seminar on private life at the Wissenschaftskolleg, Berlin

August   Primerose dies in Toulouse

October   publishes *Images de l'homme devant la mort* (Editions du Seuil)

1984 8 February   dies in Toulouse, buried beside Primerose at Castelnaudary (Aude)

Posthumous Recognitions

1986 *Histoire de la vie privée* (Editions du Seuil) published under joint editorship of Ariès and Georges Duby

1994 Institut de Recherches sur les Fruits et Agrumes renamed the Centre d'Information et de Documentation Philippe Ariès, relocated in Montpellier (Hérault)

Philippe Ariès

and the Politics of French Cultural History

1

From Tradition
into History

Ariès among the Historians

PHILIPPE ARIÈS was a singular figure in the historiography of the late twentieth century, both in France and abroad.[1] He moved from a youthful identification with sectarian royalism toward a broadly conceived perspective on a new cultural history, and so became one of the most original historians of his time. His work stimulated a sustained inquiry into the history of mentalities that would engage historians in the Western world for the better part of the late twentieth century. More than any other historian he left his personal signature on this new field. He helped to usher it in through his pioneering work in historical demography, and eventually to channel it into the broader one of the history of private life, once its usefulness as a historiographical concept had begun to wane.

From a historiographical perspective, the heyday of the history of mentalities was the 1960s and 1970s, and Ariès's *L'Enfant et la vie familiale sous l'AncienRégime* (1960) was a significant landmark in its beginnings. He offered a provocative thesis about changing perceptions of the place of children in the emerging modern family. The widespread use of the term "mentalities" as a metaphor for the new cultural history dates from about the time of the book's appearance.[2] One purpose of studying his life and work is to trace the development of this new kind of cultural history, with particular reference to its place in the historiography of the late twentieth century. Another is to remark on its relationship to the waning appeal of ideology in the politics of writing history.[3] Though Ariès abandoned doctrinaire royalism after the Second World War, he sought to reconcile his love for the culture of old France with his sensitivity to the new political realities of the postwar world. His efforts to blend the old with the new inform his historical writings in stimulating, often provocative ways.

The deep source of Ariès's interest in a history of mentalities sprang from impressions formed during the 1940s, more specifically from his youthful reckoning with the historical meaning of the Second World War, the German Occupation of France, and the Vichy regime. Such realities obliged him to come to terms with the collapse of a beloved and familiar world. In his view, the fall of France revealed not only the failure of the Third Republic but also the bankruptcy of a widely accepted interpretation of history that presupposed the unambiguous advance of modern Western civilization. It set him thinking about the way the prevailing sense of historical time—history as a linear ascent toward a more promising future—had been fashioned out of a particular conception of the meaning of historical change in the Western world.[4] What Ariès had in mind in his historiographical meditation on changing notions of historical time was not far removed from what historiographers today refer to as the dissolution of the grand narrative of history. He sensed that he was living in the midst of a sea change in historical understanding, and he wanted to interpret its historiographical significance. His interest was not in some alternative notion of history's destiny but rather of changing ideas about the meaning of historical time itself, as it had been formulated and reformulated across the ages.

Ariès's reflections on this topic during the Vichy years became the basis of his pioneering study of the way particular strands of remembrance of the French past had been woven into the fabric of a national history. In his *Le Temps de l'Histoire* (1954), a collection of essays on French historiography composed immediately after the war, Ariès contemplated how the framework of French history, as interpreted by historians writing from both republican and royalist perspectives, had been constructed over the course of the nineteenth century out of a battle over the long-range meaning of the French Revolution. Born of the Enlightenment, contested in the political struggles of royalists and republicans, advanced through the liberal policies of the nation-state, the hopes that had inspired the modern age had battened on an idea of progress promoted continuously through the nineteenth century, before being shattered in the catastrophes of the world wars of the twentieth. In the collapse of the Third Republic in 1940, Ariès saw the inadequacy of this working model of his nation's history in light of the somber realities of the Vichy regime and the German Occupation. The conceptions of history embodied in the French revolutionary tradition, he recognized, had lost much of their meaning. In sorting out the elements of French historical writing since the Middle Ages, he anticipated the reflective turn in historiography that surged into prominence during the 1970s.[5] Formerly viewed as a preliminary guide to research, historiography henceforth aroused an unprecedented interest in theoretical issues about the conceptual groundwork of historical understanding. So reconceived, historiography became a new kind of intellectual history for our times.

Many of Ariès's ideas about a new approach to history were derived from his reckoning with his traditionalist heritage. In his assessment, he was aided by his interest in the work of the rising Annales school of historiography, which was developing a panoramic conception of the geographical, economic, and social foundations of history. He had discovered the writings of Marc Bloch and Lucien Febvre during the Vichy years, and their work was a revelation for him. In their exploration of new domains of the past, he saw many of his own insights confirmed, and they inspired him to pursue his research with renewed conviction. Thus he found his way into a new kind of cultural history scorned by his mentors in the Action Française. The Annalistes who were his own contemporaries never paid much attention to his work, and he made his way as a historian independently until well into middle age. But in his last years he was able to link his scholarship directly to that of the younger professional historians at the Ecole des Hautes Etudes en Sciences Sociales, by then the institutional home of Annales historiography. There a new generation of scholars (among them, André Burguière, Roger Chartier, Arlette Farge, François Furet, François Hartog, Pierre Nora, and Jacques Revel) came to appreciate the originality of his perspective on cultural history. They found his ideas intriguing and recognized their heuristic effect upon research into the social and cultural problems of everyday life, notably the dynamics of family relations, the mores of sexuality, attitudes toward death and mourning, and the historical rise of the notion of privacy. Ariès's project for a history of private life in the early 1980s signaled the merger of their interests with his own. It was the means by which he passed on his historical inquiry to his colleagues and successors.

Ariès never completely let go of his royalist past. His discovery of mentalities as a working historiographical concept in middle age and his eventual integration into the ranks of the Annalistes in late life may be read as stages along the way in his long and troubled wrestling with his royalist attachments, which remained to the end the source of his personal values and his closest friendships. Most of his royalist friends from his university days clung stubbornly to the views they had held as militants together in the prewar Action Française, and they were intent upon renewing the royalist political struggle after the war as if little had changed. For them there was no acknowledgment of differences between prewar and postwar political culture. For twenty years after the war, Ariès joined in their journalistic ventures, all the while searching for some new way to adapt his old values to a vastly different contemporary scene. That quest brought out his originality as a historian. As he retreated from royalist politics, he turned to the history of the popular culture of old France, highlighting its personalism, sociability, and informality for a generation that worried about their waning place in contemporary social life. In his historical writings, he provides a glimpse of a vanishing traditional culture as a counterpoint to his critique of an emerging mass culture whose gloss was alluring but tawdry and unsatisfying. The royalism that he had once championed had by then lost its influence in contemporary French politics, but he was intent on making a case for a historically informed conservatism that would renew interest in the deep sources of the national identity.[6]

Ariès's contribution to academic scholarship during the 1970s and early 1980s is indicative of the diversification and growing complexity of the Annales as a historiographical movement. He was a latecomer and an outsider, with unconventional views and a suspect political past dating from his association with the Action Française in the years before the war. Here I argue that Ariès's entry into the ranks of the Annalistes, far from being the mere accommodation of an eccentric royalist, signaled a meeting of mind with other historians who contended with the political dilemmas of an age that bore few resemblances to the one in which they had received their scholarly formation. If Ariès learned from the first generation of Annales historians, a later one was prepared to learn from him.[7] His rise to prominence and his influence on Annales scholars coming of age in the 1970s challenge the prevailing notion that the emergence of the new cultural history can be explained in terms of expanding applications of the "Annales paradigm" by three successive generations of historians. Such a view treats Annales scholarship without reference to the realities of the world in which it was carried on. It ignores outside scholarly influences on its practitioners. It dismisses the political issues of the postwar era that had a decided effect on the problems these historians chose to address.

In their apologies for a new history, the Annales historians tended to downplay the importance of politics. But many in their ranks had past associations with the political left. Despite the association of mentalities with the culture of old France, most of the historians lured toward this new field of historical research had once held youthful sympathies for the revolutionary tradition, and some had been drawn to Marxism as the ideology that had fostered a heroic resistance to Nazi oppression. Some had joined the Communist party in the late 1940s and, even after their disillusionment with Stalinist tyrannies by the mid-1950s, continued to value

Marx's deepest insights into the nature of economic exploitation, as well as the materialist humanism that had been his original inspiration. Among the generation of historians that embarked on their studies after the war, such eminent exemplars as François Furet, Emmanuel Le Roy Ladurie, Michelle Perrot, Annie Kriegel, Pierre Chaunu, Jean-Louis Flandrin, and Michel Vovelle all had early sympathies for Marxism, and in some cases affiliation with the Communist party. However sophisticated their scholarship, these proponents of a new social history continued to draw on some basic Marxist presuppositions about class struggle as their historiographical guide.

By the 1960s, however, left-wing historians, too, had become restless with the pieties of a Marxist-inspired social history and began to search for new problems on which they might test their talents for research and interpretation. Like Ariès on the right, they turned to this unexplored history of popular culture under France's Old Regime. They were in search of premodern contexts against which the institutions and values of the modern age might be measured. Some wanted to understand the inertial power of inveterate custom and old habits of mind to retard the development of modernizing ways. Others struggled to form some conception of what an alternative to modern industrial society might aspire to be. Like Ariès, they recognized that a new history for the contemporary age should concern itself with differences that shed light on the problems of their current circumstances.

By the early 1970s, their interests and those of Ariès had come to converge on the mores of ordinary people in old France. Mentalities thus provided a common ground for historians coming into their professional maturity, impatient with timeworn interpretations derived from the ideological conceptions of their youth. As it had Ariès, mentalities offered left-wing historians opportunities to pursue new directions of research, drawn for the most part from topics dealing with France before the revolutionary age. François Furet and Emmanuel Le Roy Ladurie were the most prominent of these disenchanted Marxists, and they led parallel lives with Ariès as practitioners of the history of mentalities during the 1970s. Michel Vovelle, who continued to honor his Marxist heritage, openly engaged Ariès as a friendly adversary in a decade-long dialogue about the meaning of the history of changing attitudes toward death and mourning.

The new cultural history of the 1960s, therefore, facilitated a move away from the political discourse of the postwar era. During the 1950s, left-wing historiography had focused on the politics of class conflict over economic issues, notably the conjuncture between economic crisis and the demonstrative political protest associated with the revolutionary tradition in the eighteenth and nineteenth centuries. By the 1960s cultural issues were beginning to intrude into contemporary political thinking. The advent of unprecedented affluence in French society during those years blurred class lines and began to turn public attention from issues of economic deprivation to those of the quality of life. The social effects of the emerging mass culture found a place in political discussion that rivaled that of economically driven social inequality. It changed the nature of the debate about the good life and undercut the influence of ideologies devised a century before to deal with issues of economic hardship that had since eased and those of class struggle that were becoming obsolete. As historians distanced themselves from the ideological credos of their youth, they reinvested their hopes in new meanings to be discovered in the cultural attitudes toward everyday life in an earlier age. The history of mentalities, therefore, was a historiographical project in time, a cultural history of a forgotten past revisited for the historical perspective it might cast upon the dilemmas of the "present age," roughly the period from the early 1960s to the early 1980s.

My study of Ariès as exemplar of this historiographical reorientation proceeds from this crossroads of his early life as a royalist journalist and his later life as a cultural historian. As a young man, he aspired to become a man of letters in the tradition of his mentors, Charles Maurras and Daniel Halévy. But his destiny was to be remembered as a cultural historian in the tradition of the Annales school, albeit with a difference. If he remained enamored of the traditions of old France that he had known as a child, he grew in stature throughout his adult life as a historian of the modern world in which he made his way. His abandonment of doctrinaire royalism, his *agon* with the Marxists, his admiration for Annales scholarship, his astute perceptions of his own time in history, his quest to uncover the secrets of mentalities—these are the highlights of his journey as a historian. Independent of mind, he prided himself on his unorthodox interpretations while seeking to participate with grace and enthusiasm in the collaborative research projects that by the 1970s had become the Annales fashion.

Formative Historiographical Encounters

I consider Ariès's development as a historian in light of five crucial historiographical encounters along the way that he tried to reconcile with faithfulness to what he perceived to be the personal thread of his own life story. They provide the touchstones of this book as follows:

Royalist Intellectual Life. Ariès's intellectual traits were formed during the 1930s, partly as a student at the Sorbonne, partly as a journalist for the student wing of the Action Française. He brought with him to the Sorbonne his youthful conception of Capetian history, shaped by family lore, the genealogy of kings, and the traditions of old France. In keeping with his political allegiance during these troubled times, he set aside his royalist sentimentality so as to pursue the rough-edged politics in which royalists then engaged. As a protégé of Charles Maurras, the preeminent figure in royalist politics, he wrote articles on contemporary European statecraft. In imitation of his mentor, he combined intellectual elitism with a certain political parochialism and played out his modest supporting role in the grandiloquent discourse of what he later came to recognize had been Paris's rarefied and self-contained intellectual world.[8]

Though Ariès praised Maurras in his newspaper articles, he had little affinity with his most fervently held views. Maurras espoused a respect for tradition with which Ariès could in principle identify, and he tended to play up this aspect of his mentor's intellectual influence on him. But Maurras's positivism and Jacobin nationalism cut against the grain of Ariès's romanticism and federalist regionalism. Moreover, Maurras took an ahistorical approach to the royalist cause from which Ariès became increasingly estranged. He remained loyal to Maurras in his way. He paid him a visit on his deathbed in the prison to which he was condemned after the war, and he dedicated his first book to his memory. Late in life he wrote an essay about Maurras's notion of the *chemin de paradis* as a memento mori.[9] But there was little of Maurras's intellectual legacy that he could take with him on his own journey as a historical investigator of the traditional culture that his former mentor had claimed to venerate.

Later, reflecting on those years at the Sorbonne, Ariès noted that his major intellectual challenge had been to overcome his adolescent notion that his conception of history must remain an apology for the traditions that linked him personally to the past.[10] That notion had been given firmly resolved expression by Jacques Bainville, the celebrated royalist historian, whose *Histoire de France* (1924) Ariès remembered as the "breviary of my adolescence."[11] As he grew more intellectually mature following his university years, he found himself at odds with Bainville's apology for a royalist interpretation of history. Bainville argued that history is able to teach us useful lessons about the past because human nature has remained essentially the same throughout the ages. History shows us repeating the mistakes of the past, while we should have learned from them. For Bainville, the past offers a resource within which we may discover similarities with our present dilemmas. The human condition, he taught, is unchanging, and hence the past is a useful guide for teaching moral lessons about how to live. In the course of his reading, particularly during the war years, Ariès found his way to an opposing viewpoint. Historians, he came to believe, should take the present as their primary frame of reference and consider the past to understand differences between them. Far from being unchanging, human nature is a historical condition, malleable in the face of new realities. Humans define themselves in fashioning their environment, and they remodel their nature as their circumstances change, and with them their strategies for dealing with life's elemental problems—what he originally referred to as the "techniques of life and death," and later as "mentalities." Ariès also repudiated Bainville's focus on politics as the backbone of history. Bainville's historical studies concerned statesmen and politicians, and his reputation as a historian was based on his astute analysis of their purposes and his skillful depiction of their statecraft in action. As a student journalist for the Action Française during the late 1930s, Ariès wrote articles on contemporary state relations in Bainville's manner. But after the war he paid no further attention to such topics and evinced little ongoing interest in diplomatic history.[12]

Ariès's education at the Sorbonne also enabled him to distance himself from the royalist historiography of the Capetian school, permitted in part by his exposure to the new regional history with its strong geographical bent and in part by his studies with republican historians. He enjoyed his courses at the Sorbonne and learned a great deal from the regional studies in history and geography then in vogue. His friend François Leger recalls that Ariès especially admired the geographer Emmanuel de Martonne and the historian of antiquity Jerôme Carcopino.[13] In his autobiography, Ariès passed over their influence on his thinking. But the geographical approach provided the framework and set the tone of his first two historical books, one dealing with local traditions in France and the other with the French population. In both, he proceeded region by region, pointing out differences among them as a foundation for understanding the pluralism of the French past.

Ariès pursued his project on the renewal of regionalism during the early years of Vichy. In *Les Traditions sociales dans les pays de France* (1943), he inventoried the regional popular traditions of old France for indications of the ways in which they had maintained their vitality through adaptation to changing historical realities. Though the policies of the Vichy regime soon disabused him of the present prospects of regionalism as a basis for the renewal of immemorial tradition, this study marks his first excursion into a new cultural history that he hoped might sustain the profound legacy of royalism. The book's publication whetted Daniel Halévy's personal interest in his work and soon opened the way to their friendship. Halévy was a savant of the old style. Ariès admired him for an intellectual elegance reminiscent of an earlier generation of French men of letters.[14] Halévy had his reservations about Maurras and kept his distance from him. But he had intellectual interests to which Ariès was particularly attuned, notably his concern about the erosion of the folkways of rural culture. His writings have the loving, elegiac feel of a meditation on a vanishing world. For most royalists, such nostalgia served as a trap. Rather than succumb, Halévy looked for ways in which the regional cultures of rural France might be renewed. Initially, he harbored some hopes that the Vichy regime might interest itself in this cause.[15] He became the traditionalist historian as mentor for whom Ariès had been searching and never found among the luminaries of the Action Française. Halévy invited Ariès to his literary salon during the Vichy years, and they remained correspondents until Halévy's death in 1962.[16]

Ariès's friendship with Halévy suggests his ongoing need for a connection to this old-fashioned refined culture. It may even be that he saw himself preparing for a like role as an independent-minded man of letters rather than for that of the professional historian. Halévy had quirky, eclectic intellectual interests of the sort that Ariès could admire. Moreover, Halévy was committed to rethinking the meaning of the royalist historiographical tradition. His *Histoire d'une histoire* (1939, published on the occasion of the 150th anniversary of the French Revolution) may have had an influence on Ariès's early awakening to the significance of historiography.[17] His respect for Halévy notwithstanding, Ariès recognized that the world of royalism was a charming garden which he could no longer tend. Its elitism was coupled with parochialism. Out of personal loyalty, he retained his attachments to the friends and mentors who had populated that preserve. But they were no longer a source of inspiration for him. The editorial policies of the royalist newspapers for which he continued to write through the 1950s and into the 1960s were ever more remote from his present concerns, and his articles stand out as different from most of the fare that they published. He could look back at the receding shore of the royalist land he loved for the way it had once nurtured him. Emotionally he remained anchored there. Intellectually he sailed on.

Marxist Ideology. As an adversarial approach to history with which to reckon, Marxism loomed large in Ariès's thinking. Suspicion of Marxism had been part of his formation in the Action Française, and he articulated his critique in his student journalism of the late 1930s. His first newspaper article on the topic assailed Marx's quixotic abstractions, and his opposition to Marxism deepened with the onset of the Cold War.[18] In the midst of the post-Liberation purge in France, he offered an indictment of contemporary Marxists as hapless intellectuals caught in the maelstroms of these uncertain times. Having broken their ties with family, community, and social tradition, he proposed, some were in search of an ideological refuge. In that they possessed no concrete sense of a past with which they might identify, they were easily impressed with Marx's abstract scheme about the larger course of history. Swept up in the turbulent tide of war, they had decided to give themselves to its flow. Ariès believed that Marxism in its economic reductionism homogenized the human condition, eliding genuine differences among people and their particular cultures. Marxism, he argued, also ignored crucial differences between past and present in its contention that class struggle, based upon unchanging human motivation, drives the course of history.[19]

But it is worth noting that Ariès remained in dialogue with Marxist scholars throughout his life, and he learned from them. As a student at the Sorbonne, he took a course with Georges Lefebvre, a Marxist historian with broad and humane sympathies and the reigning figure in the left-wing historiography of the French Revolution during the 1930s. Lefebvre offered him a comprehensive interpretation of the multifold class struggle that lay beneath that upheaval, and Ariès used it to draw out his own ideas about the influence of secret societies on revolutionary politics and the regional resistance of the Chouans of the Vendée to Jacobin terror emanating from Paris.[20] Over time, Marxist intellectuals became friendly adversaries. As a mature scholar during the 1960s, he appreciated the expression of interest in his work by the other Lefebvre, the Marxist philosopher Henri, who shared his grim assessment of mediocrity in the everday life of contemporary mass culture.[21] Such an encounter was a prelude to his long and productive intellectual exchange with Michel Vovelle during the 1970s. Through their congenial debate, they would mourn, each in his own way, the passing of the French revolutionary tradition. The new cultural history served as a forum for this requiem.

Annales Historiography. Ariès's discovery of the scholarship of the Annales historians was the intellectual epiphany of his young adulthood. He was inspired by their unconventional subject matter and their panoramic view of the past. They widened his intellectual horizons and stimulated his thinking about new ways to approach economic and social history, topics shunned by Maurras, Bainville, and their entourage. He read avidly in this new social history and related fields of sociology during the war years, and he was especially taken with two perspectives emerging out of their research. The first concerned the notion of a history of the present. Marc Bloch confirmed his thinking about the present as the point of departure for investigating the past, and he made much of the importance of observing one's present surroundings for leavings of a lost past. The past survives into the present, Ariès recognized, in its artifacts and its iconography. A present-minded perspective on the past also makes one more aware of how different its realities were from one's own.[22] The second dealt with the structuralist thinking then popular among Annalistes attuned to the methods of anthropology. The notion of a historical epoch as a coherent structure was associated with the work of Fernand Braudel and Robert Mandrou, who presided over Annales historiography during the 1950s.[23] Within such structures, they explained, changes are so slow as to be imperceptible to the historical actors within them. But there are often dramatic differences among such structures, and it is the historians' task to identify the breaking points. Surveying the past in terms of the dynamics within its structures enables historians to understand ongoing tensions— between continuity and change, private and public life, time-worn customs and ambitious improvisations. In structuralism, nothing is ever lost, but everything is reconfigured in an ongoing process of change. What was central at one time might be marginalized at another, but rarely does it disappear. As Ariès embarked on his inquiry into the history of mentalities—beginning with *L'Enfant et la vie familiale*—he formulated such a model to plot a succession of comparatively stable mental structures over long periods of time. He was also taken with Braudel's notions about the relativity of historical time, particularly his use of the concept of synchronic time to explain the ongoing tension between continuity and change in eras of comparative stability.[24]

The Historical Meaning of the Contemporary Age. Ariès was readily disposed to rethink history in light of the problems of his own time. In the immediate aftermath of the Second World War, he commented on the brutal way in which he had been wrested from the secure prewar world that had nurtured him and thrust into the larger, more precarious postwar world. His journalism of the 1950s and 1960s reflects his sensitivity to the differences between the postwar and prewar eras, and his newspaper articles in *La Nation française* seek to identify distinguishing historical features of the contemporary age. Ariès was fascinated with the new departures of his times. He had a keen eye for contemporary trends and kept abreast of recent literature on social and cultural change. As he drew his readers' attention to contemporary events, he also offered them a broad historical context in which to place them, illustrated with references to social mores in the popular culture of traditions that had since faded. He began to refer to old France not for its continuities with the present but for differences that might contribute to a more discriminating interpretation of the richly layered cultural texture of his own times. In this respect, he explained how traditional perspectives had survived the onslaught of modernity by taking refuge in sanctuaries of privacy fashioned along the way. In the course of his historical research during the 1950s, he identified the affectionate family as the principal asylum for such values across the span of modern history. As for the present, though, he was less certain about the family's stability as an agency for the maintenance of social values. Expectations for the future among his contemporaries, he surmised, had become more modest in their accent on private life and personal satisfactions. In his late-life interpretation of the history of attitudes toward death and mourning, he reflected on the diminishing significance of the notion of collective destiny among his contemporaries. The larger problem of the historical emergence of a private life apart from a public one during the early modern era continued to serve as the organizing principle of all of his work, though he was sensitive to the widening divide between them in the contemporary age.[25]

In his last years, Ariès remained alert to the newfound theoretical and methodological interests of his colleagues in cultural history and tried to relate them to his own historical conceptions. But he never again attempted a comprehensive study of the theoretical groundwork of historical writing, which had become fashionable by the 1970s. He appreciated and learned from some innovative practicing historians, notably Natalie Davis, Arlette Farge, Jean-Louis Flandrin, Carlo Ginzburg, and Paul Veyne. One of his most rewarding connections was that with Michel Foucault, with whom he came to recognize an intellectual affinity. Both drew attention to the margins rather than the centers of power. Their interests in historical psychology converged in the early 1960s, and their work became intertwined by the early 1980s when Foucault was a guest in Ariès's seminar at the Ecole des Hautes Etudes and a contributor to his anthology on the history of sexuality in Western culture. By then they were both investigating the relationship between attitudes toward sexuality and techniques for the care of the self. Underpinning their inquiry was a common critique of the invasive "policing" techniques of public authority in contemporary mass culture.

Sentiment as the Secret of Mentalities. In his manifesto of the early 1940s calling for a new kind of history, Lucien Febvre urged his colleagues to consider the possibility of writing a history of sentiment.[26] One might say that twenty years thereafter, Ariès was among the first to heed the call, and identified the rise of the affectionate family as a crucial step in the making of the modern mentality. He grounded modernity in two sources, one rational, the other emotional. The former had been much studied. It concerned the rise of modern science and the application of rational techniques in both the political and the social order. The other source, less studied by historians, concerned the reorganization of emotional life around private forms of identity in early modern European society. Ariès found his way to this topic during the Vichy era through his research into historical demography. It was the source of his most original insight and the matrix of all his subsequent research. Ariès's pioneering work in mentalities grew out of these early studies of human sexuality, more specifically out of his interest in the emergence of new attitudes toward contraceptive practices in early modern France.

That interest had been inspired by his dialogue with Vichyite educators, who contended that the physiological decline of the French people was the deep cause of the political fall of France in 1940. Their ideas were closely linked to the eugenics movement, which gave a scientific allure to a way of thinking then popular not only in France but throughout the Western world.[27] As a young instructor at a Vichy training college (*école des cadres*), Ariès listened to his colleagues' views about the need for the biological rehabilitation of the French people. The school's director was much taken with such notions, and instruction in the principles of eugenics was integrated into the school's curriculum.[28] Ariès was uneasy with this hypothesis, and set out on a historical investigation to challenge it. He used population studies to present an alternative explanation, one based on cultural rather than biological factors and one that identified the decline of the French population not with physiological degeneration but rather with the rise of a modern mentality favoring conscious choices to further one's own well-being, that of one's family, and by extension that of society at large. Here Ariès linked his fortunes with a new school of demographers who would reshape the field in the postwar era. Led by Alfred Sauvy, they would transform the Fondation Alexis Carrel, Vichy's newly constituted center for research in eugenics, into the Institut National d'Etudes Démographiques, a highly respected scholarly institution, and to this day a major force in the social sciences.[29] Ariès was a lesser participant in this project. But his ability to transpose their findings in demography into an emerging cultural history would give this approach a visibility it otherwise would never have received. In Ariès's rendering, the rise of the history of mentalities to historiographical prominence during the 1960s marked the culmination of the inquiry into France's diminishing place in the modern world that had obsessed Vichy's leaders. Thus Ariès put the fall of France in a different historical perspective and showed the way toward an understanding of France's role in the present age in light of its cultural rather than its political heritage.

A Reflective Turn on History's Sources in Tradition. Ariès's other route into the past after the war was an excursion into historiography. It was inspired by his need to come to terms with the waning appeal of the royalist historiography that had framed his conception of history from childhood through his university years. To launch this project he composed a series of essays in the immediate aftermath of the war, which he then collated and published as a book, *Le Temps de l'Histoire.* A history of French history, it is also a meditation on the nature of historical time, and documents his growing awareness of the inadequacy of his youthful conception of a transparent connection between his own royalist tradition and a more cosmopolitan historiography.

The war had uprooted Ariès from his traditionalist world, and he came away from its trials with a newfound respect for History reconceived as the existential past, a depth that defied the historians' efforts to frame its meaning. His own royalist tradition of historiography—and for that matter the modern French historiographical tradition in which it figured—now seemed parochial by comparison. As conceptual frameworks, they were too narrow to make adequate sense of the tide of human experience. Given its scope and complexity, he remarked, History cannot be reduced to the interpretations that historians have imposed upon the past. Even in their most capacious narratives, the histories they write are only thin accounts of its realities. In *Le Temps de l'Histoire* he set out in search of France's multiple historical roots buried deep in the many traditions that issued from its past.

Ariès was a historian, not a philosopher. But *Le Temps de l'Histoire* has some thought-provoking implications for understanding the relationship between tradition and history. Proceeding from the proposition that "History" (conceived as the aggregate of past human experience) encompasses both tradition and history, he considers their relationship in terms of an interplay between two ways of understanding historical time—one as it flows through living tradition, the other as it punctuates historical reconstruction. The time of tradition is existential: it embodies lived experience as it emerges out of the past and confirms our sense of continuity with it. The time of history is hermeneutical: it interprets the meaning of the past by breaking it up into discrete units and so makes us aware of the differences between past and present. Historians interpret particular traditions in terms of their specific characteristics. One of their tasks is to show the diversity of the human experience in the variety of its traditions. But the meaning of tradition for those immersed in each of them, he argued, is incommensurable with such particularities, for it conveys an immediacy of contact with a unifying, ontological ground of human experience. That is why tradition appears to embody the presence of the past. The ambiguity of the historians' enterprise, Ariès further argued, is that historians, too, are immersed in their own traditions of historical writing, each dependent upon specific historical circumstances. They may differentiate past from present in the infinite variety of their historical interpretations. But the act of writing history is itself a lived experience that they share with their colleagues and predecessors and tends to reinforce their sense of participation in a common search for the meaning of the human predicament. Like Hippolyte Taine, who had first popularized the idea in the nineteenth century, Ariès construed the past as a living resource, deeper in the possibilities of its interpretation than any particular histories may draw forth. In this sense, the act of writing history is commemorative in that historians identify within the limits of their critical understanding a past whose meaning is otherwise continually remodeled in the ongoing revisions of collective memory.[30]

To adduce his argument, Ariès traced the particular traditions out of which modern French historiography had been constructed. These, he argued, were the matrices from which historical writing proceeds. In the making of modern history, historians composed their narratives out of the materials of ancient traditions. Modern French history, he explained, had been cobbled together in the seventeenth century out of the fragments of medieval chronicles, which in turn drew upon the collective memories of scattered oral legends. In the making of history in early modern France, these elements had been assimilated into a common narrative about the rise of the modern French state. It conflated the times of particular traditions into a single chronology, demarcated by highlights in the lives of the French kings. Ariès contended that this grand narrative imposed a new temporal framework, one that defined the time of history more abstractly and consigned to oblivion the sense of time as repetition that had informed the local traditions from which it was derived. Modern history was more than an aggregation of narratives derived from local traditions. It imposed its own sense of linear time upon tradition, and with it the way the idea of tradition itself was understood. The notion of the presence of the past within immemorial tradition was recontextualized within a history imbued with a sense of direction between a formative beginning and a projected end. In the process, he proposed, the modern understanding of tradition took on the shape of historical time.[31]

French history, Ariès maintained, had since the Revolution been interpreted in light of opposing conceptions of what France's destiny might be. Historians sympathetic to the revolutionary tradition viewed the Revolution as a series of formative events setting the direction of moral intention their nation would seek to further; those who favored the counterrevolutionary alternative construed the same events as harbingers of the collapse of an ill-conceived experiment in modern government that would eventually require a return to the political ideals of old France. But in a way, Ariès contended, these views of history are mirror images of each other. With variations of emphasis and sympathy, each contributed to an emerging national tradition of historiography. In that sense, historians inspired by the Revolution and those loyal to royalism had been tethered to one another in their efforts to reckon with France's past. The irony for Ariès was that royalist historians had as a consequence lost sight of the cultural substance of their heritage—the local traditions of old France—in favor of a conception of a national tradition that reduced heritage to political abstractions.[32] That is why Ariès turned from epic to ordinary lives in his own historical investigations.[33] Here, he believed, was subject matter ignored by political historians that is essential to our understanding of the past. It was in his musings on such sources embedded in popular culture that he formulated his earliest conceptions about a history of mentalities.[34]

Le Temps de l'Histoire was prescient in its anticipation of the deconstructionist tenor of historiography today, though with attention to the reconfiguration rather than the displacement of traditions of historical writing over time. In this project, Ariès sought to unburden royalist history of its fatalism, as he had Vichy's demography in his *Histoire des populations françaises,* by reinventing it in an alternate mode of expression. The larger significance of his work lies in his rehabilitation of the heritage honored by the French right, which over the course of the early twentieth century had slid into obsolescence and during the Vichy era into disgrace. In this respect, he played for the right wing in France at the end of the century the role played by Bainville at its beginning, though in a more subtle, less combative way. In what might be construed as an act of atonement, Ariès sought to recontextualize old social values in the making of a new civic identity that would suit the needs of the present age. Without apologizing for the shortcomings of the royalist movement in the twentieth century or more poignantly its inculpation in the shame of Vichy, he sought to portray a more authentic royalist heritage with which the French might identify. The legacy of royalism, he taught his contemporaries, lay in its mores, not its politics, and his project as a historian was to explain why. As a journalist during the 1950s, he displayed insightful perspectives on the relationship between the present and the past, though his influence was limited to a comparatively restricted readership. As a historian from the 1960s, he reached a broader audience. As a pioneer in the new cultural history that flourished in France from the 1960s to the 1980s, he opened vistas on a previously unseen past and in the process drew forth his own deepest convictions about the way the study of history can help us to appreciate what is constant and what is changing in the human condition.

I do not wish to idealize Ariès or to exaggerate his importance. But I do wish to show his originality as a historian and the marked influence he had upon the historiography of the late twentieth century. Free of the constraints of academic historical writing for much of his working life, he in the end helped to lead university scholars into new paths of cultural history and new conceptions of the relationship between public and private life. His accomplishment is remarkable given the obstacles to his vocation as a historian during his formative years, and his largely independent journey as a scholar well into his middle age. He showed a new way to integrate old France into contemporary historiography. Modern French historical writing had been dominated by the revolutionary tradition. Postmodern historical writing has been more open toward the pluralism of the past. Ariès's life and work help us to understand the transition from a historiography devoted to a conception of politics and statecraft derived from the revolutionary tradition toward one that permitted a many-faced cultural history attuned to the problems of the present age. Few historians navigated the passage with such insight and conviction.

FIGURE 1. Ariès family tree (courtesy of Marie-Rose Ariès)

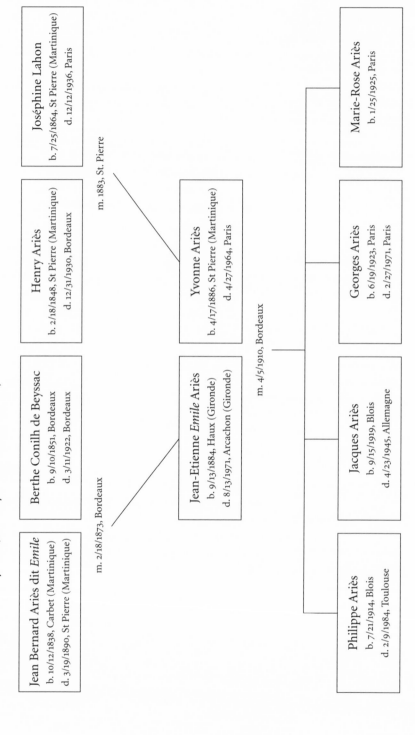

Jean Bernard Ariès dit *Emile*
b. 10/12/1838, Carbet (Martinique)
d. 3/19/1890, St Pierre (Martinique)

Berthe Conilh de Beyssac
b. 9/10/1851, Bordeaux
d. 3/11/1922, Bordeaux

Henry Ariès
b. 2/18/1848, St Pierre (Martinique)
d. 12/31/1930, Bordeaux

Joséphine Lahon
b. 7/25/1864, St Pierre (Martinique)
d. 12/12/1936, Paris

m. 2/18/1873, Bordeaux

m. 1883, St. Pierre

Jean-Etienne *Emile* Ariès
b. 9/13/1884, Haux (Gironde)
d. 8/13/1971, Arcachon (Gironde)

Yvonne Ariès
b. 4/17/1886, St Pierre (Martinique)
d. 4/27/1964, Paris

m. 4/5/1910, Bordeaux

Philippe Ariès
b. 7/21/1914, Blois
d. 2/9/1984, Toulouse

Jacques Ariès
b. 9/15/1919, Blois
d. 4/23/1945, Allemagne

Georges Ariès
b. 6/19/1923, Paris
d. 2/27/1971, Paris

Marie-Rose Ariès
b. 1/25/1925, Paris

2

Between Ego-Psychology
and *Ego-Histoire*

A Biographical Sketch

Stages of an Ego-Psychology

THE LIFE OF Philippe Ariès as an intellectual in twentieth-century France is a study in personal growth in the face of obstacles, some imposed upon him by the times in which he lived, some derived from his personal makeup, and some of his own creation. Denied his ambition to become a university professor as a young man, he pursued an alternate route as an amateur historian and achieved success as a scholar that he might otherwise never have known. He was conspicuous for his commitment to some deeply held convictions about the nature and value of historical inquiry while reformulating them with critical insight as his intellectual maturity as a historian advanced and as new realities presented themselves. He took a different view on the meaning of the past from that of his *confrères* on the extreme right, who were obsessed with the past as they wanted to remember it, and unwilling to rethink their position in light of the new conditions in France after the Second World War. Ariès took the present rather than the past as his historical frame of reference. The study of the past, he explained, enables us to assess the issues with which we deal in the present with greater nuance and deeper understanding. In the process he re-dressed the royalist legacy in the guise of a new cultural history that focused on private rather than public life. The story of his own private life is the subject of this chapter.[1]

One might easily read Ariès's biography as a story in ego-psychology in the manner of Erik Erikson—one of his lifelong personal growth as he came to terms with the challenges each stage of life presented to him.[2] Erikson's historical writings were in vogue during Ariès's own prime, and there is an intriguing parallel between Erikson's psychological model of the stages of growth across the life cycle and Ariès's historical one of their gradual elaboration over the last four centuries.[3] Ariès's own life history accords with Erikson's model to the degree that it is punctuated by decisive transformations, especially at the threshold of young adulthood and again of middle age. Here I plot what I see as the essential stages of his life: an enchanted childhood; a troubled adolescence; idyllic college years; a difficult coming of age under Vichy; a productive adulthood defined by disciplined work habits in both his professional and his intellectual life; significant recognition in middle age in both career and vocation; late-life recourse to traditional religious resources to prepare for dying. For Ariès, personal need and intellectual inquiry were closely intertwined. Exploring that relationship helps us to understand the projects he took up as a historian in the various stages of his life.

A Childhood Immersed in Centuries of Heritage. Philippe Ariès was a well-loved child, the first-born in a family of four children.[4] His parents were first cousins, both with the surname Ariès (see figure 1), and their ancestors hailed from the same small town in Martinique in the French West Indies, from which they carried nostalgic memories with them in their emigration to France in the late nineteenth century. The town of Saint-Pierre was a French colonial enclave. The Ariès families, like other overseas French in this community, made few concessions to the indigenous culture or the tropical Caribbean setting, but rather lived the style of life they would have followed in provincial France. The urban geography and popular culture of Saint-Pierre were reminiscent of small-town France as it harked back to an earlier age. These were not plantation aristocrats, but rather representatives of the middling commercial and professional bourgeoisie. Philippe's paternal grandfather Emile ran a business in the center of town and served as president of the local chamber of commerce. He died comparatively young at age fifty-two in 1890, whereupon his widow Berthe and their son Emile (Philippe's father) returned to her native Bordeaux. Philippe characterized his maternal grandfather Henry as a *bricoleur*. He possessed the skills of a craftsman, and he enjoyed working with his hands. He owned a sawmill at the edge of town, a venture that failed as did others he attempted (one an electrical service he set up with his future son-in-law). Without prospects for work on the island, he emigrated with his family to Bordeaux in 1899, settling near members of his extended family. Henry saw the move as permanent, and there could be no return anyway after the volcano Mount Pelée erupted in 1902 and its lava deluged Saint-Pierre. Soon the maternal Ariès family was joined by other relatives and friends fleeing a disappearing paradise. The volcanic catastrophe of Saint-Pierre may have ended a way of life there, Ariès explained, but it lived on as a legendary community in the memory of his parents and their fellow émigrés. For his mother especially, Saint-Pierre remained an idyllic landscape that she cherished for its *douceur de vie*. The overseas experience of the Ariès family, therefore, reinforced their provincial one. In light of their colonial heritage, they held fast to an image of old France even more fervently than did their royalist counterparts in the metropole.[5]

A Troubled Adolescence. While growing up, Philippe had a difficult relationship with his father Emile, who pushed him toward a career in engineering for which he had neither aptitude nor interest. Emile was born near Langoiran (Gironde) in 1884, and though he spent his early childhood in Martinique, most of his upbringing was in Bordeaux, where he attended Catholic schools. An unsuccessful candidate for the Ecole Polytechnique, he graduated from the Ecole Supérieure d'Electricité. As an electrical engineer, he became an apostle of the new technological culture and played a major role during the interwar years in the rural electrification of France. As an adolescent, Philippe would have no part of such a vocation and stubbornly neglected his studies until he was at last permitted to pursue his passion for history. His recalcitrance might be interpreted as a manifestation of the tension between the two cultural worlds that he had known as a child: one scientific in its practicality, the other romantic in its nostalgia. His behavior obliged his parents to try different schools and even a tutor to help him pass his baccalaureate exam. Along the way, he attended a primary school on the rue Franklin run by the Dominicans, and secondary school at the Collège St. Louis de Gonzague and the Lycée Janson-de-Sailly, all near his home in the sixteenth arrondissement of Paris. For a brief time, his father sent him as an apprentice to one of his shops in Les Andelys to teach him a lesson in self-discipline.[6] It is ironical that as a young adult Philippe would find his way into a career on the cutting edge of the new technologies of computer science, much as his father had gravitated to those of electrical engineering in his own day.

Philippe had a closer, more devoted relationship with his mother Yvonne. Her romantic memories of her childhood inspired him to search for his own, and his sense of the intimate relation between his private sentiments and his public calling owes much to her example.[7] In his first autobiographical essay on his childhood, he invoked the expression *douceur de vie* to convey his love of the imagined communities of old France, much as had his mother. He was influenced by her modest Catholic piety and admired her especially for her loyalty to friends and family, a personal trait he strove to emulate.

Idyllic College Years (1934–39). To compensate for his rocky road through secondary school, Ariès spent a year at the University of Grenoble as a preparation for matriculating at the Sorbonne. Grenoble may have been a choice he negotiated with his parents. It was considered a safe school for conservative Catholic youth. Philippe notes that he studied with Jacques Chevalier, a celebrated philosopher whom anxious conservative parents judged acceptable for the moral formation of their children in such parlous times.[8] He remembered the experience fondly, though his following years at the Sorbonne proved more intellectually liberating. He describes his years as a university student in Paris in the late 1930s as a time of contentment and personal satisfaction. He admired many of his professors. He earned his *licence* in history and geography, then his *diplôme d'études supérieures.* He had an opportunity to write a research thesis, and perhaps more important, to find a niche in a community of like-minded peers. He and his newfound friends studied, socialized, and worked together, and so forged bonds that would endure through their lives. As admiring apostles of the celebrated man of letters Charles Maurras, they edited the student newspaper of the royalist organization Action Française. In this setting, the young Ariès tested his intellectual powers in the public lectures he delivered and the newspaper articles he wrote. He had several love affairs, according to his friend François Leger. But his more enduring romance was with this way of life. On the left bank of Paris in the 1930s, he had discovered a *douceur de vie* of a different order.[9]

The Trials of Coming of Age (1939–47). If Ariès's university years were romantic in his experiences and his expectations, those that followed during the Vichy era called for a more realistic and painful reassessment of his prospects in life. This turn in his fortunes is striking, and an analysis of his way of coping with the transition goes far toward explaining the route he chose into adulthood. His fall from grace was abrupt, marked by academic disappointment. He failed his *agrégation* on his first try in 1939, ordinarily no major setback in those days. But the war with Germany intervened, and he answered the call to arms. He spent the *drôle de guerre* in officer candidate training in the French army (September 1939–August 1940). Demobilized after the armistice, he returned to Paris to study for his exam, only to fail a second time. His inability to satisfy this prerequisite for a career as a professor in the university must have been devastating for him. He tried to make the best of what Vichy had to offer. Its leaders were officially committed to the restoration of old France, a project with which he could identify in principle. He gave Vichy his solid support by participating in its experimental projects for public education in 1941–42. He may early on have been a group leader at one of the *chantiers de la jeunesse,* hastily institutionalized for the training and rehabilitation of French youth.[10] It is certain that he spent several months in early 1942 as an instructor at a Vichy-sponsored college to train their camp leaders, and that he departed disillusioned. In his memoirs he claims to have found the atmosphere at the school bizarre in the Nazi sympathies of its directors, and the Action Française, reconstituted in Lyon, a caricature of its former self.[11]

The war years disabused Ariès of his lingering illusions about the viability of the old style of royalist politics as a means of dealing with the chaotic conditions of France as a defeated and occupied nation. After his disillusioning teaching venture, he sought a different kind of retreat to wait out the war and found it as an archivist (*documentaliste*) in a documentation center that maintained data on commerce in tropical fruit.[12] The job's connection with his overseas heritage should be noted. In a practical way, he was seeking to reconnect with his family's colonial past. His work was not burdensome, and the center gave him a quiet place to rethink his plans and pursue his newfound interest in historical demography in his spare time. He settled into his job early in 1943; he found his research intriguing, a private refuge from the public turmoil around him.

Over the course of the war years, Ariès relinquished his ambitions for a career as a university teacher. At the same time, he deepened his commitment to the study of history. One might say that he privatized it, and in such a way that it acquired even more personal meaning for him. History was not to be his career but rather his vocation. Henceforth he would lead a double life: archivist by day, scholar by night. The old calling among royalist intellectuals to play a role as men of letters in the style of nineteenth-century savants was still open to him, and he may for a time during the postwar years have seen himself in that image. As I have noted, he frequented the salon of Daniel Halévy, who hosted men of letters in the old style. After the war, he became a reader for the publishing house Plon, and over the years served as editor for two important series in modern history.[13] He also returned to political journalism straightway, and in 1946 helped to edit a resurgent right-wing newspaper with Pierre Boutang, his friend in the Action Française in prewar Paris. As he later reflected, the Vichy years were crucial in his formation as a young adult. The old connections with the royalist friends of his days at the Sorbonne were renewed in this postwar foray into political journalism, and they remained firm until the Algerian crisis of the early 1960s.

Habits of Work in Adulthood (1947–60). Ariès forged his identity through his habits of work. These had a public and a private side.

On the public side, he pursued his career as an archivist at the dawn of the electronic revolution. He saw its possibilities and played a leading role in the expansion of the documentation of production and commerce in agriculture overseas, not only in the former French empire, but around the world.[14] He promoted the new technologies for collecting and sorting data, microfilm in the late 1950s, computer software in the early 1970s. His colleagues admired him for his innovations in constructing data bases, his commitment to expanding the scope and utility of the data systems devised, and his futurist vision of a new age of information whose archives would be user-friendly in the way those of the age of print had never been (in France at least). Over time, he took on new responsibilities and became an expert on international organizations in this field. In 1971, he agreed to supervise the making of a data bank of information about agricultural production in the developing world, with applications especially in Latin America and North Africa. During the 1970s, he served a five-year term as president of the International Association of Agricultural Librarians and Archivists and delivered major addresses to their congresses in Luxembourg, Rome, and Mexico City, where he outlined his proposals for the coordination of data in this field. His professional work led him to the far corners of the former French African empire, notably to Algeria, Morocco, Senegal, and Madagascar (which had held a fascination for him since childhood), and farther afield to Mexico and the Philippines. In 1978 he was chosen president of a newly constituted organization for coordinating the documentation of agricultural production in the developing world. The projects he supervised were coordinated with those of the United Nations. Shortly before his retirement in 1979, he launched a project for the formation of a worldwide data bank on tropical agriculture.[15] As a measure of the esteem in which he was held during his lifetime, his colleagues in documentation posthumously renamed the expanded information center he had helped to bring into being in his honor in 1994 as the Centre d'information et de documentation Philippe Ariès.[16]

On the private side, Ariès made his way into a new kind of demographic history. He established professional contacts in this newly emerging field and by the late 1940s had published a book and contributed scholarly articles to its leading professional journal. It was an important, if modest beginning. Working independently and alone, he saw his project as an agenda for further research that would move beyond demography into cultural history. During the 1950s he crossed that divide into a "history of mentalities," which encompassed such subjects as attitudes toward childhood and family, and death and bereavement. His scholarly pursuit of the private side of life might be sketched as a succession of interrelated projects emanating from his insights of the war years, each more panoramic than the last: 1) demography (1943–47), which involved formulating an alternative to the Vichyite perspective on population theory; 2) historiography (1946–54), in which he reflected on the meaning of historical time in light of his newfound appreciation of the scope of history's domain; 3) mentalities from the vantage point of the techniques of life (1954–60), which centered on developmental attitudes toward children within the family; 4) mentalities from that of the techniques of death (1963–74), which concerned changing attitudes toward mourning; and 5) private life (1979–84), which explored the changing understanding of the relationship between public and private life as envisioned and re-visioned in the Western world from antiquity to the present. As the culmination of his work, this last project, conceived as a collaborative venture with his colleagues in this emerging field of cultural history, was the most comprehensive of all. His scholarly achievement here parallels his culminating professional project as an archivist by setting an agenda for further work for his colleagues. He died before he was able to see either project come to fruition. Through it all, his habits of work remained much the same. One colleague at the Ecole des Hautes Etudes mentions the ease with which he could dash off a short article over a lunch break in the midst of a busy workday.[17] His dual life as a pioneer in the making of data bases for the future and a new cultural history of the past is reminiscent of that of the nineteenth-century English polymath John Stuart Mill, who is remembered for his scholarship, not for the professional career as a colonial administrator that occupied so much of his time and energies.

The Sea Change of Middle Age (1960–80). The key to Ariès's fortunes in his mature years turns on a sea change in his scholarly associations. By the late 1960s, his writings on childhood and family had aroused a keen interest among practitioners in the "helping professions" of social work and psychology as well as among university scholars in America. In 1971 he received an invitation from Orest Ranum, an American professor of early modern French history, to lecture at Johns Hopkins University.[18] Their acquaintance soon became a friendship, solidified by Ranum's frequent visits to France, where he had a summer residence in the Aveyron. With Ranum's encouragement, Ariès won a fellowship to study at the Woodrow Wilson Center in Washington, D.C., and subsequently lectured at universities throughout the United States and Canada.[19]

The ironical effect of this American connection was to prompt French scholars to give his work a belated second reading during the 1970s. They treated his new project on the history of attitudes toward death and mourning more seriously than they had his earlier venture on childhood and family. During the late 1970s, Ariès engaged in a running debate with Michel Vovelle, a historian at the University of Aix-en-Provence who was also investigating this subject. In 1977, Ariès was offered and accepted a position at the Ecole des Hautes Etudes, now the institutional home of the Annales movement whose founders he had discovered during the Vichy years. His colleagues there invited him to contribute the article on "mentalities" for their historical dictionary of the expanding interests of their research.[20] By the late 1970s, he was receiving invitations to participate in seminars and colloquia throughout North America and Europe. He brushed up on his English, and he carried on an extensive correspondence with colleagues around the Western world.[21] There was not time for him to pursue the many avenues of research he had launched, and much of his scholarship during the 1970s was cast in the form of short essays in which he revisited topics he had earlier explored. He returned to historiographical issues that he had not addressed directly since his book on historical conceptions of time, *Le Temps de l'Histoire* (1954). He began to explore the private history of his own family's heritage. These last years of his life were marked by close professional relationships and the rewards of recognition for his scholarship. He began to think of ways in which he might pass on his cherished projects to his younger colleagues. He lined up contributors for the multivolume collaborative project on the history of private life that he had planned. All the currents of a lifetime of scholarship were beginning to coalesce when death denied him the opportunity to effect a synthesis.

Reckoning with "One's Own" Mortality (1980–84). Ariès fell victim to colon cancer in the late 1970s and underwent surgery.[22] Primerose was already ill with breast cancer, though she hid the news from him for several years. In 1983 they moved to Toulouse, Primerose's natal home, to which she wanted to return to die. In their last years, they supported each other in growing isolation. Removed from their network of friends, colleagues, and associates in and around Paris, they became closer to and more dependent on friends nearby, notably Patricia and Orest Ranum, then residing in their country retreat in the Aveyron, and Nicole and Yves Castan, professors at the University of Toulouse.

Their preparations for death were intertwined with their collaboration on a last scholarly project, a book of images of death across the ages.[23] It is extraordinary that these historians absorbed for so many years in research on dying and grieving could not talk to each other openly about facing their own. Primerose's illness also created complications for their sojourn at the Wissenschaftskolleg in Berlin during the spring 1983, where Philippe was to prepare for a seminar he was scheduled to direct there in May. They returned to Toulouse as Primerose's condition worsened, though Philippe did go back to Berlin alone for the seminar. Philippe comforted Primerose in her last days. By temperament dismissive of religious piety, she nonetheless underwent a deathbed conversion. Philippe saw it as a divine blessing that he might care for her in her final reckoning with her faith so that they might share a common salvation. She died in August 1983.[24]

The fears and anxieties of facing his own death brought out Philippe's religious feelings more openly. After Primerose's death, he raised religious themes more directly in his conversations and his correspondence with his old friends. He was by this time displaying symptoms of his own physical deterioration, though he denied their importance when together with friends. Leger claims that by then he had come to see the commitments of his life from the vantage point of his own imminent death and that he regretted the absence of references to the divine in his writings. "There are two readings of life," Leger remarked of Ariès's state of mind in his last days, "one material and one spiritual. Philippe Ariès revisited the spiritual reading of his life and with striking illumination perceived that it does not end with the paragraph in which the material reading ceases."[25] Such an image of the last days of Philippe Ariès suggests his return to the transforming dilemmas of the dying in the nineteenth century, of the sort depicted so vividly in the tableaux of the hour of death by Roger Martin du Gard in his novel *Jean Barois*. Philippe died on 8 February 1984. He was buried beside his wife at Castelnaudary, southeast of Toulouse.

Signatures of an *Ego-Histoire*

When Philippe Ariès was a young man courting his future wife in the years immediately after the war, he sent her a copy of an essay he had recently composed entitled "A Child Discovers History" (1946) in the hope that it

might give her a better sense of what the study of history meant to him.
He wanted to show her that history, more than a pastime, was his vocation,
the source of his deepest convictions about the human experience.[26] Life
under Vichy had exercised its unsettling effects, and he had become more
reflective about the personal meaning his historical inquiry into the secrets
of everyday life held for him. The fall of France, the ill-fated Vichy experiment, the German Occupation, the purges of collaborators in the war's
aftermath now prompted him to rethink his understanding of history from
the vantage point of his newfound circumstances. As a witness to (and in
some ways a victim of) the disruptions, privations, havoc, and moral compromises of France's humiliating subjugation to the Third Reich, he cast
his own story within the broader historical pageant of the French people
that he sensed was underway. The war years, he claimed, had made him
aware of the scope and momentum of the historical change that was in
process, and of the parochial nature of his prewar concerns in the debates
and struggles of the Action Française. The war had wrested him from the
royalist "oasis" in which he had formed his impressions of history. Through
his observations of the ordeal of the French people during the war years,
he had come to think of History—to which he now referred with a ref-
erential capital H—not as a series of political events, but rather as the
relentless tide of human experience considered in its broadest terms, shaping us against our wishes and in ways we can never fully understand. The
ready-made royalist political history that had formed his historical conceptions as a child and even as a university student addressed in a limited
way only a moment in historical time, and one that had now passed by.
Such a parochial conception of history provided no usable framework for
understanding the realities of the contemporary age as they intruded into
the everyday lives of ordinary people. Having glimpsed the force of History
in the disruptions it had worked in his own life, he was better able to
appreciate its effects on others, and so to begin his ruminations on a kind
of social history he had never studied before.

Ariès initially referred to his still inchoate conception of a history of the
human experience in a private world apart from public life as "existential
history."[27] But he recognized that the awareness of such a divide itself had
a historical beginning, somewhere in the dawn of the early modern era.
From the sixteenth century forward, he hypothesized, people began to
make a distinction, quite tentative at first, between the public and private
spheres of their lives. Historians of the modern era had concentrated on
the former, leaving the latter to folklorists. But Ariès recognized that the
sphere of privacy was one in which ordinary people in the modern world

The Ariès children: Philippe, Jacques, Georges, Marie-Rose (circa 1926)

Philippe among friends at Arcachon (Gironde), summer 1937. Philippe is standing; his future wife Primerose sits before him; François Leger is seated, second from the right.

Philippe with his parents and siblings, 1940s

Philippe, with the women of his immediate family:
from the left, Marie-Rose, Yvonne, Primerose, 1940s

Philippe, resting in a chaise longue, 1940s

increasingly invested their hopes and ambitions, and so was worthy of the historians' attention. It was to this unexplored realm, he explained to his prospective bride, that he planned to direct his attention as a historian.

"A Child Discovers History," which became the lead essay for *Le Temps de l'Histoire,* was Ariès's proclamation as a young man that history was his vocation. In the profession of faith with which he concluded that essay, he mused on the relationship between his poetical intuition of history as a child and his critical perspective as an adult. "I wonder," he speculated, "if the modern historian, late in his career, when he has withstood all of the temptations to succumb to the desiccating science the world demands, does not arrive at a vision of History quite close to that which the child experiences."[28] In a naïve way, his remark suggests his understanding of his vocation as a hermeneutical inquiry. His poetical intuitions as an ingenuous child acceded to his critical perspective as a learned adult. But the insight of the former remained the inspiration that motivated his pursuit of the latter.

Ariès's essay may have been unusually forthcoming about his private convictions. But in all of his writings he leaves signatures that mark the secrets of the personal meaning he invested in the study of history. They lead us toward his particular preoccupations—his curiosity about his family heritage, his interest in traditional conceptions of community, his loyalty to his friends, his private convictions about faith and commitment, his identification of death with destiny, and his dedication to history as vocation. I pay particular attention to Ariès's path into history in light of these autobiographical references. It prepares the way for my larger assessment of his place in French historiography in the late twentieth century. These personal reflections help us to read his moral compass and to take a more exact measure of his intellectual convictions. They deepen our understanding of his vocation as a historian. They provide clues to his intuitions about the human condition. Here are some of the themes whose signatures appear and reappear in his historical writings:

The Heritage of His Extended Family. Although the roots of his immediate family were in Martinique, Ariès puts more emphasis in his memoirs on the sources of his extended family's culture in southwestern France. He recounts fond memories of a childhood in which he had extensive contact with his larger family on summer vacations in Bordeaux, the seaside town of Arcachon (where his father built a villa), and the hinterlands of the Gironde. He was particularly taken with his maternal grandfather Henry, the émigré *bricoleur,* courtly in his devotion to old-fashioned family rituals.

As a child, Philippe accompanied him on visits to friends and family in their ancestral homes in and around the city. These served as his introduction to traditional sociability. He also knew the surrounding countryside. His paternal grandmother's family had owned a country property near Langoiran in the Médoc region of the Gironde. Southwestern France, Philippe observed, was a conservatory of the mores of old France that one could still readily observe. Familial, fraternal, and regional communities held on there. Their old-fashioned cultural structures remained intact, particularly in the networks of tradition-minded families such as his own.

The members of Ariès's extended family were in varying echelons of accomplishment descendants of the provincial bourgeoisie, and their political allegiances were to the Orleanist dynasty. His was a traditional family with maiden aunts and bachelor uncles who played at life for want of serious vocations. In recent times, his family had produced a few noteworthy royalists with political aspirations. His uncle Nel Ariès had organized a section of the Action Française in southwestern France in the early twentieth century, while a cousin, Germaine Mauriette, had been a close associate of Marc Sangnier in the progressive Catholic social movement, the Sillon. On the whole, Ariès claims, men in the family tended to have been genteel failures, charming in their manners but ineffectual in their careers. Observing the contrast between their aimless old-fashioned lives and the ambitious ones led by his own royalist friends from school and university in Paris, he noted how striking were the differences between the social world into which he had been born and the one into which he was making his way.[29]

From an early age, Ariès recognized that his family's memories of its heritage freely mixed fact and legend. These childhood sojourns in the Gironde nonetheless secured his own sentimental appreciation of the traditions of his larger family, even if they came clothed in an idealized folklore. They inspired the social values that sustained him throughout his life. His royalism was grounded there, a commitment to a way of life and a culture rather than a politics. The royal family in the present age, he suggested, symbolized the value of family life generally, and it is no surprise to learn that his first exercise in history as an adolescent had been to construct an elaborate genealogical tree of the French royal family.[30]

At the same time, it would be a mistake to portray Ariès as lost in his family's naïve allegiance to old France. He was too aware of the reality of significant change in the present to fix his commitments on timeless values, as did so many of his comrades in the Action Française. His concern, rather, was that contemporary French people were losing their connection with their heritage as embodied in tradition, and so were vulnerable to a loss of a sense of their place in time. Ariès affirmed the need to relate his cherished past to an anticipated future.[31] In this respect, the appeal of old France for him resided more in the nineteenth than in the seventeenth century. He tended to view the nineteenth century as a golden age in its blending of the old social mores with the new. Such references to the nineteenth century appear in his writings in many manifestations: the ideal of lifelong marriage, the nuclear family nested within the extended one, the tolerance of the Catholic clergy toward heterodox expressions of popular piety, the open avenues between the rural and the urban worlds.

If Ariès's roots were in the provinces, his life was in the city of Paris. Until well into middle age, he lived in an apartment in the well-to-do sixteenth arrondissement in which his parents had settled. He retained an affection for the "old city" of Paris, in which both children and adults had room to play, though in his later years he identified the gregarious neighborhood more often with Naples.[32] He turned in his research to the historical uses of urban space because of his concern about the deteriorating quality of social life in the contemporary city.[33]

One of Ariès's last research projects was a history of his own family. Except for his essay on his mother's childhood in Martinique, none of this work was ever published. His friends Yves and Nicole Castan, however, note that he succeeded in tracing his lineage back to the sixteenth century, where his family tree disappeared into a myriad of diverse branches, confirming his quasi-religious notion about the mystery of ancestry as it descends toward what ultimately become untraceable sources.[34]

Small Communities as Models for Making the Good Society. Ariès was intrigued with the traditional conception of community, organized around small groups based on personal ties. His social ideal was a community large enough to extend beyond kin networks, yet small enough to foster the values of mutual trust and civic responsibility. Ariès's earliest writings focus on this theme. His thesis for his *diplôme d'études supérieures* at the Sorbonne concerned the personal ties within the judicial corps of Paris in the sixteenth century.[35] He argued that this professional network of magistrates, lawyers, and their entourage used their corporative solidarity wisely in the administration of justice. The possibility of reinventing such traditional corporatism in his own time appealed to him as a young man in the Action Française, and he envisioned practical applications for it after the fall of France. During the Vichy years, he gave much thought to the notion of regional identity. His first book, *Les Traditions sociales dans les pays de France* (1943) was a history of regional differences, but with an emphasis on how such a decentralized society might be revived under Vichy. The political indifference of Vichy's leaders to the possibility of implementing such a federalism was a major factor in his disillusionment with that regime.

If Ariès was sympathetic to this old-fashioned conception of community, he was not insensitive to the rapidly changing society in which he lived. In his newspaper articles from the 1930s to the 1960s, he placed the changes of the contemporary age in historical perspective. This was a time in which French society was undergoing a modernizing transformation on several planes. The rural society of villages and small towns was relinquishing its way of life, as its youth fled to the expanding cities to seek their fortunes. The tenacious influence of the agricultural economy, lingering longer in France than in other western European countries, was at last giving way to the dynamic new urban economy driven by the power and money of industrial production. The old-fashioned rough-and-tumble politics of rural notables and small-town clerks was being supplanted by the sophisticated new managerial style of a well-educated elite, products of an expanding system of *grandes écoles* that trained for public service. At risk, he believed, were the small-scale communities that the old way of life had once embraced. Their passing, he suggested, signaled a profound change in social mores. The new model of public life brought with it a more intrusive state that prided itself on its efficiency and organizational oversight. But it also contributed to the emergence of a new model of private life that cultivated intimacy, affection, and personal identity, especially within the context of the family. This emerging distinction between public and private life, he argued, had grown so wide over time that it undercut the traditional forms of social intercourse that enabled communities to function in harmonious and humane ways.

Sociability as the Light Side of Personal Loyalty. Sociability for Ariès was about the present, not just the past, and friendship ranked near the top of the hierarchy of social values that mattered to him. Close and affectionate relationships with kindred spirits were central to his conception of the good life. He cultivated friendships and continued to make new friends all his life. He liked to flatter others. In keeping with his gregarious nature, he enjoyed informal intellectual exchange. His colleagues remember him for his mirth. He had a profound sense of loyalty to friends and family, a virtue he believed to be in short supply in the contemporary world. In his autobiography, he hints at a secret compact among his friends from the

Sorbonne during the 1930s.[36] They continued to interact closely in their shared participation in political journalism in behalf of right-wing causes and stayed at the task until the early 1960s. Over time, Ariès built other networks of friends, one among the intellectuals who frequented Daniel Halévy's gatherings, another among professors as he was drawn into university circles in his later years. In taking the measure of his appeal as a historian, one must not discount his considerable personal charm.

The High Ideal of Indissoluble Marriage. Marriage for Ariès was also about long-term friendship and the profound bonds that its intimacy promotes. He liked to think of his own in that way, and it provides a clue to his historical interest in the concept of "indissoluble marriage" and its vulnerability in the contemporary age. In 1947, he married Marie-Rose (Primerose) Lascazas de Saint-Martin. They had been acquainted since adolescence and were distant cousins. In his memoirs, Philippe describes their shared experiences of research and travel, but has little to say about the nature of their relationship. Their friends and colleagues confirm their close personal harmony, but also remark on the eccentricity of their relationship given the sharp differences in their personalities. Primerose was punctilious, highly organized, obsessive about decorum. She prided herself on a rational and scientific stance on life in imitation of her father, a prominent physician in Toulouse, and she took little interest in religion. Philippe, by contrast, was more spontaneous and informal, in keeping with his love of conversation and his penchant for laughter among friends and colleagues. He held a more romantic attitude toward life and displayed more sympathy for religious piety. Somewhat uneasy with each other at the outset of their marriage, their friends report, they became remarkably attuned over time, deeply intuitive of the other's needs and interests. To those who knew them well in their later years, they were an indissoluble unit.[37] In his late-life writings, Philippe makes references to legends of great loves across the ages, and one gets the sense that these images lived on in his own. The secrets of marital intimacy, moreover, may have been the intuition that led Philippe to his insight as a demographer into the hidden revolution in birth control practices in seventeenth-century France. It is worth noting that he formulated his thesis about the time of his own marriage. Ironically, this couple, so closely identified with the history of childhood, had no children of their own.

Living with One's Mortality. Ariès's attitude toward death was closely tied to his intuitions about human destiny. For him, death is the ending that defines the nature of our search for meaning in life. He himself mused on this theme for much of his adult life, and early on sought a historical perspective on it. In one of his first newspaper articles, written in the late 1930s, he recounts the passage from Fyodor Dostoevsky's *Brothers Kara-mazov* concerning the edifying death of Markel, the elder brother of Father Zossima, surrounded by friends and family.[38] It became the model of his depiction of the "tamed death" (*la mort apprivoisée*) of traditional society in his later writings on the subject. This reflection may have been inspired by the death of his grandparents at about the same time. A decade later, he recalls his grief over the death of his brother Jacques on the battlefield in the last days of the war as his first traumatic encounter with death's existential reality. Such reflections played into his first inquiry into the "techniques of death" in connection with his demographic studies, and would later become the subject of his major scholarly project on historical attitudes toward death and mourning. In his later years, his thoughts on death as destiny for the present age stressed modesty of expectation, in contrast with the more extravagant hopes for spiritual salvation of his ancestors. At the same time, he liked the trappings of old-fashioned attitudes about coming to terms with one's mortality gracefully. As he grew older, he favored black clothing in imitation of the practice of those over fifty in traditional French society, a memento of one's acceptance of human mortality. Such a gesture serves as a clue to deep feelings hidden beneath his outgoing personality and his ongoing zest for life, for his last years were his most productive and rewarding as a scholar.

The Consolations of Religious Faith. Ariès was a religious believer, though the nature of his convictions is not easily deciphered. He thought of religious attitudes in terms of tacit understandings, and he put his accent on piety rather than theology. He was a practicing Catholic in a nondogmatic way. Though educated by the clergy, he could be critical of them, especially of the posturing of their more progressive element during the 1950s and 1960s. This was the era of the Second Vatican Council, and he read *Le Monde,* with its liberal Catholic leanings, every day for examples of religious innovations that vexed him. From his perspective, these progressives wanted to project the meaning of religion into the future, whereas he preferred to associate its consolations with the past. Our religious sentiments, he allowed, well forth in our acknowledgment of the mystery of a hidden past that beckons us to search out its secrets. It fills us with childlike awe to the end of our lives. We do not choose our religious heritage, he remarked. We are born into it, and it is nourished (or not) as children by our parents. We may choose to cultivate it as adults by observing its customary rituals and prayers. In this respect, he was sad to see the passing of the old rites of the Catholic Church, notably the use of Latin in the Christian Mass. He had no use for new liturgical fashions and viewed prophets of a reformed church such as Hans Kung with suspicion. Nor had he any patience with theological speculation, and he found the cult of Pierre Teilhard de Chardin that gained such popularity during the 1950s to be absurd.[39]

Ariès's appreciation of religion, therefore, mixed piety toward Catholic traditions with skepticism about modernizing them in socially fashionable or politically progressive ways. His deepest religious beliefs were intertwined with his sense of history. He argued that the historical nature of the human condition is itself a basis for religious belief. One of his key working concepts for approaching the history of mentalities was that of a "collective unconscious," which he construed as the tacit understandings that link us in the present with the practical wisdom of our ancestors. As he argued in "A Child Discovers History," he stood with humility in the face of History conceived as the unknown past. His inspiration to study history was his desire to recapture "that lost Eden" of which intimations survived in immemorial tradition.[40]

Autobiographical Reflections

As he gained public recognition during the 1970s, Ariès began to divulge more explicit details about his personal life in interviews with the press and magazines of commentary.[41] These culminated in his interview with Michel Winock, which served as the basis for his autobiography, *Un Historien du dimanche* (1980). As the reminiscences of an old man about the highlights of his life, it complements the "A Child Discovers History" essay that he had written in young adulthood. It provides his critical assessment of how his intuitions had played out along the way.

Ariès's autobiography spoke to his readers in a variety of ways.[42] In the years immediately following its publication, he received letters from old friends and acquaintances from different stages of his life, admirers of his journalistic and historical writings, and new enthusiasts who converged in their appreciation of a memoir in which he linked his personal makeup to his interests as a historian and his scholarship to his pursuit of life's meaning.[43] Some mentioned the courage of such an exposé within a profession that traditionally had carefully bracketed authorial intention. Ariès showed his readers that they might appreciate a historian as one would a writer, a poet, or an artist—for personal perspectives on the human predicament. One might argue that Ariès displayed a candor that appealed to the late twentieth century in a way analogous to that of Jean-Jacques Rousseau in the late eighteenth.[44] Ariès never aspired to Rousseau's transparency. But across a boundary between private and public life whose historical nature he was the first to define, he did convey a sense of honesty about himself and his path into history that beckoned his colleagues to cross that divide themselves. Over the following decade, the most prestigious among them began to imitate his model by publishing confessional memoirs of their own. By the late 1980s *ego-histoire* had become a popular genre among readers of French history. Among the historians themselves, composing such a work had become an announcement that one had arrived.[45]

From a historiographical perspective, *ego-histoire* signified the distancing of historians from the schools of historical writing with which they had identified for the better part of the twentieth century. Royalism and Marxism had been major emblems of such allegiance early in the century, and the Annales movement might be regarded as a last major expression of professional solidarity among French historians. With the weakening of ideological allegiances among historians amidst the diversification of their interests in the late twentieth century, collective identification under particular historiographical banners lost its appeal. With the growth and diversification of the historical profession in France, the power of patronage its most illustrious practitioners had once dispensed diminished significantly. Historians were choosing to go their own ways, priding themselves on their independence of mind. In their personal reflections on their paths into history, though, many reminisced fondly about their apprenticeship in one ideological movement or another. In this respect, Ariès was prototypical in breaking free of the ideological commitments of his youth, though atypical in his independent journey toward recognition of his work. Earlier than the others, he had meditated on the personal factors that had contributed to his formation as a historian. While *ego-histoire* was a phenomenon of the 1980s, Ariès had anticipated the genre in the autobiographical sketch of the circumstances and convictions that had led him into history some forty years before.[46]

3

The Politics of a
Young Royalist

The Two Journeys of Philippe Ariès in Vichy France

IN HIS AUTOBIOGRAPHY, written in 1980, Philippe Ariès, by then a member of the faculty of the Ecole des Hautes Etudes, evokes a tableau of his discovery of the writings of the Annales historians during the dark days of Vichy France, when Paris was under the Occupation. Conscripted immediately at the outset of the war in September 1939 and as precipitously demobilized after the armistice of June 1940, he returned to Paris, his life disrupted and his plans for the future uncertain. Still hoping to pass his *agrégation,* the qualifying examination for an appointment to the university faculty, he turned once more to his studies in history. Since classes at the Sorbonne were few, he spent his days beneath the high, vaulted ceilings of the beautiful reading room at the Bibliothèque Nationale. "I lived at the Bibliothèque Nationale as if it were a monastery," he reminisced years later.[1] There he first read the works of Marc Bloch and Lucien Febvre, who during the 1930s had pioneered a new kind of social history not yet appreciated within the university, and of Maurice Halbwachs, a sociologist of the Durkheim school whose investigations of social structures were poignantly ignored in the intellectual circles of the extreme right in which he moved. These readings fired his imagination as a historian, just as the legends of Capetian kings and their courtiers had first kindled his interest in his nation's past when he had been a child.

To Ariès, writing his memoirs from the vantage point of his latter-day integration into the everyday world of the Annalistes, the point of departure for this intellectual journey seemed clear. The Bibliothèque Nationale had been a refuge in which he had salvaged something good from the terrible times of France during the Second World War. In this retrospective view, the Vichy years had been a moratorium, and in an ironical way a fortunate fall from the comfortable milieu that he had known as a student during the 1930s and in which he had nurtured his affection for a royalist politics and culture in which he then fervently believed. Paradoxically, the disruptions in his life permitted him to discover a new kind of history, and his openness to its possibilities was an important step in his move toward intellectual maturity.[2] He later speculated about the predictable career as a competent but conventional history professor he might have pursued but for this turn in his fortunes. "I would have become a university historian . . . somewhere not far from Roland Mousnier and his school. With a little luck, I would be teaching at Paris IV," he quipped.[3] "That is why the year 1940–1941 was crucial in my development," he later explained.[4]

But long days at the Bibliothèque Nationale are only part of the story of Ariès's formation as a historian during the Vichy years. For all the charm of the tableau that he conjures up for our appreciation, his sojourn there was comparatively brief and unsuccessful in terms of his immediate objective. In 1941 he failed his *agrégation* for a second time. Shortly thereafter, in the winter of 1941/42, he made another journey, this one out of Paris north to La Chapelle-en-Serval, a chateau enclave in the valley of the Oise River, surrounded by the forests of Senlis.[5] There he took up a post at the newly established Ecole Nationale des Cadres Supérieurs. If his idyll at the Bibliothèque Nationale had been a refuge from the war, his tenure as an instructor at La Chapelle was his moment of *engagement* in the project of Vichy leaders to promote a new kind of education for the youth of France.[6]

In his memoir, Ariès discusses the experience with candor but makes light of its importance.[7] But this observation was offered forty years after the fact, when the Annales school launched by Bloch and Febvre had established its historiographical preeminence and Vichy's educational projects were enshrouded in shame. His remarks do not adequately explain his motives at the time. In its way, this experience as a teacher at La Chapelle was as important in his formation as a historian as had been his halcyon days at the Bibliothèque Nationale. If the Annales historians had acquainted him with new historical methods, the concerns of his colleagues in the Ecole des Cadres prompted him to consider historical topics about everyday life that would preoccupy him for the rest of his life. He stayed at La Chapelle for some six to eight months, about the same length of time that he had spent at the Bibliothèque Nationale preparing for his examinations.

From what we now know of the Ecole des Cadres at La Chapelle, Ariès had thrown in his lot with one of the most radical educational experiments promoted by the new Vichy regime. La Chapelle was a school for the training of the teachers and directors of the youth camps (*chantiers de la jeunesse*) recently established by the Vichy government. It was the lesser-known counterpart in France's occupied zone to the Ecole d'Uriage in its free zone. Both schools were key institutions in Vichy's project for coping with France's newfound status as a defeated nation. They stood at the apex of a hastily designed apparatus to prepare youth for the new moral order envisioned by the Vichy head of state, Philippe Pétain, the aging hero of the First World War upon whose shoulders had fallen the responsibility of leading a defeated and occupied nation. France's future, Pétain believed, lay in the education of the generation of French youth that was coming of age to a new sense of its civic responsibilities.[8] The écoles des cadres stood at the top echelon of the institutional hierarchy created to accomplish this task. One of their purposes was practical—to train unemployed youth for places in the work force. The other was moral—to inspire them to take up the civic responsibility of restoring the self-esteem of France as a nation. The écoles des cadres were intended to serve as an alternative to the regular educational system, which had been a mainstay of the Third Republic and was resistant to accepting Pétain's vision of France's destiny. The directors of the écoles, therefore, recruited both their faculty and their students from among outsiders to the university system. Ariès's first and until late in life only experience as a teacher came via this route.[9]

The Ecole d'Uriage, established shortly after the creation of the new regime, has recently been reappraised by several historians as a noble experiment in educational reform.[10] The Ecole de la Chapelle, by contrast, has a less savory reputation, for it is tainted with the stigma of collaboration.[11] Uriage sought to refurbish a unique identity for France; La Chapelle was more disposed to favor an educational system that would emulate that of Nazi Germany. The founder and for a time director of La Chapelle was Jacques Bousquet. *Agregé ès lettres,* he had been a teacher of grammar at the Lycée Voltaire in Paris before the war. He was a man of personal strength, energy, and ambition. He was also an opportunist. For him, the German Occupation offered a chance to explore alternatives to the Third Republic, which he blamed for France's ruin. Immediately upon the naming of Pétain as head of state in June 1940, Bousquet founded a youth movement, les Jeunes du Maréchal, to boost support for the regime.[12] He was a protégé of Abel Bonnard, minister of education under Vichy, and his project for the Ecole at La Chapelle, launched in late 1941, was the most important among several ventures he pursued to promote a revolution in the French educational system.[13]

Ariès makes particular mention of Bousquet's seductive charm. He describes him as a university man, a dilettante, an excellent pianist. "He replaced the Catholicism and spirit of Péguy of Uriage with a Nietzschean romanticism that rendered him vulnerable to the magic of Hitler's Germany," he commented.[14] Bousquet admired the dynamism of national socialism, and looked for ways to inspire like sentiments in French youth.[15] He was particularly taken with the model of the German Free Corps that operated in the Baltic after Germany's defeat in World War I, and he envisioned that a similar French movement might renew France's imperialist role in Africa. In time, he found Pétain's policies too cautious and defensive. Indeed, his pro-German sentiments came to alarm officials in Vichy's Ministry of Youth, who in 1942 described him in official correspondence as a neo-pagan, hostile to Christianity and increasingly cool toward Pétain's leadership.[16]

Bousquet ran the school much like a military college. The students were kept busy all day long with classes and manual labor. They wore uniforms and learned close-order drill. Instructors were addressed as "chief" (*chef*). A physical education program, which included long hikes in the surrounding forests, was an integral part of the curriculum.[17] According to Ariès, Bousquet himself dabbled in Celtic folklore in his search for the deep sources of the French spirit, and its mysteries were a subject of after-dinner discussion among the faculty. Such a program might seem as innocuous as the Scout movement but for Bousquet's desire to bring French educational policy into line with German thinking. Here he was aided by his second-in-command, Philippe Lavastine, who succeeded him as director of the school in June 1942 when he himself moved on to the Ministry of Education. Lavastine, like Bousquet, was an enthusiast for educational and intellectual collaboration with Nazi Germany. He participated in ventures to promote Franco-German cultural exchange and contributed to the review *Deutschland-Frankreich*.[18] Also mentioned in official reports from the school's director was Chief Heller. This may have been Gerhard Heller, a cultivated, French-speaking German army officer with responsibilities for cultural liaison in Paris. His course focused on "Jewish problems" and dealt with such themes as the biological foundations of culture, demographic weakness, eugenics, and the protection of the French race.[19] There were some thirty instructors in all, none of particular notoriety, though Ariès mentions that two later became well-known university professors.[20]

To the historian's good fortune, records of the program at La Chapelle, including nine course syllabi for the long-term internship, remain intact at the Archives Nationales.[21] From these we may reconstruct a fairly complete profile of the curriculum of the school under Bousquet's leadership.

Bousquet himself set forth its objectives in detailed memoranda to the Ministry of Education early in 1942. His program included plans for long-term as well as short-term internships (*stages*). The curriculum was designed around civics lessons for the new moral order, dressed up as studies in history and literature.[22] It embodied three principal themes:

An Education for Activism. Bousquet's curriculum was designed to inculcate a sense of duty through an authoritarian formation. It also professed to teach principles of leadership through practical training in public speaking and the dissemination of propaganda. As he pointed out, this was an education for the average citizen of reasonable intelligence and motivation, not for sports heroes or intellectuals. One theater he proposed for this activism was France's empire overseas—in anticipation of France's renewed role there once its place in Hitler's new European order had been regularized.[23]

The Importance of Racial Anthropology. Bousquet called for an education that would cement the German-French connection in the new European order. It would pay attention to themes central to national socialist ideology. He proposed studies for a "new conception of man" that acknowledged psychological and racial differences as they had developed historically.[24] Many lectures were to be devoted to the topic of racial anthropology, with special attention to the status of Jews. At La Chapelle antisemitism was outspoken, and Jews were prohibited from membership on the faculty or admission to the school's programs. The school itself was housed on a property confiscated from its Jewish owners.[25]

History Reconceived. History was the glue that held the curriculum together. All the instructors addressed historical issues in light of the possibilities for reinterpretation that France's recent defeat raised. Bousquet's scheme called for the reconsideration of the meaning of history from the perspective of the present. Teaching history at La Chapelle, therefore, meant revising its conventional presentation. For the champions of Vichy's national revolution, the past held a different meaning from that taught in the schools of the Third Republic.[26] The history conceptualized by the professors of that regime, a history of the rise of liberalism and the making of democracy out of ideals enunciated during the French Revolution, was to be invalidated. Vichy France required a different genealogy, and its instructors at La Chapelle traced an alternate route to its sources in France's deep historical heritage. The lectures they devised provided an interesting mix of contemporary and ancient history calculated to reveal the hidden meaning of France's many-faceted past. Particular attention was given to the nature of revolution, even though the French Revolution was conspicuously ignored.

Here is where Ariès fit in. He had little influence on the school's policies, but he was a mainstay of the instructional staff in history. At twenty-eight, he was comparatively young. His duties were varied. He taught camp instructors in the long-term internship, but he is also listed as having lectured to primary school children. He also had at least a marginal connection with the Jeunes du Maréchal, Bousquet's movement for adolescents that was by then proselytizing in lycées in various parts of the country.[27] For the encampment of this group at the school in April 1942, Ariès lectured on regional exploration, a practical method for understanding the decentralized country that France might become.[28]

The syllabus for Ariès's course in the long-term internship (see figure 2) was one of the documents that Bousquet forwarded with his curricular program to the Ministry of Education.[29] Even though it is only an outline, the syllabus reveals Ariès's early thinking about how the grand scheme of history might be reconceived. Indeed, the theme of his first lecture was the history of history, a preface to his repudiation of the interpretation of the course and meaning of modern history taught in the universities of the Third Republic.[30] Herein we find his first reference to the ideas about historiography that he would develop into *Le Temps de l'Histoire* after the war.[31] In that book he mentions the way in which he questioned his students at La Chapelle about their memories of their own heritage, testimonies about local social histories sheltered from the force of the more imposing political history that was presently shaking the foundations of their nation. In the spirit of starting over, of reconsidering historical issues from the vantage point of present circumstances, he was already thinking about the neglected histories of ordinary people in their everyday lives, so different from the conventional grand narrative of France's past.[32]

Ariès's views were attuned to those of Bousquet to the extent that he conceived of the present age as a time for the reconsideration of the reigning conception of history taught in the public educational system because of its sources in republican ideology. His course for the long-term internship centered on a historical critique of the liberalism that had served as the ideological underpinning of France's republican tradition. Liberalism was an English invention, he proposed, and corporatism was its French alternative. Extrapolating from his outline, we may surmise that he pitted English liberalism, whose fortunes he believed to be in decline, against

FIGURE 2. Program of the Ecole Nationale des Cadres Supérieurs à La Chapelle-en-Serval (Oise), for the six-month internship, April–October 1942 (prepared 17 June 1942)

Instructors: Jacques Bousquet, Philippe Lavastine, Heller, Jean Roy, Grau, Ariès, Parias, Etievan

Sequence of lectures for the course offered by Philippe Ariès:

1) The history of history: Titus Livy, Bossuet, Taine
2) Modern conceptions of history—the abuse of erudition—the constants of history
3) The nation in the science of modern history
4) Liberalism—its English origins—liberalism and capitalism
5) The end of liberalism—the foundations of the new state as outlined in the initial speeches of the Marshal [Pétain]
6) Economic liberalism and its transformations at the beginning of the twentieth century
7) The committees of organization
8) The idea of corporatism across the nineteenth century—the different schools [of thought]
9) The Charter of Work
10) French demography
11) The transformations of the colonial ideal in the nineteenth century
12) The elements of empire
13) Present-day problems of the [French] Empire: the new exotic powers
14) The French Empire and the political and economic compartmentalization of the planet
15) The French Empire and autarchy

French nationalism, which he portrayed as the leading ideology of the present.[33] For Ariès, this nationalist ideology turned on the pillars of corporatism within France and imperialism in French spheres of influence overseas. He traced the rise of corporatism from the nineteenth century, which found its fulfillment in the Charter of Work (*Charte du Travail*) ordained by Pétain's government in 1941.[34]

Ariès offered some five lectures on the colonial ideal and the French empire, with references to historical stages in the economic and political division of the world. His close attention to this topic is the biggest surprise in his syllabus, for it is not one that he later pursued as a historian.[35] It does, however, have links with his own family's colonial heritage in the French West Indies and with the career he would subsequently choose in the colonial milieu. Indeed, he got his lead for the job he took in 1943 as the director of a documentation center for tropical fruit through contacts made at La Chapelle.[36] Far from being an oddity, as Fernand Braudel once surmised in poking fun at him as a "banana merchant," his job was a memento of his own dream of France's role overseas.[37]

Ariès also makes tantalizing mention of a lecture on French demography. There is no telling from his syllabus how he approached the subject. But it makes clear that he was already at this early date intellectually preoccupied with the topic that would eventually lead him into the history of collective mentalities. Demography was a major theme of discussion at La Chapelle. There, as in intellectual circles of Vichy sympathizers generally, the decay of the French population was believed to be at the heart of France's sudden defeat.[38]

It is not clear when Ariès departed from La Chapelle. In his autobiographical memoir, he mentions that many instructors left the school at the time of the formation of the second Laval ministry (April 1942), and he may have been among them.[39] But documents from the Ecole itself suggest that Ariès stayed on. He was still officially listed as an instructor in June in a variety of the school's programs.[40] It is likely that he left sometime in the summer or early fall, as the school fell on hard times. Launching such a venture had proven to be infinitely more difficult in practice than in design. Reportedly, the drop-out rate from the first internship was high, and recruitment for the second long-term internship did not fare well. By then Bousquet had moved on to the Ministry of Education, though he tried to micromanage the school from a distance through his successor Lavastine.[41] The ministry replaced their leadership at the school completely later in the year. Bousquet's venture had failed for lack of support, time, or enthusiasm for its objectives on the part of the students.

Ariès, then, was among those recruited to serve what was the most direct and obvious effort to refashion education in France along lines attuned to the German Nazi model. My purpose is not to identify Ariès with the collaborationist attitudes of the educational reformers at La Chapelle. There is no evidence to suggest that he shared the pro-German sentiments of Bousquet and others on his staff. There is no mention in his syllabus of race or eugenics, and certainly no expression of sympathy for German imperialism or national socialism. But he was teaching in a school that was the leading wedge of collaborationist indoctrination in Vichy France. One cannot avoid asking questions about what he was doing there.

One must put Ariès's decision to participate in this educational experiment in perspective. There are some obvious short-range factors. The coming of the Vichy era had precipitated a crisis in his dissatisfactions. He had for some time been critical of the educational system of the Third Republic, particularly the teaching of history. He turned to this theme in an article he wrote for *L'Etudiant français* shortly before the war. The history curriculum, he charged, was specialized and technical. It abdicated its responsibility to nurture in the young a capacity for moral judgment. It focused almost exclusively on modern political history. It reduced ancient and early modern history to a litany of royal genealogies, thereby ignoring the history of popular culture to be found in the customary fabric of everyday life.[42] The young Ariès was searching for some alternative that would illuminate the heritage of traditional French society. Herein his appreciation of the lectures on regional history by his professors at the Sorbonne, as well as the spate of books on the subject during the 1930s, provided him with concrete models for interpreting social and cultural topics neglected in the national histories. Still, he envisioned such curricular innovation within the intellectual framework of his conservative formation. It is worth noting that from the prewar years into the Vichy era, Ariès participated in the activities of the Cercle Fustel-de-Coulanges, a society dedicated to preserving a curriculum for higher education that gave priority to the traditional claims of classics and the humanities over new approaches in the social sciences. The Cercle included a number of intellectuals who would become key figures in public education and intellectual life under the Vichy regime.[43]

Then, too, Ariès failed his *agrégation* twice. One wonders why. His sister Marie-Rose remarks upon his nervous sensibility. He became flustered under this kind of pressure, she suggests, and did not always do his best.[44] His friends assert that he was too independent-minded to give the stock answers the examiners expected.[45] The subtext of this claim is that his republican examiners may have found his royalist bias too strident. The consequences of failing such an examination were not then of the moment that they are today. Many failed, and one could always try again. Ariès might have, but for the war. As it was, this disappointment must have contributed to his uncertainties about his future. After his second failure, he was offered an appointment as a professor at the lycée at Rennes, which he considered a forlorn outpost.[46] La Chapelle was close by, a consideration in times in which families were thrown back on mutual support for the essentials of everyday life. Moreover, what was there to lose in such an adventure?

Finally, the personality of Bousquet himself ought not to be discounted.

Herein we confront a psychological issue, and it may be the most important one of all. Ariès had a tendency all his life to be drawn into ventures to which he was not completely committed by virtue of his attachment to forceful personalities. It is the reverse medal of what was one of his most attractive traits: his loyalty to his family, friends, and heritage. His "particular friendships," in this case his choice of mentors, sometimes led him into political activities with which he did not completely identify. Such *fidélité* is a key to Ariès's politics. It helps us to understand not only why he lingered at La Chapelle, but why he conceived of his political ideal as he did: as an extension of the solidarity that sustained the network of his personal associations.[47]

Journeying Back: Friends and Mentors in Prewar Paris

To understand the nature of Ariès's political commitments during the Vichy years, we must look back to the way in which he formed his loyalties before the war. As a student at the Sorbonne in the late 1930s he moved in a closely knit world of mentors, friends, and their families. A royalist enclave in the midst of republican Paris, it was an intimate world of gregariousness and personal sympathies. He remembered these years as a particularly happy time in his life. He had been a recalcitrant student in the lycées, but redirected his energies more positively in a university milieu that he came to love. He followed his courses with enthusiasm, especially those in history.[48] He had first come to history steeped in the lore of his family's legends of old France, and he never completely abandoned the insights of that first encounter.[49] But through his university studies, he came to see the limitations of the Capetian history in which his early conceptions of the past had been formed. He learned to appreciate adversarial positions advanced by historians identified with the political left. But his growing powers of intellectual discrimination led to a deepening of his earlier perspective, not an abandonment of it.

We may take some measure of his interests and his viewpoint at this time from his thesis for his *diplôme d'études supérieures,* a rough equivalent of the masters of arts degree in American universities. Based on the archives of the commissioner-inspectors of Le Châtelet de Paris of the sixteenth century, it considers the functioning of a judicial corporation in traditional French society, where the lords of justice exercised far-reaching policing as well as judicial responsibilities.[50] Nobles with a commitment to public service, they played a particularly effective role in public life as an intermediary body between the king and his subjects.

Ariès idealized the civic virtue of this ancient corporation. The nobility of their commitment, he argued, was derived from their fidelity to the archaic tradition out of which their politics had emerged. It was a politics of delicate balances between public and private responsibilities typical of the corporations of early modern France, each with its particular traditions. In their ensemble, they provided a countervailing force to the rising absolutist pretensions of kings in that era. In this tradition-bound, more decentralized political world, Ariès contended, the king served as an arbiter among the great vested interests of his realm by easing their minor frictions. But the practical work of government was carried out by these corporations among the various constituencies that were beholden to them.[51]

Such a politics worked well, Ariès claimed, because of the social harmony among these lords of justice. The line between their public and private lives was hard to draw, so thoroughly were they intertwined. As Ariès presents them, the lords of Le Châtelet were a circle of friends and the personalism of their relationships enhanced their capacity to dispense justice in this society. To enter their ranks was an apprenticeship in which newcomers adopted their mores while learning their judicial code. As a judicial corporation, Ariès argued, Le Châtelet had emerged out of a more primitive politics of families to whose traditions it remained true. The vigorous role of these magistrates of the sixteenth century contrasts with the emasculated one of the courtiers of the absolutist kings of the seventeenth century. In his way, Ariès was suggesting the possibility of a corresponding role in public service for the professional classes of his own day.[52]

Ariès's study of the judicial lords of Paris marks his passage from the royalist mythology of his childhood to the royalist history of the prewar era. At the same time, it is unabashedly an idealization of corporatism in a politically decentralized state. Therein he espouses a conception of politics derived from immemorial tradition yet revitalized as it was revised to meet the "modern" conditions of the sixteenth century. In his commitment to corporatism, he showcased the shared endeavor of a small society whose ethos was characterized by the solidarity of its members and their loyalty to its traditions. It would become a focus of his research as a cultural historian in the 1960s, as it had earlier been his guiding ideal as a royalist activist in the 1930s. In Ariès's view, such an association was a developmental step beyond the politics of families. Herein we may note Ariès's first discussion of his notion that the family is the historical matrix of politics and as such the prototype of its workings. As a historical outgrowth of a politics of families, the corporation was for all practical purposes an extended network of clients, personal acquaintances, and intimate friends.

As Ariès interpreted the lives of the lords of Le Châtelet, the network of their associations seemed not unlike his own. His deepest friendships were formed during his university days at the Sorbonne in the mid-1930s, and he held fast to them throughout his life. His circle was composed of young men of his own age, background, and aspirations. They were drawn together through shared participation in the youth movement that rallied to the Action Française. In retrospect, he acknowledged their elitist attitudes. "We were imprisoned inside a closed culture of mandarins and a canon of literary masterpieces," he allowed, "in which the arts, the music, were not pursued for enjoyment, but rather appropriated as a repertoire of symbols, metaphors, and analogies." But the relationships formed in this *petite église* had profound and enduring meaning for him. "What I would cherish especially about [those years]," he reminisced, "is that it was a time of friendship [*amitié*]. My authentic choices in those days were those of my friends."[53]

Ariès's closest friend was François Leger (b. 1914), a talented young intellectual who played the animating role in leading the activities of this movement, notably its newspaper and its political studies group. His formal studies at the Sorbonne were in classics. He later went on to a successful career in international commerce in mahogany. He lived for a time in Thailand and wrote an interesting study of the emerging societies of southeast Asia in the era of decolonization.[54] But all the while Leger kept his hand in political journalism, and he wrote for royalist magazines of commentary throughout his adult life. Skeptical, intelligent, charming, he epitomized the old-fashioned man of letters whose erudition was closely tied to his wide-ranging intellectual interests. Late in life, he wrote two biographical studies of the famous nineteenth-century historian Hippolyte Taine (to whom his wife Margueritte was related), for which he received prizes from the Académie Française.[55]

Ariès was also close to Pierre Boutang (b. 1916), a polemical champion of the prewar royalist cause to the end of his days. Hailing from Lyon, Boutang matriculated at the Ecole Normale Supérieure in 1935, and passed his *agrégation* in philosophy four years later. He had a reputation for brilliance among his fellow students in the Latin Quarter. Intellectually self-confident, an imposing presence in any gathering, he exercised a magnetic influence upon his friends and acquaintances. In his memoir, his friend Raoul Girardet ruminates on his enigmatic power of appeal.[56] Robert Brasillach, a slightly older, more infamous militant in the Action Française, recalls his "absolutely prodigious zest for life, full of anger and of vigor" on the eve of the war.[57] François Brigneau, another comrade in the Action Française, remembers him for his "still ingenuous pride and even his irritating self-confidence in all areas of philosophy."[58] With his friends, he was active in the student journalism of the Action Française in the late 1930s. Upon the fall of France in 1940, he became one of the principal organizers of Les Amis du Maréchal, a booster society formed to support the cause of the Vichy regime. He taught briefly in Clermont-Ferrand, then took refuge in North Africa, where he became the principal adviser to Jean Rigault, a leading figure in the Group of Five, who negotiated with the Allies for the liberation of North Africa.[59] Returning to political journalism after the war, he briefly published with *La Dernière Lanterne*, an underground newspaper calculated to compromise aspiring republican leaders of the new regime.[60] He remained an inflexible, often acerbic publicist of the ideas of the Action Française until its demise in the mid-1960s. Along the way, he wrote an enormous volume of newspaper copy, always erudite, but often obscure. More than his friends from university, he carried their circle's style of writing and speaking into the postwar era. Simultaneously Boutang pursued graduate studies in philosophy. He taught in the university from the mid-1960s, in 1973 successfully defending a doctoral thesis at the Sorbonne entitled *Ontologie du secret,* and going on to a controversial career as a professor there.[61]

Another academic was Raoul Girardet (b. 1917), the child of an army officer. H was raised in Paris and attended the Lycée Voltaire. He was a bold young man and led an adventurous life. He enlisted in the militant fascist Camelots de Roi during the late 1930s. Girardet entered officer training with Ariès at the outbreak of the war in 1939; he was active in the Resistance during the Occupation. Arrested and interned by the Germans at Drancy, he was awaiting deportation to the death camps when the war ended. Returning to graduate study, he became a respected professor at the Institut d'Etudes Politiques de Paris and the author of several books dealing with French nationalism and the army. During the Algerian crisis of the early 1960s, he gained some public attention as a journalistic defender of the cause of *Algérie française,* for which he was briefly arrested and imprisoned. Gilbert Picard (b. 1913), with whom Ariès studied for his *agrégation,* also pursued a successful academic career. A protégé of the historian of antiquity Jérôme Carcopino, he spent the war years as a teacher in Tunisia. He was professor of archaeology at the University of Strassbourg from 1955 to 1959, then was named to the chair in Roman archaeology at the Sorbonne, which he held from 1959 to 1983, following in the footsteps of his father Charles, renowned in this field.[62] Philippe Brissaud was of a more aesthetic bent, a painter by avocation. He too trained to be a professor, but accepted a post as administrator at the Institut de France. The

most romantic figure among the group was Jean Bruel, who also participated in the Resistance, though he is better known for having launched
the fleet of bateaux mouches after the war to ply the Seine as one of Paris's
most popular tourist attractions. A certain glamour followed him as he
directed his flotilla into old age. Ariès held fast to these friendships all his
life. They sustained him through good times and bad.

Ariès's friends might be characterized as rebels and aesthetes, drawn to
the Action Française for its pugnacious antirepublicanism but also and
especially for its intellectual elitism. It was a training ground for young
intellectuals bent on playing a role in public life. Girardet and Leger have
written memoirs about this youthful association. Therein they reminisce
about the way their lives as students in the Latin Quarter provided a sociable setting for their political beginnings. Several recall delivering lectures
at the conference hall of the Action Française on a back street in the Latin
Quarter under the tutelage of the society's elders, Henri Massis and Charles
Maurras among them. Others evoke the romance of street fighting with
their political adversaries on the left, though it is difficult to imagine Ariès
in this role.[63] More to the point in his formation were the gatherings he
attended at the homes of these friends. These contributed to his sentiment
that his circle of friends constituted an extended family. It suggests why
these friendships played such an enduring role in his life, long after he had
become estranged from their more intransigent political opinions.[64]

The circle had a mentor in Charles Maurras, who exercised considerable
influence on royalist youth with a penchant for politics during the 1930s.[65]
He was the icon of a dying royalist movement that had taken on a surprising vitality in the twentieth century as a forum for right-wing intellectuals. In the mid-1930s, he was imprisoned for a time for libelous remarks
about governmental leaders, and so became in the eyes of his young admirers a martyr for the royalist cause. At other times, he was an Olympian
presence at the lectures sponsored by the university section of the Action
Française in Paris. Ariès and his friends identified him with a venerable
classical tradition of learning, and they found his intellectual conservatism
particularly appealing. Maurras spurned new intellectual trends. He taught
his followers to trust in the wisdom of the classics of the French literary
tradition and of ancient Greece and Rome. In this respect, Ariès prided
himself on his knowledge of Latin, and as a student he wrote essays on
nineteenth-century literary figures, such as George Sand and Honoré de
Balzac.[66] As for Maurras's own writings, his young disciples took them quite
seriously.[67] He epitomized a style of intellectual leadership that they wanted

to emulate. In an age before university careerism, many students aspired to be men of letters who could influence public opinion in his way.[68]

Ariès, too, contributed to the common praise of Maurras. In the years before the war, he published several articles in the newspaper of his youth group, *L'Etudiant français,* commending Maurras for his courage and his stature as a political leader in troubled times.[69] He respected him for his insights into the pragmatics of tradition: the search for the authentic sources of the good life in land, families, and ancestors.[70] Maurras's views on the authority of tradition tended to confirm his own beliefs. At the same time, Maurras could be didactic and ahistorical in ways of which he disapproved. Nor was he sympathetic to Maurras's integral nationalism as an ideology for the political right in the present age. Ariès acknowledged the appeal of nationalism, but kept his distance from it. Probably the most direct intellectual legacy he received from his mentor was a suspicion of Romanticism for the sentimental illusions it projected. Ariès always favored the concrete over the abstract in his historical interpretations.

All his life Ariès held a place in his heart for Maurras's insights into the nature of tradition, as if his mentor had helped him as a young man to find his *chemin de paradis,* the route toward his destiny.[71] After the Liberation, Maurras was prosecuted and imprisoned as a collaborator. Ariès nonetheless remained faithful to him to the end. In 1946, he, together with François Leger and their future wives, made a pilgrimage to their dying mentor's bedside in his prison at Clairvaux.[72] Maurras may have helped the young Ariès to understand more clearly the dimensions of the intellectual world he inhabited. But unlike his mentor, Ariès came to see the world with a historian's analytical eye. Whereas Maurras believed that tradition discloses timeless truths about society, Ariès would instead come to argue that tradition studied critically reveals the historical evolution of our social attitudes. This historical perspective on tradition served as the point of departure for his exploration of tradition's place in the process of modernization. So considered, tradition embodied the evolving common sense of humankind in its ongoing response to changing historical realities.[73]

The notion of friendship also figured prominently in Ariès's journalism during that era. Consider his series of articles on the French Revolution, in which he focused on the importance of comradeship in the making of the good society. Herein he contrasted the social conceptions of Jacobin revolutionaries with those of Vendéen insurgents. Personal ties meant little to the Jacobins, he argued, whereas the Vendéens shared a common stake in their work and in their land. He therefore characterized the Jacobins as a sect, the Vendéens as a fraternal band. The politics of the Vendéens was concrete, practical, tailored to present needs, while that of the Jacobins was abstract, doctrinaire in its conceptions of social remedies, fashioned to the vision of some future social paradise. Such sectarian notions had pernicious consequences, he contended. The Jacobins conjured up abstract enemies to populate their fantasy of revolutionary struggle, and this imaginary discourse served as their justification for the policies of terror they pursued in 1793. The Vendéens, by contrast, took up arms only to defend themselves against Jacobin intruders. Afterward, they returned to the ordinary activities of their everyday lives.[74]

Ariès's essays on the French Revolution provide us with a glimpse of his prewar conception of history.[75] One notes that here he interpreted the past within the conventional historiographical framework of the day: as the saga of the ideological contest between the right and the left. In the 1930s as in the 1790s, counterrevolutionary royalism was directly engaged in a struggle with revolutionary Jacobinism. Modern French history, he contended, might be read as the enduring saga of the conflict between these irrevocably opposed viewpoints. Here he linked Jacobinism with Marxism, contending that they sprang from the same matrix and led logically to the same self-destructive impasse in a search for ideological enemies and for traitors within their own midst. The classless society was one more romantic illusion, an unattainable "mystical city built upon freestones." It lacked the stuff of life that is its mortar.[76]

It is also interesting to note how Ariès groups his critique of left-wing ideology with that of fascism, which he characterized as a species of romanticism. For him, fascism was doctrinaire and therefore artificial, "constructed" in the same way Jacobinism was. Hitler was a sorcerer of sorts, a mentor unworthy of the calling who mesmerized the people of central Europe with a nationalist dream. For Ariès, fascism and communism were two faces of the same threat, the doctrinaire demand for the reconstruction of society to fit some imaginary ideal. Both ideologies devalued tradition. In a series of articles on state relations in Europe in the 1930s, he pointed to the trouble created when institutions grounded in immemorial tradition are discarded in favor of romantic new creations. In this way, he tied the crisis in central Europe to the demise of the Hapsburg empire.[77] The states of eastern Europe created after the First World War, he argued, were artificial constructions, and fascist politicians had taken advantage of their vulnerability. In commenting on the historic role played by the Hapsburg monarchy, he speculated generally on the role monarchs might play in the contemporary world. In France as in Austria, a king could be what he had been historically: an emblem for the allegiance of the nation, an arbiter among its constituencies, a bulwark against doctrinaire trends.[78]

Journeying Forward: Old Friends and New Colleagues

Surrounded by his friends, content in his studies, confident about the perspectives he offered as a journalist, the young Ariès enjoyed a sure sense of royalism's place in the politics of prewar France. He had already become an articulate spokesman for traditionalism, and he had formulated pragmatic political conceptions to which he would always remain committed. If such sentiments predisposed him to take seriously the opportunity that the educational experiment at La Chapelle seemed to offer, they also prepared him to be suspicious of the doctrinaire fascism of Bousquet and his allies once he had witnessed it first-hand.

Whatever hopes Ariès may have originally had for Vichy, he was soon disabused of them. Like most of his countrymen, he became disillusioned with the Vichy leadership and abandoned active participation in its causes.[79] It is unlikely that he ever took seriously the more excessive teachings of the doctrine proffered at La Chapelle. What is clear is that in time he found the approach of its directors to be doctrinaire in the same pernicious way he had found that of republican leaders to be. The sectarian nonsense of the rituals at the forest encampments staged by Bousquet sent him in search of alternative conceptions, grounded in the common sense that sustains ordinary people in their everyday lives. For that reason, Vichy was the seedbed of his search for a new conception of history, and his subsequent work in the history of mentalities grew out of his reflections on that experience. Increasingly his interests turned to how people actually lived, apart from intellectual theories or state-sponsored educational experiments.[80]

As for his initial support for the Vichy regime, Ariès had no apologies. In his mind, the political significance of Vichy was inconsequential in light of what the war signaled about the larger tide of History that had coursed through the world that he had known.[81] In *Le Temps de l'Histoire*, he noted its effect on intellectuals who had no ties to tradition and who sensed themselves swept away by its turbulence during the war years.[82] Without such attachments, he argued, they had no sense of belonging to a particular community, and hence no concrete sense of a social identity. In Ariès's terms, these were people without a circle of friends such as his own. Often compromised by their wartime allegiances, wandering in the no man's land of the postwar purge, they were susceptible to any ideological fad—fascism yesterday, communism today. They gave themselves to public confession in the desperate hope of currying favor with public opinion. Ariès saw them as harbingers of a coming mass society, one in which the political solidarity born of particular friendships would lose its meaning while public professions of newly acquired ideological faith before a faceless public would become all-consuming. As political types, they harked back to the Jacobins during the French Revolution. These, the Jacobins' modern-day counterparts, augured the reappearance of like radicals in equally turbulent times. For Ariès, his circle of friends served as a salvage ship amidst the wreckage of his youthful political dreams.

Some forty years later, Ariès took one last sentimental journey among his friends, this one a voyage in 1981 on a bateau mouche, one of the tourist boats that ply the Seine from the Pont de l'Alma to the far side of the Ile Saint-Louis and back again.[83] The event had been arranged by the director of the boating company, Jean Bruel, once Ariès's companion in the youth movement of the Action Française, now touted by his old friends as "the prince of the Seine."[84] The ostensible purpose of the trip was to fete Ariès on the publication of *Un Historien du dimanche*. The unpublicized purpose was to provide a setting for his wife Primerose, dying of cancer, to say good-bye to old friends.

Ariès by then had two circles of friends to invite: his newfound colleagues at the Ecole des Hautes études and his companions from his former days in the Action Française. They had not mingled much before. Playfully he arranged for them to sit side by side at the dinner tables on board, each before a place setting marked "red" or "white," mementos of the vastly different intellectual worlds from which they hailed. The world of the Annales scholars was the one to which Ariès now ostensibly belonged. But the aging militants of the Action Français remained his closer friends. My point is that Ariès's growing maturity as a historian should not be construed as an abandonment of his right-wing past. His loyalties, if not his attitudes, were too deeply embedded in the royalist heritage from which he had come. Along the route that he had traveled toward a historical appreciation of his youthful politics, he had been able to lead his old friends only so far. But their friendship remained dear to him. They provided him with a sense of place in the particular community from which he had come.[85]

In this respect, it is worth noting Ariès's historical observations about that time on the psychology of his lingering attachments to the right-wing friendships of his youth. In one of his last essays, one dealing with homosexuality, he ruminated on changing historical attitudes toward male friendship, attributing the current attention paid to homosexuality to the declining importance of "particular friendships" among men in the modern world. As formal contractual relationships have come to displace informal social ties, he explained, the range of sentiments that used to inspire male friendship has contracted, thereby exaggerating the present-day perception of the sexual element in male bonding. "Friendship once bulked large in people's lives," he noted. "It seems to me that a history of friendship would show its decline during the nineteenth and twentieth centuries among adults."[86] Still counting the "web of sentiment" among friends as the source of community, Ariès held fast to his own as consolation for the passing of that world.

The importance Ariès attached to friendship helps us to understand why he was originally intrigued by the educational experiment at La Chapelle. But it does not explain the lessons he drew from the experience. If he was loyal to his friends and mentors, he was not beholden to their opinions. The crisis of the war years in general and the sojourn at La Chapelle in particular provided him with an incentive to deepen his understanding of history. In wrestling with the viewpoint of his colleagues there, he would over the following years formulate original responses of his own, and through them the sum and substance of his approach to the history of collective mentalities.

In this sense, it was not the Bibliothèque Nationale but La Chapelle that was the place of Ariès's fortunate fall. At the former he may have widened his historical horizons. But it was at the latter that he was inspired to pursue a particular path of historical inquiry. At La Chapelle, he was exposed to the moralizing generalizations of his colleagues about the historical causes of the fall of France, which focused on the decay of the French population and the decadence of French society generally. To their call for moral regeneration, he responded with his own research into the history of popular culture.[87] To their biological explanation for the demographic crisis of the present, he replied with his own historical analysis of the revolution in social attitudes that prepared the way for limiting population growth through family planning. To their efforts to impose a heavy, fatalistic framework upon the past, he posed his own highly original study of the pluralistic sources of French history in the collective memories of old France.[88] My point is that Ariès's experience as a teacher at La Chapelle was crucial in his passage from the folklore of the extreme right to a new kind of cultural history. As he later remarked, "It was he [Bousquet] who in his way inspired me to consider cultural influences on demography."[89] He had made his journey to La Chapelle out of loyalty to his traditionalist heritage. But in his journey away he began to put that heritage in historical perspective. That is the key to his originality as a historian.

Ariès was among the last of a disappearing breed of right-wing intellectuals identified with the Action Française. That was the role for which he, as a royalist, had trained from his university days, when he first took up political journalism. His rise as a historian was in some measure a response to the declining possibilities that postwar French society provided for playing such a role. His work as a historian of mentalities was in effect a refuge for a royalism which was no longer politically viable, but which remained as a stance toward trends in contemporary culture. The way in which royalism found a haven in cultural history from the 1960s has not received the attention it deserves. Nor has Ariès's crucial role in promoting it. The rise of the history of mentalities was more than a "third stage" in the development of quantitative methodological techniques, as some students of the new history have claimed.[90] Rather this new cultural history emerged out of the incomplete and unsatisfactory reckoning with the war years and the closing ideological combats of young intellectuals of the left and the right in the waning days of what we now characterize as the modern historical era. Mentalities as practiced by Ariès provided a critique of that modern age. The tragedy of the royalism that he had espoused is that Vichy became its final testing grounds. In the failure of Vichy, its political fate was sealed. Though it was a regime without honor, Ariès refused to concede that the values of old France on which it had battened were destined to share its fate. In writing of their history Ariès sought their redemption.[91] He reinterpreted the mores of old France for the present age, and in this history of mentalities royalism found a sanctuary.

4

Royalist Politics
after the War

A Man of Letters in the Twilight of Royalist Politics

DURING THE FALL 1941, Philippe Ariès, an aspiring man of letters, attended the salon of Daniel Halévy for the first time. Halévy was a renowned intellectual with broad and eclectic interests, formed in the style of the savant of the nineteenth century. He wrote old-fashioned narrative essays on France's political heritage, with subtle insight into correspondences between past and present. As a man of letters, he epitomized refined, lingering attachments to old France. These were somber days in Paris, and the city's normally vibrant intellectual life had been largely stilled. But Halévy's salon on the quai de l'Horloge was a place where intellectual exchange was carried on much as it had been before. In the midst of Paris under the Occupation, his home was a sanctuary where the surroundings were elegant, the guests learned, and the conversations thoughtful.

The young Ariès had come to Halévy's attention because he had been scheduled to preside at Ariès's lecture to the Cercle Fustel-de-Coulanges, a scholarly forum loosely affiliated with the Action Française that favored traditional conceptions of the curriculum for higher education and that was generally sympathetic to Vichyite educational policy.[1] Halévy was unable to attend, but a week later he sent Ariès an invitation to one of his own gatherings. Halévy chose his guests carefully with an ear to the conversations the right selection might stimulate. On this first visit the aspiring young intellectual seems to have made little impression on the grand old man of letters. But two years later, he was invited back, this time upon the publication of his *Traditions sociales dans les pays de France,* a historical geography of French regionalism and his take on what a decentralized nation under Vichy might have been in the best of circumstances. Henceforth, he was a frequent guest at Halévy's soirées. As an aspiring man of letters in the royalist tradition, he must have sensed that he had arrived.[2]

Halévy was famous for his study of the eclipse of the political power of the notables, the monarchist faction that had fought an unsuccessful rear-guard action against the emerging republican leadership in the early years of the Third Republic.[3] In Ariès's mind, Halévy was not only their historian but also their inheritor. He spoke for traditional values of the sort in which Ariès himself believed. Is not our shared commitment today, he wondered, like that of the notables whom Halévy described? Did not their struggle then lend insight into our predicament now, in these uncertain times when the Republic has fallen because of the incompetence of its leaders and the hapless Vichy regime seems the only hope for the future? Ariès took Halévy as a mentor to follow and a model to emulate. "His friendship shepherded me henceforth as a guardian spirit," he reminisced in looking back on those years.[4] Like Halévy, he retained an affection for the mores of old France. The difference between them was that Ariès eventually relinquished his aspirations to influence politics as a man of letters, and settled instead for the honest, modest, but ultimately testimonial role of professional historian. Here he left his mark, and one might say preserved the only legacy royalists might have hoped to maintain—a sympathetic historical representation of the traditions of old France for a generation that had no living memory of them.

But Ariès never forgot his origins, or the attachments they implied. All his life he reverenced the traditions of old France that had been an inheritance of his childhood and the friendships formed during his university years in their shared struggle to advance the royalist cause. Most students of contemporary French historiography are familiar with Ariès's ascent as a cultural historian during the postwar era. But few are aware of the degree to which he simultaneously remained actively engaged in a rear-guard defense of royalist politics. From 1946 to 1966, he was an editor and a journalist for newspapers that tried to adapt the perspectives of the prewar Action Française to the changed circumstances of the postwar world. In his later years, he made much of his difficulties in emancipating himself from the political commitments of his early adulthood.[5] But I argue that his maturation as a historian owed much to his persistent if ultimately futile effort to redefine a role for the traditionalist right in contemporary French politics. In a way the history of mentalities became his consolation for a royalist politics that he recognized was no longer viable.

That a reinvigorated cultural history should have become the refuge for a royalist politics on the verge of disappearing is one of the most poignant ironies of contemporary French historical writing. Only gradually, painfully, and reluctantly did Ariès break the political ties that had sustained his youthful ambitions. As his possibilities as a royalist man of letters diminished, he went on to pursue others as one of the most original cultural historians of his generation. His journalism of the 1950s and 1960s mediated these two vocations. Herein he offered a historical perspective on the mentality of the contemporary age. His essential insight concerned the way ordinary people had come to find more significant meanings in the pursuit of what they perceived to be their private destinies than in the public ones with which their predecessors had more openly identified. In the process of these investigations, he fashioned a destiny of his own. Here I trace that route in light of his gradual abandonment of political journalism in behalf of a dying royalist cause.

Ariès's Particular Friendship with Pierre Boutang

Ariès's renewed dedication to political journalism from the mid-1940s through the mid-1960s—years in which he led other lives as archivist, editor, and cultural historian—owed much to the influence of Pierre Boutang, whose youthful energy and sense of purpose had flagged little since his days in the prewar Action Française. After the war, he returned to that cause with renewed vigor, resuming his role as an editor, political director, and lead polemicist for a succession of newspapers identified with the political right, and sustaining it over the following twenty years.[6] Although he went on to become a professor of philosophy at the Sorbonne in middle age, he never retreated from the doctrinaire royalism of his youth or his fervor for political combat in its behalf.

Ariès and Boutang had gone their separate ways during the war. While Ariès stayed in Paris, Boutang accepted a teaching post in Clermont-Ferrand, then moved on to North Africa where he participated in the negotiations with the Allies for the terms of its liberation. They corresponded regularly during those years, however, and in a way their friendship deepened. At the war's end, Ariès was especially touched by Boutang's moral support during his grieving for the death of his brother Jacques in one of the French army's last campaigns. Subsequently, Boutang encouraged Ariès in his scholarly research in demography.[7] Ariès had been disappointed with Vichy, and might have retired from politics altogether after the Liberation, but for Boutang's appeal to him to persevere.[8] Still, they shared many of the same concerns about present-day France. Ariès judged the purge that followed the Liberation excessive. The left, he believed, was bent upon settling old scores, and he was appalled by the reprisals taken against Vichy's sympathizers. He also recognized that Communist partisans

were rising to intellectual prominence and threatened to play a more imposing role in French politics than ever before. His own traditionalist right,
compromised by Vichyite acquiescence to German demands during the
war years, was once more vulnerable to the assaults of its old enemies
identified with the revolutionary tradition.[9]

As for intellectuals in public life in postwar France, Ariès was particularly
bothered by the appearance of a new breed of opportunists. He identified
them as products of the totalitarian politics of the contemporary age. Before and during the war, he claimed, they had used their talents to advance
extremist ideologies—fascism on the right, communism on the left. Now
as emotions surrounding the purge ran high, they sought to curry popular
favor through public confession of their errant ways or to reinvent themselves in the guise of the left-wing politics that had come into vogue. For
Ariès, they represented a disturbing trend. He had always thought of public
intellectuals in terms of the political traditions in which they were
grounded. Tradition set the course and the limits of the intellectual positions they might take. For example, one could reckon with the Marxists
because one knew the terrain on which they took their stand. But this new
type of intellectual displayed no such loyalties. Ariès characterized them as
"reprobates, heroes without a past." They looked to the whims of public
opinion for the positions they would adopt. They were harbingers of a new
politics of propaganda, drawing on the new modes of publicity to support
what he prophesied would become a manipulative authoritarianism practiced by the modern state.[10]

Anxious over the excesses of the purge, Ariès was persuaded to enter
the fray of postwar politics. With Boutang, he agreed to coedit *Les Paroles
françaises* in late 1945. It was a venture designed to contribute to the emerging politics of the Cold War, and it brought together unlikely allies. This
newspaper was owned by André Mutter, a moderate republican elected to
the Constituent Assembly for his role in the Resistance. Boutang viewed
him cynically, and as managing editor quickly took possession of the newspaper's editorial policy. He surrounded himself with a staff of journalists
that included veterans of the Action Française, some of whom had been
wartime collaborators. The coalition was too unstable to last very long.
Their major story was an exposé of the massacres of Poles by the Red
Army at Katyn as it advanced toward Berlin in 1945. By late 1946, Boutang
and his entourage were in open disagreement with Mutter and collectively
resigned.[11] Boutang went on to serve as political director of *Aspects de
France,* the organ of the reconstituted Action Française. Ariès turned to his

work as an editorial reader for the publishing house Plon, and more deeply into his own research and writing in historical demography.

The collaboration between Boutang and Ariès in this venture nonetheless set the style of the working relationship they would resume a few years later. In 1955, they launched a newspaper of their own, *La Nation française,* aided by the moral support of Daniel Halévy.[12] In both papers, Boutang wrote boldly and polemically in the style of his mentors of the prewar Action Française. No issue appeared without his lead editorial. At *Les Paroles françaises* Ariès's role had been modest by comparison. He carried out editorial tasks behind the scenes and contributed only a few articles of his own.[13] At *La Nation française* Boutang served once again as the managing editor and the more prolific journalist. But this time Ariès contributed articles more frequently, and in the end they counted for more. Boutang remained obsessed with the causes advanced by Charles Maurras and his followers before the war, and much of this resurrected fare was remote from present-day concerns.[14] Ariès, by contrast, addressed the issues raised by the new realities. As a journalist he sought to identify modern contexts in which traditional values might find fresh meaning. He soon acquired a following of faithful readers.

The Journalist as Historian of the Present Age

Between 1955 and 1966, Ariès wrote some 130 articles dealing with the contemporary scene.[15] They constituted what he characterized as a "history of the present," a way of evaluating the circumstances of his own times by emphasizing their differences from the past, not their similarities as was the more common practice among historians.[16] This project paralleled and provided an important complement to his historical studies of family and childhood, and he soon won admirers among the more open-minded readers of his columns. These topical essays reveal Ariès at a crossroads, leaving behind the familiar path of the royalist apologist for the uncharted territory of the cultural historian. Indirectly, they evince his own painful and reluctant abandonment of his traditionalist politics while seeking to remain true to the more profound convictions on which they were based. As a man of letters bent on making a difference in politics, he witnessed the vanishing of his cause. As a historian, however, he was more successful in explaining the role that tradition continues to play in the contemporary world. The two projects were intertwined. But for his journalistic meditations on the present, he might never have plumbed so deeply the historical issues that marked his appeal to his contemporaries. It was not just that he would write a history of the family. He would do so in light of the crisis of the family in his own times.

In launching *La Nation française,* its editorial staff professed a desire to give the traditionalist right a new direction. In their preface to *Ecrits pour une renaissance* (1958), a separate collection of essays intended to promote this journalistic venture, they claimed that the veterans of the campaigns of the Action Française were hopelessly lost in old quarrels, incapable of appreciating new realities or of modifying their viewpoints even if they wanted to. By contrast, they professed to be open to new ideas.[17] In his contribution to this anthology, "Une Civilisation à construire," Ariès asserted the need for the right to move beyond the "sacred sociology" of the nineteenth century elaborated by Georges Sorel, Charles Péguy, and Charles Maurras, for that past had "irremediably disappeared."[18] In scanning the issues of the newspaper over the years, however, one cannot escape the conclusion that Ariès was alone in taking this manifesto seriously.[19] In this respect, he took the opportunity to offer his own reformulation of the timeline of history. To the distinction between the Old Regime and the modern age, he added another, to which he referred as the "present age." It augured new beginnings, but at the same time invited a reconsideration of the enduring wisdom and vitality implicit in the social values of old France, spurned by the makers of the modern age, and of their application in these newfound circumstances.[20]

Ariès's essays for *La Nation française* tend to fall into two phases: an optimistic opening (1955–60), in which he explored social and cultural trends with an eye to the future, and a more pessimistic closing (1961–66), in which the crisis in Algeria tugged him back into unresolved political conflicts dating from the Second World War. He took up topics as they presented themselves in the news, but some recurrent themes stand out:

Demography and the Historical Secrets of Living Traditions. Ariès offered glimpses into his work as a historical demographer and the significance it held for him. Demography was appealing because it considered the vast biological, environmental, and cultural forces that promote long-range change. It opened pathways into a secret world. It focused attention on man and his mores. It drew out the hidden meaning of dry-as-dust statistics about birth rates and death rates, marriage contracts and last testaments. Here was contained the human experience considered in its complexities and its visceral contact with basic life processes. Ariès wanted to convey to his readers the realities of change that such a history might enable them to understand—not just in the past but in the present, a time in history that was beginning to display its own distinctive traits and its new psychological needs.[21] Demography, he averred, provided signposts to shifts in cultural attitudes about life's most elemental meanings, as they surface on the boundary between recurrent anxieties and practical remedies. In his articles he alluded to the pioneering initiatives in population studies by Alfred Sauvy, the demographer who after the war salvaged and redirected the work of the Fondation Française pour l'Etude des Problèmes Humains, the demographic institute Alexis Carrel had founded under Vichy.[22]

Equally important for Ariès, demography provided a counterpoint to economics in making sense of social history. Through demography he hoped to construct a vision of history that would stand as an alternative to Marxism, whose popularity among left-wing historians was enjoying a renaissance in the aftermath of the war. By comparison, the Marxist vision of history seemed to Ariès to be simplistic and one-dimensional. As he remarked in one sweeping summary, "Far more powerful than economic determinism and the dialectic of class struggle—because they make and unmake the great masses of humanity, rejuvenating or aging populations—[demographic trends] now appear to us as long-standing and profound forces that we perceive to lie at the boundary between the sociological and the biological, and that modify the laws of the ages of life and death."[23] Ariès sought to intrigue his readers with observations about the historical journey on which he was embarking. His destination was not yet clear but in his project he would seek to interpret the historical meaning of the attitudes of ordinary people toward everyday human experience as these were modified over time. On his way toward formulating his concept of collective mentalities, he wanted to attune his readers to the possibilities of this new approach to history, which promised to reveal secrets of the human experience hitherto known only in the inchoate and idealized reconfigurations of living traditions. In this sense, Ariès believed, historical demography would provide its practitioners in the mid-twentieth century with a route into hermetic knowledge, much as Marxist-inspired economic history had its followers a century before.

A Critique of Marxist Class Analysis. In the contemporary age, Ariès observed, the mores of the bourgeoisie were changing. Class society had been a product of the rapid development of urban concentration in nineteenth-century industrial society. But even then, he explained, economically inspired class consciousness had never totally shaped the attitudes of the bourgeoisie. Posing Honoré de Balzac as an alternative to Marx, he argued that bourgeois mores had been formed long before that epoch and owed as much to culture as to entrepreneurship. In their heyday, he maintained, the best among the bourgeoisie had been generalists. They prided themselves on refined sensibilities—a knowledge of fine wine, a taste for *haute cuisine*, an appreciation of good literature and art. The idealists among them were civic-minded and contributed their talent and energy to the public causes of the day.[24]

The working class, too, was for Ariès a social type that needed to be understood within a broader historical context. He considered its emergence out of the older strata at the bottom of society, *"les gueux,"* the mix of vagabonds, drifters, and others on the margins of urban life. In this respect, he was favorably impressed with the recent study by the social historian Louis Chevalier, who analyzed Parisian society in terms of the geographical and biological conditions of its urban environment and sorted out its lesser strata into "laboring classes" and "dangerous classes."[25] The Marxist proletariat today, Ariès contended, survived only in the imagination of left-wing intellectuals, a vestige of the guilty conscience of the bourgeoisie. "Is there not among these intellectuals," he opined in a mocking way, "something akin to the transfer of Christian pessimism, as if the worker had become the original sin of capitalist society?"[26] Marxism, he asserted, was at best an inadequate sociology of nineteenth-century conditions, and certainly no harbinger of the new society in the making in the mid-twentieth century.[27] In imitation of his mentor Halévy, he proposed that Joseph Proudhon offered a better model of workers' attitudes than did Marx, noting that the corporate spirit of trade-union solidarity, not class consciousness, gave workers what identity they had in the present age.[28]

The New Corporatism. What Ariès found to be new in contemporary society was the reconfiguration of its hierarchies, in which social power was redistributed through the descending echelons of large organizations. Technocrats and technicians, not entrepreneurs and laborers, provided the cadres of a new kind of labor force for a changing economy.[29] With the coming of an unprecedented affluence in the postwar era, class distinctions were beginning to lose their meaning, and class struggle its once central political importance. The entrepreneurs of the industrial age were yielding place to the managers of the large business corporations that had proliferated since the war. These corporate executives, Ariès argued, formed their identities around their professional responsibilities, not their class interests.[30] In this respect, he was much taken with the book by the American journalist William Whyte, *The Organization Man* (1956). As managers, the new corporate leaders had recourse to different skills from those of the old captains of industry: teamwork replaced rugged individualism, and charm and flexibility were better qualities for success than abrasive competitiveness and stubborn resolve. Driven by their work, they sensed themselves to be specialists rather than generalists. Adept at working their way up the organizational echelons of the enterprises they served, they invested their loyalties there rather than in society at large.[31]

What intrigued Ariès about the new corporatism was its evocation of the older conception of the term that he had espoused in his thesis for his *diplôme d'études supérieures* on the judicial corporations of Paris in the sixteenth century.[32] Taken with the social solidarity and political cooperation that prevailed among these professional jurists, he wondered about present applications of their old-fashioned theory of corporatism. Certainly he recognized that the old corporatism was derived from notions about static communities that had prevailed in traditional society, whereas the new was a product of a dynamic economic trend toward large business organizations. But in its way, he observed, the new corporatism promoted the kind of social rapport that he had perceived in the intermediate bodies of traditional society; perhaps it contained the seeds of social renewal in its reconfiguration of social relations in the workplace. Ariès was not naive about the shortcomings of the new corporate culture. He saw its potential for a new kind of tyranny in the workplace. But he also noted that the new corporatism encouraged planning rather than competition, and in its way opened the possibility of a new forum for sociability. Might it not serve as an antidote to the isolating individualism that had been the bane of modern society?[33]

Ariès was not arguing that class society had completely disappeared. But he did wish to challenge the Marxist notions that mentalities are simple reflections of class interests and that class struggle holds the key to the dynamics of contemporary history. More specifically, he was taking issue with those Marxist critics who identified corporatism as a late stage in the coming crisis of industrial capitalism. For Ariès, the advent of the new corporatism suggested rather that class consciousness had been a historically ephemeral phenomenon that was passing quietly with the industrial age.

The Perils of a Mass Society. The question for Ariès was whether the new corporatism could stem what he saw as an ominous countertrend: the

dissolution of class society into an amorphous, homogeneous, and ultimately conformist mass society.[34] As class identity weakened, he contended,
so too did respect for the political traditions with which that identity had
been associated. In fact, society at large was losing its identity altogether,
and that posed a new set of problems. A mass society, he argued, was one
without roots in particular traditions. Its needs were shaped by consumerism, an unfortunate by-product of Western society's newfound material
prosperity. Such a society was acquisitive in an open-ended way, protean
in its tastes and interests, vulnerable in its susceptibility to newly invented
psychological needs.[35] It quickly disposed of all appreciation of heritage.[36]

Here Ariès chastised the leading intellectuals of the day for their doctrinaire left-wing posturing and their refusal to address pressing issues with
fresh insights.[37] In an article entitled "The Braying of the Beasts," he ridi-
culed the reductionist stereotypes on which they battened.[38] Too many
among them remained slavishly faithful to a Marxist orthodoxy and so
failed to recognize concrete ways in which labor and society were being
transformed.[39] In this and related articles, Ariès expressed his early insight
into "the decline of the public intellectual in his political role," a topic that
has since become a major interest among French historians.[40] In such circumstances, he asked, was it any wonder that the public had lost interest
in the intellectuals' political discourse?

Ariès made much of this concomitant drift toward political indifference.
The educated public was losing its interest in open debate and controversy.[41] The terms "right" and "left" that had defined French politics from
the time of the French Revolution had since the war lost much of their
meaning.[42] The Revolution had given birth to political ideology and a role
for the modern man of letters.[43] But now ideology was losing its *raison
d'être,* and so was yielding place to the new fascination with public opinion
polls. Calling for instantaneous responses to questions posed outside recognizable contexts, such polls elicited unreflective, even simple-minded answers. They ignored the living traditions that provide us with our bearings.
Borne by the whims of the moment, they quickly became a technique of
political manipulation for those who would mold popular attitudes to serve
their own ends.[44]

The Consolations of Private Life. Ariès's assessment of the diminishing possibilities for participation in public life suggests why he attached such importance to the family as a contemporary institution. As people found
fewer public causes with which they might identify, more of them turned
to the consolations of private life. The family was its principal sanctuary.

It was a milieu in which intimacy, personal rapport, and sociability survived in an otherwise impersonal world.[45] It was a place where the aspirations of children for the good life might be encouraged and nurtured. It was also a place that safeguarded traditional social values that were being sacrificed in the society at large.[46]

Ariès was not unaware of the ambiguities of contemporary family life. In many respects, he acknowledged, the family fostered society's newly acquisitive ways, permitting its children to indulge new psychological needs for material satisfactions without adequately inculcating in them the discipline they would need to lead responsible lives as adults.[47] The problem, he believed, was especially visible in the crisis of adolescence, to which he paid increasing attention in his articles of the 1960s. Historically a recently emerging stage in the developmental conception of life, adolescence was now one in rapid expansion, crowding aside both childhood and young adulthood as it took possession of a larger segment of the life cycle. Prolonged adolescence exaggerated all the problems associated with growing up in the present age. He noted the straying of adolescents into antisocial behavior. Raised in a permissive milieu, they lacked both models and incentives for crossing the threshold into the identities of adulthood.[48]

Given all these trends, Ariès was intrigued by the widening gap between public and private life. He noted a paradox. The role of government was expanding with the advent of the welfare state. In a way, government was intruding more than ever before into the private lives of its citizens.[49] But correspondingly he noted how people were investing more of their hopes and dreams in their personal pursuits. Since early modern times, he explained, private life had been seen as a refuge from the tyranny exercised by public authority in the name of society.[50] But at present, he contended, the idea of destiny itself was being redefined in terms of personal aspirations. Thus privacy, in an earlier age identified primarily with the experience of the family as a collectivity, had come to be centered more exclusively on the needs and ambitions of the individual. From a historical perspective, he contended, the notion of privacy was being drawn into that of the self. This was his signal insight into present-day culture. A trend long in the making, it had become strikingly visible since the war.

Ariès and the Algerian Crisis—The Return of the "Vichy Syndrome"

The Algerian crisis wrested Ariès from these musings on contemporary society and culture. Like many of his countrymen, he found himself confronted with unresolved political issues left over from the era of the Second World War. By the early 1960s, most of his articles were devoted to the plight of French nationals living in Algeria and their sympathizers in metropolitan France. With the coming of the Fifth Republic, he had for better or worse placed his faith in Charles de Gaulle's leadership. From a historical vantage point, de Gaulle seemed to Ariès to be what he claimed—the inheritor of the mantle of national leadership.[51] In this sense, he took seriously what de Gaulle said about himself. Like André Malraux, he believed that de Gaulle rode the tide of "History," a conception of the inertial power of the past on which he had ruminated in his earlier book on time and history.[52] Whatever its shortcomings, executive authority in de Gaulle's Fifth Republic provided an alternative to the parliamentarism that had crippled the Third and the Fourth. He had taken on the cause for which the traditionalist right had struggled for more than a century.

Ariès was even prepared to accept de Gaulle's master plan for the dissolution of the French empire overseas. This was not an easy concession for him to make. He had never hidden his sympathy for France's imperial role. His job as director of the documentation section at the Institut de Recherches sur les Fruits et Agrumes was a remnant of his own dream of what that empire might be. Given the technological advantage of the West, he had long believed, there was no alternative to the Western model of modernization in the non-Western world.[53] His work as an archivist of agricultural production and commerce there served that end. At the same time, he conceded that de Gaulle was right in recognizing that the nationalist revolt against the French empire could not be stayed.[54] But he never suspected that de Gaulle would abandon Algeria with the rest of the empire. In this respect, de Gaulle surprised him.

Ariès had never possessed the heart of a *frondeur*. Dismayed by the Evian accord (1962) that granted Algeria its independence, he was still unable to support his friends in their open opposition to de Gaulle's decision. Caught between a sense of the futility of defying the government's policy and a desire to remain loyal to his friends, he tried to find a middle ground by criticizing governmental arbitrariness and ineptitude.[55] In explaining his current dilemma, he drew a parallel with the attitudes he had held following the armistice of June 1940. During that era, he noted, he had tried to steer a course between open support for the Vichy regime and resistance to it.[56] Now he sensed himself caught in a like predicament. He defended his position by taking an impassioned stand against the government for its reprisals against its own citizens.[57] He castigated de Gaulle for his hardness of heart and his lack of compassion for the plight of those on the losing side.[58] He came to the defense of his old friends Philippe Brissaud and Raoul Girardet, who had been arrested and imprisoned for complicity with the defenders of *Algérie française*.[59] He himself was even arrested for having written an article about the French army's use of torture against their opponents, though he was never indicted.[60]

Ariès's stance on de Gaulle and decolonization had already strained his relationship with his old friends, and they were not appeased by this belated flourish of solidarity in defeat. The crisis threatened to compromise attachments that dated from his university days. Leger, Girardet, and Brissaud now wrote for a rival newspaper, *L'Esprit public*, and they openly repudiated his viewpoint. Even Boutang established his distance from him.[61] Years later Ariès and his friends were reconciled. But the Algerian crisis killed what little was left of Ariès's enthusiasm for politics. In the waning days of the crisis (the mid-1960s), though, he wrote essays on the historical meaning of these events that are among the best of this, his last stand as a journalist. He ruminated on the new forms of terrorism employed by the French government, borrowed from the Algerian nationalists and used against its own citizens. For him, it was a brutal manifestation of the state's ever more invasive intrusion into the private lives of its citizens.[62] The omnicompetent state was promoting a cultural conformism that threatened to sever ties with France's ancient regional traditions. In Ariès's view, it was no longer a mere threat to its political opponents. In a more profound way, it militated against cultural pluralism in the mores of contemporary life.

As Henry Rousso has argued in his study of the "Vichy syndrome," the Algerian crisis roused repressed memories of the unresolved tensions between Pétainists and Gaullists during the Second World War.[63] The rift between Ariès and his old friends confirms his thesis. The commitment of most of his old friends to the defense of Algérie française confronted Ariès with painful reminders of the compromised Pétainist cause with which he had identified through the Vichy era and beyond. Having broken his compact with them now over the issue of Algeria's place in the French national identity and having sided reluctantly with the Gaullists, he recalled other troubling memories of a past with which he may long have been uncomfortable. Though he had written a memoir in the immediate aftermath of the war about the larger forces that had shattered his traditionalist world, thrown his personal life into chaos, and forced him to rethink his basic conception of history, he remained strangely silent about specific aspects of the French experience under German Occupation. In none of his journalism on the contemporary age or his autobiographical writings does he mention the misguided policies of the Vichy regime, its collaborationist politics, or most poignantly, its complicity in the suffering of both foreign-born and French-born Jews. While admitting and in some measure repudiating his early Vichyite sympathies as naïve, he never analyzed them critically.

Ariès's stance on antisemitism, therefore, remains a puzzle, for he never commented publicly on the subject. Among his royalist friends, there may have been little that he could say. Antisemitism had been deeply ingrained in the social milieu in which he had moved as a young man.Indeed, it had taken on a sharp edge in the rhetoric of the university circle of the Action Française. In the face of rising antisemitic sentiment, one of his friends on the staff of *L'Etudiant français* wrote an unfortunate article about options for dealing with the "Jewish question."[64] While dismissing the notion of a Jewish race, he chided French Jews for refusing to assimilate more completely to French culture. He also expressed concern about the influx of foreign-born Jews into the metropole. Such sentiments were institutionalized under Vichy when discrimination against Jews took on legal force.[65] As noted above, the école des cadres where Ariès taught operated on an estate confiscated from its Jewish owner and enforced the official antisemitic policies of the government.[66]

The antisemitic discourse within the Action Française before the war was reprehensible; after the war it becomes incomprehensible in light of revelations about the deportations of both French-born and refugee Jews to the Nazi extermination camps. Still, some of Ariès's comrades remained unrepentant and once more took up the Maurrasian antisemitic rhetoric as if the plight of the Jews had never touched the French experience of the war and the Occupation. Conspicuous were the inflammatory remarks of Pierre Boutang. In the editorial offices of *Les Paroles françaises,* he openly mocked the Jews in his banter.[67] Such invectives peppered his postwar journalism, as he revisited the antisemitic rhetoric with which he had inveighed against the Popular Front before the war. In the columns of the newspaper *Aspects de la France,* he repeatedly attacked Pierre Mendès-France as he had once attacked Léon Blum—as the republican leader of a Jewish entourage that had hijacked the French government.[68] In 1949 he published *La République de Joinovici,* in which he pilloried Joseph Joinovici, a Jewish merchant who had spied for the Germans during the war while afterward posing as a French patriot. Boutang's satire was reminiscent of the press copy that had incited antisemitic hostility during the Stavisky affair of 1934.[69] Boutang may have been unusually strident in his antisemitic views. But others within Ariès's circle continued to maintain cozy relationships with notorious Vichyite antisemites in the postwar era.

Why was Ariès a silent witness to this embarrassing discourse? To his credit he never participated publicly in it. On the other hand, he did nothing to condemn it or for that matter to distance himself from its spokesmen. He remained an active member of the reconstituted remnant of the Action Française into the 1960s. It is true that hardly anyone offered an analysis of the wartime plight of the Jews in Vichy France in the decades following the war. Only in the late 1960s did victims begin to talk publicly about their experiences, and only in the 1980s did Vichy's role in the Holocaust become a major political issue, thanks in some measure to the book by the North America historians Michael Marrus and Robert Paxton. Since then, public discussion of the issue has intensified, as some of the most notorious perpetrators were brought to justice in trials that Ariès did not live to see.[70]

Along the way, Ariès was not completely immune to criticism for his reluctance to speak out on the subject. In a private letter, his friend and neighbor Joseph Czapski, a painter and Polish émigré, chided him for his silence on the fate of the Jews in France.[71] I do not know how Ariès replied to Czapski privately. But in his public role as journalist and teacher he seems only to have borne the reproach, save for oblique references to his lifelong solidarity with Jewish intellectuals. In various late-life lectures and memoirs, he made much of his intellectual debt to Daniel Halévy and Gabriel Marcel. But both were part of his own right-wing intellectual entourage, and the latter a convert to Catholicism as a celebrated "Christian Existentialist."[72] Upon publication of Ariès's autobiographical memoir in 1980, Dominique Schnapper, one of his admiring colleagues at the Ecole des Hautes Etudes, confronted him directly on the absence of any reference to the suffering of the Jews reviled by groups with which he had been actively associated. "Is it propriety [*pudeur*] or obstinacy [*refus*]?" she asked.[73] In terms of the public record and even the private correspondence that I have examined, his answer to such queries remains a mystery, vanishing with other unseemly secrets of the right-wing milieu to which he remained loyal despite its corruptions.

A Historian at the Dawn of a Politics of Culture

As a journalist in 1945, and even in 1955, Ariès had been looking for ways to redefine a political role for the remnants of the Action Française that still maintained an attachment to traditionalist values. By 1965, however, he was prepared to concede that the Gaullist state had thwarted the politics he had hoped to renew. Given the public's acquiescence in the face of the state's power to mold public opinion, he had come to question whether an old-fashioned man of letters such as he could continue to play a meaningful political role.[74]

Consolation came from an unexpected quarter. Student discontent with the conditions of higher education had been brewing for several years, and in May 1968 it erupted into student strikes and demonstrations in French universities, conveying an aura of insurgency. The political pundits were quick to identify the agitation with the political left and to look for its antecedents in France's venerable revolutionary tradition. But Ariès was struck by the distance that student leaders established from the Marxist old guard of the Communist party, and the freshness of their commitment to the emerging ecology movement, a cause whose nature and significance the conventional politicians of both left and right had been slow to acknowledge. It was as if the wayward adolescents about whom he had worried during the previous decade had at last found their cause. Were not the interests of this youth movement, he wondered, like those of his own in the years before the war? Their cause, he suggested, was the intellectual analogue to that of his own generation, for their environmentalism now seemed close in conception to his regionalism then. Both groups spoke of the need for conservation within communities conceived on a smaller scale. The boundary between their interest in ecological equilibria and his own in social acculturation, he believed, was easily crossed, and their causes closely allied. For Ariès, the student protest of 1968 signaled an underlying crisis of culture. It dramatized the conflict between the high culture of a rationalizing and transforming science and technology and the popular culture that harked back to the customs and mores of old France. The former was triumphantly embodied in the Gaullist welfare state as an instrument of paternalistic social management. But the latter endured as a subterranean movement of resistance, sustained by the conviction that free societies thrive upon diversity, local identities, and respect for privacy.[75]

Ariès found the student uprising of 1968 personally liberating in two ways. First it provided a new venue for the politics he had pursued unsuccessfully for much of his adult life. The "moribund right," he proposed, could pass its banner to the "dynamic left" he saw reborn in this youth movement, secure in the knowledge that they shared suspicions about the overweening power of the state. He could let go of the present in favor of the past, to devote himself exclusively to a history of private life that he believed contained the secrets of France's deeper identities. It was in these circumstances that he began to refer to himself as an "anarchist of the right." His anarchism signified his opposition not simply to Gaullist policies now, but to the underlying trend toward the homogenization of culture under the beguiling auspices of the big state.[76]

Second, it enabled him to acknowledge openly the political meaning of his vocation as a historian. As a young man of letters, he had expressed his awe before the ineluctable power of the forces driving modern history.[77] Now as a more mature historian, he reconsidered that reading. In a lecture to a group of students in 1973, he spoke of a "tendentious" interpretation of the history of mentalities. His studies in that history, he claimed, had reinforced his respect for the enduring power of popular tradition and the importance of collective memory. Tradition, he observed in a way reminiscent of his essay on the subject in 1943, was the bedrock of pragmatic ways. It embodied concrete attitudes toward everyday life, an antidote to abstract public discourse. Through the history of mentalities, he explained, he would show the ongoing appeal of a countervailing tendency issuing from the past. That history, precisely because it explored the values of traditional society obscured in the making of modern history, was an essential inquiry in the search for an alternative to the moral bankruptcy of modern mass culture.[78] Whereas he had hitherto identified his political opposition with his journalism, he would henceforth associate it solely with his historical scholarship. The importance of the distinction between public and private life that had been the inspiration of his turn to cultural history after the Second World War seemed confirmed by all that he had since learned. His insights into the nature of this field, he believed, were the deep source of his original contribution as a historian.[79] A younger generation of Annales historians agreed. Whereas the Annalistes of Ariès's own generation had ignored his historical scholarship, their younger colleagues were more receptive to his insights. By the early 1970s, he was being invited to lecture at their seminars and conferences. These scholars were more open to influences from beyond their own ranks, more willing to acknowledge originality wherever it emerged.[80]

It would be naïve to explain the rise of Ariès to prominence among academic scholars as their simple discovery of his work. One might argue that Ariès himself played a certain part in promoting its importance. His files of correspondence for the 1970s convey that impression. By 1971, the moment was opportune for him to make a leap from his tiny circle of cultivated royalist friends to the wider community of scholars. His fortunes as a historian were rising. He had gained recognition, even admiration abroad. In France, Michel Winock, an editor at the Editions du Seuil, saw the potential readership of Ariès's early writings and published new, slightly abridged additions of both *Histoire des populations françaises* and *L'Enfant et la vie familiale sous l'Ancien Régime* in 1971 and 1973 respectively. For the latter, Ariès contributed a new prefatory essay in which he placed his work in the context of the burgeoning interest in the topic. Nor was he shy about publicizing the reappearance of these studies. He sent copies with personal dedications to many of the leading historians of the day, in France and abroad. There is a fine line between gift-giving and self-promotion among academics. In the old-fashioned world of men of letters, sending one's book to friends and admirers may have been considered a courtesy. In the expanding realm of contemporary professional scholarship, it served a more practical need for building a network of scholars aware of one's work. Ariès's feelings about this effort may have been mixed. He often made self-effacing remarks in his dedications, though obviously he was looking for approval. Most of his recipients politely gave him the acknowledgment he wanted.[81] A few even engaged him seriously on the issues he raised.[82] Either way, his books won an important French academic following during the 1970s and the respect of the community of scholars. All of this was a prelude to his entry into the faculty ranks of the Ecole des Hautes Etudes en Sciences Sociales in 1978.

Ariès's rise as a cultural historian from outside the academy, seemingly out of nowhere, has since puzzled the historiographers of our day.[83] He did not fit the Annalistes' own description of their evolution as a historiographical movement. The secret of Ariès's originality as a historian was in the tradition that he brought with him out of his intellectual exile. While he was integrating his scholarly work into academic historiography, the traditionalism that he had championed as a journalist for the Action Française from student days well into middle age remained his deepest source of inspiration.It is not surprising, therefore, that he should have paid homage to his mentor, Daniel Halévy, in his inaugural lecture at the Ecole des Hautes Etudes.[84] Harking back to their first meetings during the Vichy years, he noted their shared appreciation of an intellectual style that would disappear with them—one calculated to bring to public discourse their broad learning in the defense of the particular tradition from which they had come. Thanks to Ariès's scholarship, however, such traditionalism would become an element of the new cultural history. Halévy's work as a man of letters had been an epitaph for the notables of the late nineteenth century; Ariès's contribution as a cultural historian was an epitaph for the men of letters themselves.

If Ariès's evolution from man of letters to cultural historian in these postwar years is original, it is not without parallels with others of like stature. His interpretation of the historical meaning of the present age is very close to that of certain American scholars who worried about the same trends—Richard Sennett, Daniel Bell, and especially Christopher Lasch, to mention the most prominent. Indeed, it was among the Americans that Ariès's work received its warmest reception. Such recognition prepared the way for Ariès's visits to American universities in the mid-1970s.[85] Thus was constituted his American connection. The popularity his work enjoyed in the United States in turn stimulated a more serious consideration of it among French scholars.

The waning role of the public intellectual in the postwar era is currently a topic much discussed among historians.[86] They tend to put their accent on the left-wing intellectuals and the way Marxism eventually led them to a dead end. The right-wing intellectuals, those whom Ariès characterized as "men of letters," fared no better. Most clung to the anachronistic attitudes formulated by the prewar Action Française, as exemplified by Pierre Boutang. But the notion of a declining role for intellectuals needs qualification, for ironically some of those who abandoned the conventional mode of learned journalism found a better forum in the new cultural history. Ariès for one reached an audience far broader than any to which he might have aspired as a journalist. In this passage, he was not alone. The new cultural history also became a refuge for intellectuals on the left, such as Emmanuel Le Roy Ladurie and François Furet. For most of them, this migration entailed a repudiation of their youthful political ideals.[87] Ariès's journey, by contrast, is interesting because he used it to reconfirm his belief in his traditionalist heritage. In a subtle way, his exchange of the role of man of letters for that of cultural historian was a political act, for in the present age culture itself has become an object of political contention. This rendezvous of intellectuals from the extreme left and the extreme right in this new, highly popular genre of history, therefore, may suggest less a diminishing role for intellectuals than its reinvention in a manner better suited to our times. Ariès's personal trajectory is a particularly compelling example of how and why it occurred.

5

Secrets of the History
of Mentalities

The Secrets of Private Life in Vichy France

IN THE WINTER OF 1943 Philippe Ariès, by then an unemployed teacher coping with the travails of life in Paris under German Occupation, made a pilgrimage to Lyon to visit with the remnant of the Action Française that had gathered in exile there. He was looking for some validation from his former associates of his fragile hopes for the movement's renewal under the Vichy regime that had taken on the responsibility of governing a defeated nation. The war years had been miserable not only for their privations but also for their deceptions. Ariès had just resigned as an instructor at a Vichy-sponsored training school, where he had felt uncomfortable with the collaborationist stance of its director. But the visit to Lyon did little to lift his spirits. The Action Française had retreated into narrow-minded and self-defeating sectarianism. If anything, he was obliged to acknowledge that the royalist cause was dying and incapable of resuscitation.[1]

On his train ride back to Paris, he reflected on the difficult route he had traveled since his days as a student, when Paris had been his enchanted garden and his intellectual paths therein had been clearly marked and easy to follow. He had pursued his studies in history and geography with enthusiasm and surrounded himself with friends who shared his idealized vision of old France as the best source for national renewal. As a journalist for the student newspaper of the Action Française, he had been an apologist for Charles Maurras, who still exercised a certain mystique over the generation of right-wing intellectuals that was then coming of age. Like many other bright and idealistic youths, Ariès had been captivated by Maurras's high-minded erudition, his classical literary tastes, and his uncompromising opposition to the politics of the Republic. He remembered himself as happy in that setting, confident in his convictions, secure in his royalist world in the midst of Paris's intellectual and student life.

That way of life had come to an abrupt end with the beginning of the Second World War and the fall of France. At the outset, the Occupation seemed only an unpleasant moratorium that the Vichy regime would bring to an acceptable conclusion. But as its leaders became more beholden to their Nazi overlords, he was obliged to concede Vichy's moral bankruptcy and the illusions of his political apprenticeship in the Action Française. The train ride from Lyon to Paris, therefore, served as a sobering moment of recognition. His youthful royalist ardor had burned into ashes. But the phoenix of his ambitions would rise again, for this first experience with mourning his losses would inspire him to undertake a historical inquiry into the mores of the traditional world from which he had come. The history of mentalities that he would pioneer was conceived amidst the disappointments of the war years.[2]

Ariès had left La Chapelle and its youth camps behind. But he took with him the seed of an idea for a new kind of history dealing with the secrets of private life. Most of the instructors there had lectured to their students following a detailed syllabus. But Ariès had also listened to the students' stories, and he found them fascinating.[3] He, so deeply immersed in the lore of his family's heritage, had been struck by how little most knew of their own family histories. Among those from the working-class *banlieue* of Paris, few could trace their lineage beyond the three generations that they knew through living memory.[4] Yet they readily divulged the secrets of their own pasts, their ordeals and their suffering, their disappointments and transgressions. Of particular interest were their revelations about unresolved issues in their personal lives, notably their responsibility for the premarital liaisons in which many of them had become entangled. As Ariès later recalled: "I listened to their stories of abortions, of abortionists (*faiseuses d'anges*), of curettages at exorbitant expense in private clinics for fear of the painful consequences of going to a public hospital." Here, he recognized, was an unseen history of sexual behavior about which no one spoke, "except in hushed tones, pillow talk that could not be overheard by public authority, or even the clergy, and that nonetheless swelled or hollowed out the statistics of the population. I asked myself, why not draw them [these secrets] forth from this hidden realm?"[5]

The Annales pioneers had not addressed the history of sexuality in family life in this explicit way. Nor had royalist historians been much interested in such problems. Jacques Bainville, the most prominent among them in the era in which Ariès came of age, devoted himself to the political history of the royalists' rear-guard (and for the most part losing) battle with republicans for a place in the political life of modern France.[6] For these historians, the popular culture of old France was a sentimental memory to which they paid little critical attention. But in the remote forest encampment of La Chapelle north of Paris, Ariès had seen the possibility of lifting the shroud of royalist sentimentality to expose the chaotic realities of everyday life in old France. If today's students told revealing tales of their sex lives, he wondered, why should one not expect that those told by their ancestors were every bit as turbulent, anarchic, and compelling? Was there not a history to be written based on their secrets? To explain the decline of the French population since the seventeenth century, why not remove the moralizing shroud of Vichyite resignation and begin where ordinary people in old France began—in the choices they made in the prime of life about the passions of their daily lives?

With Paris still under Occupation, Ariès turned to historical research as a respite from his administrative work at the documentation center for commerce in overseas tropical fruit. Though he had reports to write and a bibliography to compile, he had plenty of time to pursue his own research to see whether he could uncover the secret history of private lives to which the stories of his students had given him his first clue. It was not easy, he explained, for he carried on his research amidst the curfews of the Occupation, the unrelenting difficulties of daily life, and endless rumors about approaching catastrophe. "And yet," he recounts, "I persisted in my search among parish records and demographic statistics for love stories, for facts about private life, for the inexhaustible sources of our culture, that is, for man's essential ties with nature, his body and that of others. In a solitude sheltered from the misfortunes of war, I discovered subterranean forces stronger than wars and nation-states."[7]

Ariès stressed the obstacles the German presence presented to his project. But in an ironical way, the Occupation may have contributed to his decision to pursue this line of inquiry. Most of the political topics to which French historians had typically devoted themselves in the prewar era were too sensitive to address, notably the long-standing debate between historians of the right and left about the meaning of the revolutionary tradition. In this historiographical void from which politics had been banished, culture presented itself not only as a topic that would escape the scrutiny of German censors, but also as one that permitted a search for a deeper foundation of the French identity. In a late-life interview, Ariès argued that the Vichy era was crucial in inspiring historians to make a distinction between the history of politics and statecraft and that of culture and society.[8]

In taking up this project, Ariès was intruding into a political debate that had raged since the beginning of the century about remedies for the long-term decline of the French population. It pitted natalists, who favored fecundity to expand the quantity of the population, against neo-Malthusians, who preached the virtues of birth control to improve its quality. As William Schneider, a historian of the politics of the eugenics movement in France, has pointed out, both groups were anxious to manage the population in the hopes of improving its health and well-being. Without explicitly favoring the neo-Malthusian position as a public policy, Ariès was intent upon tracing its deep sources. His research took him back to the seventeenth century and to his first insights into the "revolution in sentiment" that prepared the way for family planning.[9]

Ariès worked on the project for some five years, from 1943 to 1947, scouring myriad sources from different regions of France—some quantitative, such as parish registers, and demographic statistics, but others anecdotal, notably the seventeenth-century memoirs and letters in which highly literate women confided "their stories about the brute facts of life, the indelible sources of our culture." He offers us glimpses of these secrets first divulged in this new literature of intimacy by correspondents such as Mme. Françoise de Sévigné, who tactfully counseled her friends about how the perils of childbearing might be avoided.[10] One key to this new history, Ariès recognized, was to look for others like her who long ago gave such secrets away, and so unwittingly provided historians today with routes into the inner sanctum of private behavior.

Family life had been much on the minds of Vichy educators. In their sympathy for the natalist position, they had tended to attribute population decline to infertility, delayed marriages, abortions, alcoholism, and family instability.[11] In official reports, they expressed their concerns about an aging nation that had lost its energy (goût de vivre) and its initiative (esprit d'entreprise). They believed that the decline of the French population had become critical in light of France's military defeat. Their remedy was the rehabilitation of family life, in its material means but especially in its social values.[12] This was to be an era of moral regeneration, and the directors of La Chapelle were among their most ardent apostles in the quest for the restoration of the physical fitness and moral improvement of French youth. They shaped their educational program to serve that end. They prescribed for their students an elaborate regimen of physical education and a moralizing curriculum in civics and history.[13] They also drew upon the recent interest in eugenics to give a scientific allure to their teachings about the biological decline of the French people. Was not the success of the Germans testimony to their vitality, they inquired, and was not the current German experiment with national socialism a model to be emulated?[14]

The biological fatalism from which such an argument sprang had been most fully articulated by Alexis Carrel, a renowned physician whose *L'Homme, cet inconnu* (1935) was a best-seller and a highly influential apology for eugenics. Carrel had spent most of his adult life as a researcher at the Rockefeller University in New York, but returned to France in 1940 to help leaders of Vichy find constructive solutions for the rehabilitation of the French people in light of their devastating defeat. He, too, worried about the biological decline of the French race, and he proposed a bold program for its "regeneration." Given the recent development of techniques in the life sciences to prolong the lives of the aged and remedy the deficiencies of the infirm, he speculated, humankind was also in a position to reconstruct its own genetic condition along more positive lines. Carrel envisioned ways to improve human stock generally, and even to fashion a potential elite.[15] For him, the latter need had taken on a certain urgency in light of France's defeat, and he offered his services to Vichy officials with that in mind. The first task, he argued, was to understand the history of France's demographic decline and to use that knowledge as a basis for the rehabilitation of the younger generation. In 1941, with Vichy's subvention, he founded the Fondation Française pour l'Etude des Problèmes Humains. Carrel's program in eugenics had many dimensions. Some of his work on organ culture anticipated techniques for transplanting living organs that have become commonplace today. But his ideas about disposing of recidivist criminals and the incurably insane through euthanasia struck his critics as uncomfortably close to Nazi eugenic policies. Cited in the purge following the Liberation, he died shortly thereafter. But his foundation for population studies, divested of such excesses as its eugenics program, survived in only slightly altered form under new direction as the Institut National d'Etudes Démographiques (INED).[16]

Carrel's efforts to institutionalize the study of demography is important for our purposes because it was to this research that Ariès turned toward the end of the war. It is uncertain whether he had any dealings with Carrel. But he did establish scholarly contact with the INED's new director, Alfred Sauvy, shortly after the war, and with his encouragement completed his book, *Histoire des populations françaises* (1948), and contributed three articles concerning his research to the INED's learned journal *Population*.[17] Ariès, too, was seeking an explanation for France's long-range demographic decline. At La Chapelle he had listened to endless discourse about the biological degeneration of the French race.[18] Increasingly skeptical of this argument as his own research progressed, he advanced an alternative interpretation in which he contended that mentalities, not biology, is the key to understanding demographic trends in modern France. This insight set the future course of his scholarship, as he sought to explain the rise in expectations about life's opportunities that we have since come to identify with modernity.

In his *Histoire des populations françaises*, Ariès took seriously Carrel's notion about using the techniques of life to human advantage, but grounded these in cultural practices that had long since been adopted, not in a eugenics program yet to be enacted. Here he acknowledged his debt to Sauvy and especially to Adolphe Landry, both pioneering demographers, for their insights into the relationship between profound changes in cultural attitudes and long-range population trends.[19] He explained how the emergence of these new attitudes paralleled the rise of the modern life sciences and reinforced their efficacy. Rather than accept decrepitude and early death fatalistically, the well-born among the French people in the early modern era had taken control of their own bodies on these interrelated planes. The revolution in attitudes about birth control he labeled new "techniques of life." Correspondingly, he discussed the advances in medicine that were prolonging life and enhancing its quality as the "new techniques of death."[20] Together they contributed to the rise of the culture of modernity.

For his formulation of a method of historical investigation, *Histoire des populations françaises* is arguably Ariès's most important book. In a late-life lecture, he notes that "it contains the program of my working life up to now." It marks his shift from comparative regional studies to what he then characterized as the history of "techniques of life and death."[21] In this book and in related articles in the learned journals on demography, he took issue with the Vichyite claim about the moral and biological decline of the French people by offering an alternative explanation of a secret revolution in social mores dating from the seventeenth century.[22] "Within these stubborn [demographic] data," he explained, "were encoded the secrets of the bedroom, the ambitions of families, the route of migrations."[23]

Ariès placed these topics within the context of a historical process that had been under way since the seventeenth century.[24] He contended that the decline of the French population had less to do with biological infertility, moral degeneracy, and dysfunctional families, and more with the conscious decisions made by married couples in the secrecy of their sexual relations to practice birth control. The widening use of contraceptive practices signaled not lascivious hedonism, as Vichyite moralists believed, but rather a deepening sense of family care among an ever larger portion of the population. Beginning in the seventeenth century, he noted, married couples became more sensitive to the burdens and the risks of endless childbearing. Recognizing that they had choices, they made private but conscious decisions to practice birth control as a way of improving the quality of their own lives and those of their children.

Such efforts to limit unwanted pregnancies, Ariès suggested, served as a rudimentary beginning to family planning and as evidence of humankind's newfound willingness to take responsibility for its own future. Ironically, it was not a lack of will, as Vichy apologists claimed, but this willful revolution in attitudes, quietly conceived in secrecy, that had contributed so significantly to the leveling of the French population in the modern age. Family planning, he explained, was a defiance of fate, expressive of a determination to exercise a greater measure of control over one's individual destiny as well as the future well-being of one's family.[25] This long revolution rippled quietly through modern society in the making, its effects passing from the well-to-do to the humble. The "techniques of life," inaugurated by middle-class couples in the seventeenth century, were introduced among working-class populations only in the mid-twentieth century, as Ariès had come to understand through his conversations with his students in the youth camps of Vichy.

Ariès had yet to find a conceptual label to characterize his research into the secrets of the conjugal bed. He referred to it only as a visit to an "unknown continent, a strange, mysterious, fathomless history."[26] But in these writings on historical demography of the 1940s he was already using the term *mentalité nouvelle* to identify this revolution in sentiment.[27] By the late 1950s, moreover, he saw that his investigations were converging with those of scholars who were giving the term a broader historiographical meaning to characterize a range of studies dealing with the history of popular culture.[28] The term had been in use since the late nineteenth century, and may have taken on some significance as early as the 1920s in the writings of Lucien Febvre, the famous pioneer of Annales historiography.[29] Set aside during the depression and the war years, mentalities as a historical interest surfaced again during the 1950s.[30] Noteworthy was Robert Mandrou's *Introduction à la France moderne, 1500–1640* (1961), a social and cultural history based upon notes left by Febvre, who had been his mentor.[31] Like Febvre, Mandrou put his accent on resistance to innovation—inveterate customs, deep-seated fears, the inertial power of time-worn ideas. His point was that the success of the scientific revolution of the seventeenth century was all the more remarkable given the tenacious cultural forces that opposed it.

Mandrou's studies in "mentalities" gave Ariès a perspective on his own work. He recognized that "mentalities" was the apt title that had so far eluded him, but with a decided difference. His own emphasis was on the emergence of a modern mentality in the midst of but not yet displacing one still deeply ingrained in the domestic life of traditional culture. These opposing mindsets coexisted from the seventeenth to the early twentieth century, an era in which there was considerable accommodation between the two. The distinguishing feature of the emerging modern mentality, he contended, is that it presented itself under the guise of privacy, for the first time conceived as a realm of experience apart from public life.

Ariès explained his position in "Interprétation pour une histoire des mentalités," an article that appeared in 1960 as a contribution to an anthology on birth control practices.[32] Here he recapitulated his argument about family planning from a demographic perspective, but this time recast as the central problem of this new cultural history. His originality was in linking a problem in historical demography to a broader revolution in sentiment out of which the affectionate family emerged, with its far-reaching implications for family planning and the careful nurturing of those children spouses chose to conceive. The family, he contended, was the pivotal institution in introducing modern attitudes to the population at large, and it did so by creating a private life apart. The secret decision to practice birth control, he argued, signaled the emergence of a "Malthusian" mentality, a new mental structure that housed a new set of interrelated attitudes. As a way of thinking, it promoted the new self-awareness that ordinary people brought to choices in their personal lives.[33]

Ariès concentrated not on mere birth control practices, but rather on the broader commitment to rational measures calculated to improve the quality of human life. Here he pointed out the rising accord between family planning and the new science of medicine. Parental decisions to limit the size of families coincided with medical advances that ensured that more offspring would live to maturity.[34] He noted especially the significance of Edward Jenner's introduction of inoculation against smallpox, a preventive measure that middle-class parents soon demanded for their children.[35] In adopting a Malthusian mentality, people chose to take control of their destinies and those of their children. The fatalistic mentality of traditional society that taught the inevitability of endless childbearing and high infant mortality was discarded.

For Ariès, the hidden cultural revolution also involved a change in feelings about the satisfactions of married life. He loosely construed this emotional reorientation as the "pursuit of happiness," derived from the uncoupling of the tie between sexual intercourse and procreation in marriage.[36] As the widening use of contraceptive practices weakened that association over the long run, the pursuit of pleasure became an end in itself. He linked this notion, in turn, to the emergence of a new economy of the family reconceived as a unit of affection. It included the love of spouses for each other and, more important, parental love of children demonstrated in nurturing their talents and encouraging them to take charge of their own futures. Parents showed more interest in the individual personality traits of their children and paid more attention to their schooling as a preparation for adult responsibility. Such notions underwrote Ariès's study of the history of childhood and family, which appeared in the same year as this article. Its visible sources were portraits of families and their children, as well as manuals on childrearing; its invisible ones were the demographic data that had first suggested to him this fundamental change in the dynamic of family life.[37]

There is a wonderful irony in this historiographical turn. Ariès, the traditionalist, royalist, and former Vichy instructor, had become the historian of the rise of the modern mentality in the private culture of everyday life that centered on progressive attitudes about preparing children for adulthood. By contrast, Annales scholars continued to stress the inertial power of extant mental structures as a drag on progressive change. Mandrou was by 1961 collaborating with the medieval historian Georges Duby, another Febvre student, in an effort to formulate a more precise definition for this new field, and it is interesting to compare Ariès's article on mentalities with one written by Duby at roughly the same time.[38] Following Febvre, Duby offered a broad review of issues in historical psychology, particularly as they reinforced resistance to innovation. He tended to dwell on the early pioneers, Febvre and Marc Bloch, and their allies among the sociologists of the Durkheim school, with particular attention to the inertial power of timeworn myths, rituals, and other symbolic gestures. He presented a comprehensive overview, but in an open-ended, even tentative way.[39] Ariès, by contrast, focused concretely on the sources of the modern mentality in an emerging culture of private life. In effect, he made the family the matrix of the many facets of the history of mentalities: love, marriage, sexuality, the process of growing up, growing old, and dying, all recast around the transactions between private and public life in the modern world.

Ariès's intervention received little attention in this incipient scholarly discussion about the meaning of mentalities as a field of history, which, despite the rising prestige of Annales historiography, was still attuned to the revolutionary tradition as the primary historiographical frame of reference for new research.[40] For most academic historians, "mentalities" concerned the reverse side of progress. It told of tradition-bound attitudes and stubborn credulity that militated against the open-minded and inventive ideas of the Enlightenment and the rational reforms institutionalized during the French Revolution. The dean of such studies, Albert Soboul, characterized the history of mentalities as a perplexing problem in collective psychology, knotted in the complex interplay between class sentiments and those of society at large. At the same time, his renowned colleague Ernest Labrousse suggested that the historical study of mentalities introduced a "third level" of sophistication in the quantitative analysis of social structures.[41] Among such historians, there was not yet any thought that the conceptual framework of history identified with the revolutionary tradition might eventually be questioned.[42] Within a decade, though, the history of mentalities would present such a challenge, and the political stakes of the new cultural history as a rival to a social history still contextualized within that historiographical paradigm would have become more visible.

Secrets of the Revolution of 1968: The Politics of Mentalities

It was not until the early 1970s that Ariès revisited mentalities as a historiographical concept. This time one notes a subtle change of emphasis and a somewhat more polemical tone in his discussion. In his 1960 article, he had presented a neutral view of the way the modern mentality of rationalizing techniques accommodated the old one of time-tested customs by absorbing them into the mores of family life. But since then mentalities had become the historiographical fashion of the day. Historians of the left were setting aside the old discussion of revolutionary movements for a new conversation about issues relating to this little-known cultural history. Exemplary of this transition is the work of Michel Vovelle, a professor at the University of Aix-en-Provence and a rising star among historians of the French Revolution, who now sought to integrate mentalities into a sophisticated Marxist interpretation of history.[43] Like Ariès, Vovelle during the late 1960s took up the history of attitudes toward death and mourning, a topic they debated over the following decade. Their exchange raised the issue of endings, and by implication the destiny not only of individual lives but of modern history. To put it differently, the Ariès/Vovelle debate showcased the politics of the new history of mentalities by problematizing the concept of progress embedded in the historiography of the revolutionary tradition.[44]

It was in this context that Ariès offered what he characterized as a "tendentious" interpretation of the history of mentalities.[45] He shifted focus from the practical advantages of the modern mentality to its demonstrated inadequacies in comparison with the traditional one it superseded. It was about this time that he borrowed the poetical phrase of the Cambridge University social historian Peter Laslett, who had referred to traditional society as "the world we have lost."[46] For Ariès, the phrase conveyed less a nostalgia for the Old Regime than an indictment of contemporary culture for having neglected such social virtues as sociability, friendship, and loyalty, which he identified with that bygone era and which he believed to be eroding in the face of the calculated strategies and rationalizing imperative of modern life.

Ariès had by then retired from political journalism, and he was ready to find in his studies in history what recompense he could for a royalist politics that was no longer viable. As he abandoned politics, he gave his history a more visibly political turn. He was still recovering from the debâcle of the failed efforts of his royalist comrades to stay the independence of Algeria in the early 1960s. The crisis had led to some bitter divisions with his old friends, and the rancor died slowly. He had therefore taken some comfort from the students' protests of 1968, particularly in their championing of environmental issues as an essential project in the making of a counterculture. In the demonstrations of these left-wing students he recognized a rebellion against the overweening power of the nation-state not unlike that which had animated his own right-wing youth group in the 1930s.

In "Une Interprétation tendancieuse de l'histoire des mentalités" (1973), Ariès sought to explain the deep motives beneath the revolution of 1968, which he identified as dissatisfaction with the Gaullist welfare state and repugnance for a consumerist mentality that pandered to the materialism and superficiality of contemporary mass culture. These students, Ariès contended, demanded that France's leaders show some sensitivity to the distinction between a material standard of living that was rising and a quality of life that was beginning to fray. In the mentality of the counterculture he noted a youthful anarchism with which he readily identified. It harked back to his own perception as a student of the threat of modernization to what was best in traditional culture: the pluralism of small communities, free and unconstrained by conformist discipline; regional variations in culture; and public space in which ordinary people could play.[47]

Ariès suggested, too, that the turn of so many historians to this new cultural history expressed a growing disenchantment with the modern credo of progress dependent upon the benevolence of the modern nation-state. Their growing tendency to shun political history bespoke the bankruptcy of a concept of linear progress over time whose ironies had become more obvious. The road to progress, he contended, was strewn with the detritus of a consumer culture that was ravaging the quality of life. In effect, he was reinvesting his royalism in a cultural history that exposed the inadequacy of the politics the welfare state. "Suddenly we noted the ransom we were obliged to pay," he proclaimed. "The decay of our cities and of our countryside, the urban and rural landscapes fashioned over the centuries, sometimes millennia, the erosion of sociability, the boredom of man in his family and his work." Henceforth, he asserted, he was unwilling to accept complacently the proposition that this was the "irreversible course of scientific progress."[48] About this time he began calling himself an "anarchist of the right."[49]

Hidden Royalist Signatures within the History of Mentalities

Late in life, Ariès gave one final turn to his explanation of the deep sources of the field to which he had devoted himself as a historian. For his inaugural lecture as a faculty member at the Ecole des Hautes Etudes en Sciences Sociales in 1978, he chose as his topic secrecy as a realm of understanding on a historically emerging boundary between traditional and modern culture during the seventeenth century.[50] Secrecy, he observed, had become an inviting topic for historical investigation.[51] Until recently, few historians had ventured into this obscure realm, and those who had tended to look for peripheral groups whose activities more often than not led to intellectual dead ends.[52] But Ariès argued that secrecy offered historians a portal into the making of modern culture, for it served as a passageway into the mysteries of private life considered as a realm of experience apart, and so would open a whole new domain of cultural history. To explain, he drew a distinction between the invisible and the visible in historical inquiry. The former, he argued, is the domain of the "collective unconscious" (*inconscience collective*), the latter of "conscious awareness" (*conscience claire*). The collective unconscious is a reservoir of tacit understanding on which people draw in their everyday lives. It is the "common sense" of living tradition. Conscious understanding, by contrast, concerns open discourse about public issues. It is the stuff of law, literature, and politics, and has long been the primary subject matter of history. On the transitional boundary between the two, he located a "hidden consciousness" (*conscience opaque*), a realm of knowledge to which only particular groups were privy and which served as a basis for their solidarity and social identity.[53] Law and literature emerged out of this realm in the crossing from orality into literacy, while secret political societies were way stations between the "enlightened despotism" of eighteenth-century monarchies and the mass parties of parliamentary politics at the end of the nineteenth century.[54] On one level, Ariès was talking about secrecy as subject matter for the new history of mentalities that dealt in mental structures as they rubbed edges in those border regions between the unstated and the stated, silence and discourse, orality and literacy. But on another he was making a veiled reference to the secret of his own path into this new kind of history. Here he alluded briefly to his experience under Vichy, when he had been inspired to search out the secrets of the private lives of the youth of that era, the venture that had first led him into the history of mentalities.[55]

Ariès elaborated on his conception of the history of mentalities in an essay he was asked to write in 1978 for an anthology on the "new history," edited by Jacques Le Goff, Jacques Revel, and Roger Chartier, prominent among a younger generation of Annales historians. His article in this collective assessment of the current state of historical research in France signaled the end of his isolation as a freelance historian and his rapprochement with academic historiography. Here his tone is collegial.[56] His essay was long and comprehensive. He treated all aspects of the historiographical emergence of the field, reaching back to pioneering work dating from the 1920s and reaching out to allied fields in the social sciences. Nonetheless, he unobtrusively embedded in his survey the principal elements of the argument about the hidden sources of the history of mentalities that he had enunciated in his early essays, notably demography as the essential method of entry into the secrets of mentalities, and the politics of culture of the 1960s as the inspiration for the "reinvention" and growing popularity of this field.[57]

In this respect, it is interesting to disassemble the components of Ariès's argument for its underlying rhetorical strategy. First, he minimized the importance of the prewar pioneers in historical psychology. Certainly he made reference to the studies by Lucien Febvre and Marc Bloch, founders of Annales historiography, and also to those by Henri Pirenne, Johan Huizinga, and Mario Praz, scholars admired as pioneers in cultural history in the era before the Second World War.[58] But he questioned their influence upon the postwar renewal of cultural history, which he ascribed rather to contemporary cultural currents. He also discounted the role of scholarship in related disciplines, such as ethnology and oral tradition. The new historians of mentalities pursued their own original research, he explained, and correspondences with these allied social sciences, while they might appear striking, had been noted only in retrospect.[59]

Second, Ariès insisted more emphatically than before that the new history of mentalities marked a turning point in contemporary historiography, signaling the end of a way of conceiving of historical time that dated from the era of the French Revolution. In its way, he claimed, the rise of this new cultural history marked "the end of the Enlightenment" in which the "religion of progress" held sway. We find ourselves, he argued, in a present-day world that requires a different stance on historical time, one that notes our present departure from the past rather than our fulfillment of its presumed destiny.[60]

Finally, Ariès took up once more the notion of the "collective unconscious" that his colleagues Duby and Mandrou had first used in the early 1960s to characterize the subject matter of mentalities, but then abandoned in deference to their scholarly critics.[61] The term smacked too much of the suspect psychohistory that had then been in vogue, and more to the point its association with Carl Gustav Jung's notion of a free-floating collective unconscious governed by eternal archetypes. It was also uncomfortably close to essentialist notions about qualities of mind invoked by folklorists and historians in the 1930s to characterize regional and national temperaments.[62] Here Ariès retitled the term the "collective non-conscious" (*non-conscient collectif*) to disassociate the study of mentalities from such essentialism, and to ground it instead in the pragmatics of habits of mind and tacit understandings derived from the concrete dealings of everyday life. On this topic, he might have said more.

Still, this reflection on "mentalities" did summarize his larger interpretation well, and in one respect was suggestive of what would become a major historiographical interest of the 1980s. In closing, he offered the historiographical observation that in the present age historians investigating this boundary between the conscious and the non-conscious were drawing forth the secrets of a "profound collective memory" of an earlier age.[63] It was because of his curiosity about this forgotten world that he had begun his demographic research, inspired by the secrets confided by his students in the Vichy youth camps in 1942.

Mentalities and the Secrets of "the World We Have Lost"

In closing discussion of this topic, I would mention two little-noticed connections between Ariès's projects in the history of mentalities and new directions in cultural history following his death in 1984. The first concerns historians' more frequent substitution of the term "history of private life" for "mentalities" from the mid-1980s. By then, the consensus among the Annales historians was that the term "mentalities" had outlived its usefulness.[64] Many had been suspicious of it anyway and stressed the limitations of the approach.[65] Ariès had invested more in mentalities as a historiographical conception and accordingly drew more meaning from it. But he, too, had become more sensitive to the way in which social mores in the contemporary age were changing, and with them his understanding of the relationship between public and private life. In some of his late-life writings he devoted himself to the recent reconfiguration of that relationship. Here he noted two characteristics of the present age: the ever more imposing managerial role of public authority in setting the standards for the mores of daily life; and the tendency of individuals to retreat more deeply into a privacy divorced from the larger public world.[66]

Ariès did not live to pursue his inquiry into the history of private life to its conclusion. But he did launch the collaborative research project on the topic that led to *Une Histoire de la vie privée,* a five-volume anthology published in the late 1980s in both France and the United States. As a synthesis, it might be thought of as the culminating work of a generation of research in the new cultural history. As surviving coeditor, Georges Duby brought Ariès's project to fruition. But one notes that the conceptual framework for this venture, with its stress on families and their secrets, is close to that blocked out by Ariès in his definition of mentalities twenty years before. The puzzles of sexuality, family life, and privacy first noted by Ariès as the germ of a new kind of history are pursued by the contributors to these volumes along the guidelines he had first envisioned.[67] In summing up the historiographical meaning of the history of mentalities, one might argue that an interpretation of popular culture that put the accent on the differentiation of private from public life had won out over one that stressed class consciousness, and so established a historiographical divide between the social history of the 1950s and 1960s and the cultural history of the 1970s and 1980s.[68]

His second legacy concerns the rising importance of the topic of collective memory in the historiography of the 1980s and 1990s. Ariès never wrote directly on the topic, which mushroomed into historical discourse suddenly about the time of his death in the mid-1980s. But he had much to say about tradition, and in one late-life article he did suggest why memory was likely to become an imposing historiographical topic in the near future. The gist of his argument is that tradition has given itself up to history because we in the contemporary age have given up on particular traditions as repositories of our wisdom and even of our folklore. "The diversity of culture [*la bigarrure*] has disappeared, as modernity has effaced its colors with its dull, gray mantle of uniformity."[69] Under such circumstances, images of exotic cultures are reduced to the kitsch of promotional advertising. What was once unique is rendered commonplace. The authentic sources of our identity are replaced with images that are light and contrived.

Ariès was suggesting that a society does not live easily deprived of its collective memory, and that the collapse of tradition may be the source of our current confusion about our social identity, in the way it had been for his students at La Chapelle in 1942. "One may wonder," he observed, "if our malaise today does not arise from the brutal hypertrophy of the sphere of the known and the spoken, and of a corresponding shrinking of the sphere of secrecy. Formerly, one's deepest convictions were those least avowed because they were the least noticed. But once they surface in our collective consciousness they lose their universal power and come to be judged from outside, criticized, condemned, or forbidden."[70] What distinguishes the present, he concluded, is the demand for the disclosure of the secrets of private life, hidden at the threshold at which they emerge from tacit understanding. This erstwhile royalist turned "anarchist" had neither the ability nor any longer the desire to stay such a trend. Indeed, one might argue that in his commitment to the study of mentalities he helped to further it. But he continued to believe that the search for the secrets of the "world we have lost" might enable us to grasp the historical meaning of the ones we currently possess, just as he, long before in an out-of-the way teaching assignment in Vichy's failed experiment in moral regeneration, had come to discover those of his own time in history.

6

Decades of Debate about
Centuries of Childhood

The Autonomous Life of *Centuries of Childhood*

PHILIPPE ARIÈS'S *L'Enfant et la vie familiale sous l'Ancien Régime* (1960), better known to its American readers as *Centuries of Childhood* (1962), is a revealing example of how a work of history, like one of art or literature, may take on a life of its own among its critics. Assessing its significance has become as much a matter of its readership as its authorship. *Centuries* was Ariès's fourth book, and the one for which he first gained international recognition. As a historian, he had never before received more than marginal notice. He had struggled to find publishers for his earlier books and had to settle for a modest circulation and occasional reviews. Originally published under the imprint of the respected Plon publishing house (for which he had been a reader for more than a decade), then in English by Random House, *Centuries* enjoyed such a warm reception during the 1960s among scholars, students, and the public generally that it opened his way to scholarly fame.[1] Such success was a mixed blessing. It gave him an opportunity to mature as a historian in new ways, to establish a wider network of scholarly associations, to win public recognition in France, to travel to academic conferences, and to lecture at universities at home and abroad. But it also tied him to a place in his own scholarly development, as if he were an actor stuck within a well-remembered character role from which his audience was reluctant to let him part. While Ariès moved on to other projects, *Centuries* remained the reference point to which he was tethered by his critics, who have based their judgment of his authorship on their analysis of its text. From the outset, *Centuries* was provocative in its thesis about a profound change in family sentiments during the early modern era, and in recent decades the book has served as a target for scholars proposing alternative paths into the historical study of family and childhood. But the judgment imposed on Ariès for *Centuries* is too narrowly conceived, for it is only one work within a corpus of articles, essays, and books that he drafted before and after its appearance. Childhood was only one aspect of his broader interest in the family, and the family in turn one topic among many in his broader interest in the history of private life. While *Centuries* deals with themes that remained central to his concerns, standing alone it does not adequately convey his ongoing inquiry into these topics. Here I consider its place in the larger context of his life and work.

As presented in *Centuries,* Ariès's thesis about the changing dynamics of family life might be likened to a triptych. The first panel concerns the emergence of a new conception of childhood among the well-born of the sixteenth and seventeenth centuries. In the long-range transition from the medieval family of the fourteenth and fifteenth centuries to the modern one of the eighteenth and nineteenth, he contends, children gradually displaced adults as the object of the family's attention. Here his principal interest is in the family in its transitional form—the traditional family of Old Regime France. As the center of an extended kin network, it constituted a small community and included servants and clients as well as blood relatives. It exercised some power in local affairs, as the family policed its own members and safeguarded its prerogatives for independent action in the community at large. In a society constructed as a web of interdependency to ensure its survival, family loyalties and obligations counted for more than the particular aspirations of its children. Children resided on the periphery of family life and were subordinated to its collective interests. Too many died young for their parents to fret inordinately about their futures. They mixed in the family and were initiated into adulthood through imitation of adult ways. Among the nobility, the young were often placed at an early age as pages and ladies in waiting in allied families. The typical lot of children in humble families was to be sent away to apprenticeships. The benign indifference of parents to the personal advancement of their children stemmed from social attitudes deeply ingrained in immemorial tradition, which greatly favored pride in the social lineage of ancestors over concern for the personal expectations of the younger generation.

The modern family, by contrast, operated according to a different dynamic. By the eighteenth century, it was growing smaller as it closed ranks around its immediate blood relatives and came to value its privacy more. The parents of modern families took contraceptive measures to limit the number of their offspring and concerned themselves more conscientiously with the welfare of those they chose to bear. Parents showed them more love and affection, and sought to advance their fortunes in life in more calculated ways. Adulthood as a status in life was reconceived as a stage for which children had to be more elaborately trained. Imperceptibly, the notion of coming of age, once conceived in terms of initiation into the obligations of adult life and work, was reconceived as a developmental process in which the child was transformed into an adult. During the sixteenth and seventeenth centuries, the new conception began to take hold within the families of the well-born, and over the course of the nineteenth century it became pervasive throughout society. The family had become a unit of intimacy, more solicitous of its children in the hope of instilling in them a greater measure of confidence about improving their possibilities in life.

The second panel explores the way education contributed to the new conception of childhood in family life. Once identified with intellectual curiosity that was not age-specific, education, too, came to be closely associated with the child's development in the early modern era. Whereas children had once been assigned to serve in other households or apprenticed in the trades, more of them were thenceforth sent to school. The Jesuits prepared the way in the seventeenth century as they took charge of the education of children in greater numbers. Other religious orders followed suit, and like models soon developed in the secular sphere. By the nineteenth century, the education of the young had become a public responsibility, tied to training in literacy and the technical skills needed to carry out the tasks of a more complex, efficient, and disciplined society. The expansion of public education and lengthening years of study became an ongoing trend that continues to this day.[2]

Along the way, school classes were redesigned to correlate with the ages of the children. The curriculum became more specialized and practical. As surrogate parents, school teachers furthered the project of preparing the young for the specific responsibilities they would assume as adults. Over time, schools became the nearly exclusive training ground for the vocational needs of the young, and so institutionalized the modern notion of life as a developmental process. Like families, they encouraged the young in their ambitions to better their lot in life. Education and upward mobility became closely intertwined in light of the liberal reforms inaugurated during the French Revolution, as the principle of equality before the law made it possible for the humbly born to aspire to a higher calling in life. With training and a little luck, a child might go far toward shaping his own future, based on his own conception of the career for which he was destined. Through education, individual wishes for one's own fortunes gradually came to assume precedence over social obligations to family. Rising personal expectations became a hallmark of modern life.

The third panel examines the implications of the changing relationship between parents and children in modern family life. In one sense, the family was losing its influence in the public sphere. By the late eighteenth century, it was growing smaller, and its private life centered on the nuclear family, sometimes surrounded by a few unmarried relatives and servants. The family household, once a center of sociability, was becoming a refuge of privacy and so fostered a new conception of household space configured to meet changing needs. Within its walls, the family segregated itself from society at large, and in turn from one another through the designation of individual rooms for specific purposes. As a compensation for the waning of the gregarious extended family, the waxing nuclear family came to enjoy a deepening intimacy. Over the long run, the modernizing family of the Old Regime served as the leading edge for a revolution in sentiment that fostered romantic love and family affection. For children, the household had become a home, a "haven in a hostile world," the place where they acquired the emotional resources to go out into the world at large.[3] For adults, it was a loving sanctuary to which they returned at the end of the day.

While the modern family had become sensitive to a new conception of child-rearing, it also came to honor its heritage in more sentimental ways. As a unit of affection, it cherished not only its offspring but also its ancestors. Family traditions were confided from one generation to the next, as children were inculcated with anecdotal memories of the family's history. So an idealized image of old France was relocated in the collective memory of family life, and family traditions came to provide an emotional link between past and future. In this way, nostalgia for the past became a romantic resource that reinforced family affection. Family traditions were, in effect, a modern invention. In the values they instilled, the modern family betrayed an ambiguity. In its solicitude for its children, it helped to form the modern mentality that favored self-mastery and individualism. But in its sentimental memories of its deeper heritage, it fostered a private respect for the mores of a sociable world that had largely disappeared from the public sphere. The modern family, Ariès suggested, was of two worlds, adapting to modern times in prizing individual ambition, yet holding fast to old-fashioned traditions anchored in memories of an idealized past.

Centuries of Childhood as a Book for the 1960s

Centuries captured wide scholarly attention and remarkable popularity among readers over the course of the 1960s, especially after it was translated into English. In that latter guise, it was such a success that its English rather than its French title is the one by which it has come to be known. For students of history it provided new subject matter. For general readers, it provided a fascinating perspective on differences between family life in the present and in a past only a few centuries old. Few historians had written on this subject before, and even the sociological studies were sparse. The French historian Michelle Perrot, who edited one of the volumes in the *Histoire de la vie privée* series during the 1980s, points out that the burgeoning scholarship on the new social history during the 1950s had focused on social stratification and class analysis. The family was a neglected topic, and so Ariès's book took on particular significance in the conceptualization of historical changes in its role since the sixteenth century. In this reorientation from class conflicts to generational differences, the prism of social history refracted in a different light.[4] Not since Frédéric Le Play's study in the late nineteenth century had such an approach to the history of the family been attempted.[5]

The early reviews of *Centuries* were scattered, but tended to be sympathetic. Reviewers liked the book because it addressed issues about the psychology of childhood that were increasingly at the center of contemporary public discussion. It is interesting to note that Jean-Louis Flandrin, in one of the first major reviews of *Centuries,* analyzed it in conjunction with two works that were more visibly psychological in approach, those by the French psychohistorian Alain Besançon and by the Dutch psychologist Jan Hendrik van den Berg.[6] Nor is it surprising that *Centuries* found its warmest reception in America, particularly within the emerging ranks of the "helping professions," clinical psychologists and social workers, as well as professors of sociology and psychology. In this respect, it is worth noting that the popular English translation dropped mention of "family" from its title, and so reinforced the identification between the book and the particular concerns about childhood among its readers.[7] The book was published shortly before preoccupation with alienated youth and their rebellion against parental authority and the prevailing conventions of society became widespread, in the heyday of the counterculture in the United States, of the "revolution" of university students in the 1968 protest in France, and of a new generation of political dissidents in eastern Europe. For youth, it was time for a new romanticism, of lyrical flights of fancy as they sought to pursue their own, more personalized dreams. "Personal growth" became the watchword of a burgeoning interest in ego-psychology. Families seemed more sensitive than ever before to generational differences. "Youth" became a principal topic of psychological attention, and some historians turned to the concept of "generations" as an interpretative principle.[8]

The appearance of *Centuries* not only coincided with this rising interest in ego-psychology; the book indeed provided it with a much-needed historical context. Ariès showed how the developmental principle itself had emerged in the long-range transition from medieval to modern family life, and so offered insight into the complex tensions that lifelong psychological growth entailed in contemporary society. In his exploration of the idea of personal development as "progress" in the private side of life, he spoke to issues historians had hitherto addressed only in the political sphere, and these became a point of reference for public discussion. Here was a new and highly original historical approach to collective psychology. In *Centuries* Ariès plotted the stages of the historical emergence of the developmental life cycle, and thus provided a historical explanation for the model of stages of lifelong growth then being popularized by ego-psychologists such as Erik Erikson.[9] While he never punctuated the human ontogeny quite as schematically as had Erikson, Ariès showed the way in which the stages of life conceived as a developmental process had emerged in the mentality of Western culture: childhood as an invention of the sixteenth century; youth of the eighteenth, adolescence of the nineteenth. The developmental cycle of life, he suggested, was an ongoing elaboration of a modern conception of the human condition. While he did not speak directly to the issue of troubled youth in *Centuries,* he was aware of the contemporary sense of crisis about the problem of their place in the modern family. In his articles for the newspaper *La Nation française* during the late 1950s and early 1960s, he moved beyond the subject matter of his book to explore these present-day concerns.[10]

The Critical Eye on *Centuries* since the 1970s

As the scholarship on childhood and family sparked by Ariès expanded during the 1970s, students of the subject began to offer more critical judgments about *Centuries.* Though Ariès had initially been treated sympathetically by left-leaning historians in the United States, probably because they knew little about him, some of them came to wonder about his youthful association with the Action Française, details of which he began to reveal in interviews in which he spoke openly about his royalist past.[11] His candor provided them with fodder. The most publicized criticism was that of the Princeton historian Lawrence Stone in a review entitled "The Massacre of the Innocents" in the *New York Review of Books* in 1974.[12] Stone called attention to what he regarded as flaws in Ariès's methods and conclusions. With his own study of family life in early modern England underway, he was on the lookout for holes in Ariès's argument. Conscious of Ariès's traditionalist Catholicism and his youthful association with the Action Française, he presented his critique in light of what one might have expected were Ariès's convictions about family life and childhood in light of such a background. Conceding the pioneering nature of Ariès's model of the evolution of family life, he nonetheless construed it as an anti-modernist argument, drawing upon the Christian notion of a fall from grace. Ariès, he contended, offered a pessimistic view of family life, caught in a process of degeneration from medieval sociability, in which people of all ages intermingled freely, toward modern individualism, which set boundaries to the intercourse between adults and children and so fostered an isolating social discipline.

Accordingly, he was unable to recognize, or unwilling to acknowledge, Ariès's insight into the role of the family as an agency of modernization or into the nature of childhood as a developmental process. Whereas Ariès accorded the new primary schools of the seventeenth century the role of surrogate parents, Stone underscored the difference in their purpose. "The rise of the school is best seen not as part of the same process as the growth of the child-oriented family," he argued, "but as its very antithesis, the transfer to an impersonal institution of a socializing function previously performed by the family." Stone also faulted Ariès for his inattention to class differences, and he questioned whether the rise of the affectionate family proceeded as a unilinear process.

Given the tenor of Stone's remarks about *Centuries of Childhood,* one is surprised to see the degree to which his larger interpretation in his *Family, Sex and Marriage in England, 1500–1800,* published a few years later, accorded with that advanced by Ariès.[13] Stone may have discriminated among the attitudes of the different social classes more directly and skillfully. But he agreed with Ariès's view that the rise of the affectionate family emerged first among the well-born, and he presented the long-range trend toward the reorganization of emotional life within the family much as Ariès had. In their interpretations of the "revolution in sentiment" that spread among the social elite of the early modern era in western Europe, they share an essential common ground.[14]

More heavy-handed was the critique by the English historian Adrian Wilson in the learned journal *History and Theory* in 1981. Wilson entitled his essay "The Infancy of the History of Childhood: An Appraisal of Philippe Ariès" to suggest that, Ariès's scholarship notwithstanding, the historical inquiry into this topic had hardly begun.[15] He mocked Ariès's self-deprecating reference to his status as an amateur historian, the implication being that such a weighty topic would have been better left to professionals. The more serious side of Wilson's critique turned on historiographical grounds. He invoked Herbert Butterfield's famous attack on "Whig" history to accuse Ariès of anachronism for having adopted a present-minded perspective. Wilson claimed that Ariès construed family relationships in the past as if they were no different from those in the present. It was an odd critique, given Ariès's thesis about the comparatively recent "discovery" of childhood. Wilson's recourse to Butterfield's argument was derived from the proposition that the historian should study the past for its own sake. Ariès's purpose was more pragmatic.[16] Arguing from a premise not unlike that of the Annales historians, he had sought to show that privileging the present moment as a historical frame of reference makes one more sensitive to the ways the past differs from it. So brutal was Wilson's indictment that Ariès never bothered to reply to it. But it must have had its effect in shaking professorial confidence in Ariès's scholarship, at least in the English-speaking world.

More judicious was the review in the same journal by the Wesleyan professor Richard Vann a year later. Vann entitled his article "The Youth of *Centuries of Childhood*," a clever play on the title of Wilson's article and, more to the point, on the life of its own that the book had acquired over two decades. While suggesting some grave reservations about the consistency of Ariès's argument and the adequacy of his evidence, he was struck by the popularity the book had gained, and reviewed the reviews in that light.[17] At the heart of his critique, Vann noted the ambiguity of Ariès's argument in its seemingly contradictory allegiance to traditional and modern ways. The ambiguity, he pointed out, might reflect the flaws of an argument insufficiently well thought out. On the other hand, he observed, ambiguity was sometimes the hallmark of a classic whose appeal lay in its capacity to harmonize opposing perspectives and so to universalize the subject matter. Was *Centuries* a classic in that sense, he queried? While demurring before an explicit answer to his own question, he expressed his doubts that this work approached such an exalted status. He wondered whether *Centuries*, its popularity notwithstanding, might not soon fade into oblivion. "Will the book quietly succumb to the acid in the wood pulp that is slowly eating away at its pages?" he asked, ". . . except as a document in the history of historiography?" But the appeal of Ariès's book, Vann conceded, lay in the paradigm of family life it offered, and "no paradigm dies until a superior one is born, and the creation of that will be a formidable enterprise indeed."[18]

That daunting task has not dissuaded scholars from trying. As the Tulane historian Linda Pollock recently observed, "The history of childhood has moved a long way from Philippe Ariès's early influential claim that the past lacked a concept of childhood, that childhood was an unimportant phase in the life-cycle, and that the frailty of children precluded any great parental attachment to them."[19] Still, judging from the recent reviews, the Ariès thesis today looms as large as ever, as scholars continue to turn to it as a target for their own interpretative claims.

At the turn of the twenty-first century, historians of childhood and family tend to stress continuities in attitudes and child-rearing practices dating back to the Middle Ages. The case for continuity has been stated boldly by Steven Ozment. A Harvard historian who has published widely on the family in Germany in the era of the Reformation, he recently wrote *Ancestors* (2001), a summary overview of scholarship on families built around a critique of what he characterizes as the "Arièsian myth" of childhood.[20] Ozment couches his argument in broader terms than did Ariès's earlier critics and identifies some, including Flandrin, Stone, and Edward Shorter, with the Ariès thesis. His critique challenges a generation of scholarship issuing from Ariès's proposition about the "revolution in sentiment" underpinning attitudes toward family life in early modern Europe. Ozment worked with quite different evidence, derived from his scholarship on the culture of the German Reformation, and his purpose is more to point out the perils of presenting a covering thesis for parent-child relationships for an era in which they were complex and varied.[21] Culling the letters of German merchant families dating from the Middle Ages, he marshals impressive evidence of their intimate and loving relationships. His discussion of the debates of the Reformation on issues such as marriage, celibacy, childbirth, and education reveals how conscientiously church leaders had thought through family issues and were sensitive to their problems. If parents did not always love their children adequately, it was not for ignorance of what the ideal of a loving family might be.

One might argue that Ozment presents the Protestant reply to Ariès's Catholic analysis of family life in the early modern era. From a methodological perspective, however, he goes further in contending that no covering thesis is better than one that distorts the record.[22] His approach at the turn of the twenty-first century suggests a retreat from the structuralist model with which Ariès and the Annalistes worked. Suspicious of abstractions, he challenges arguments based largely on demographic data and judicial records, the evidence on which Ariès and other historians of mentalities had made their claims. He draws attention to the insights to be gained from the anecdotal surprises in family archives, especially letters in their spontaneity and informality, and concludes that family affection appears to have found constant expression amidst the travails of life in the early modern era.

One might counter that from a structuralist perspective a chronology of change is difficult to pinpoint, given that the tension between the old indifference and the new affection in family life was ongoing. One might expect to find anecdotal evidence of both. Only by looking at the dynamics of family relations *à la longue durée*, Ariès suggests, might one be able to discern the larger trend. In the closing pages of *Centuries*, he takes pains to convey his sense of the balance the family of the early modern era had succeeded in establishing between its aspirations for its children and its sentimental respect for traditional ways.[23] Had he been around for today's historiographical controversy, he would surely have agreed with Ozment about the value of family archives. His last project in the last year of his life was an investigation of the histories of his own and his wife's families, based on just such sources.

His telling argument notwithstanding, Ozment's case for continuity seems overstated to many scholars in the field, as their research draws them into murky complexities. As the English medievalist Nicholas Orme puts it, the main difference between our understanding of medieval and of modern family life is more a matter of evidence than of attitudes. For medieval families, the record reveals not their lack of affection but rather a lack of data from which we might generalize about what they thought and how they behaved. The written record is so sketchy, and the more we study it the more variegated the experience appears to have been. The evidential record thickens as we approach modern times, and so we may reach more certain conclusions about modern parental attitudes toward offspring. But about most parents in those earlier times "we know nothing at all."[24]

It would be astonishing if the decades of research stimulated by Ariès's *Centuries* did not result in an ever-more complex discrimination of contexts and experiences. But for all the richness and detail of this research, there is no shared sense of an emerging paradigm to replace Ariès's model, as early critics once presumed there would be. Considering the enormous scholarly energy devoted to articulating or contesting the paradigm advanced in *Centuries*, one might conclude that it may be in the nature of paradigms to take shape in early insight rather than later reflection. Today's scholars have exposed the reductionist character of Ariès's thesis. Still, they return to it incessantly as the reference with which to signal their own new departures. Pollock therefore suggests that the debate about the Ariès thesis has led us to an interpretative impasse, and that we should look for other avenues by which a "more well-rounded approach" to the topic might proceed.[25]

The complaint of these historians about the Ariès thesis concerns not only his claim about parent-child relations within families, but also, and more important, his underlying conviction about a revolution in sentiment. Ironically, Ariès's intellectual adversaries of the 1970s—Stone, Flandrin, and Shorter—are now grouped with him as proponents of an interpretation they themselves had once disputed or at least qualified.[26] Whatever their differences in those days, Ariès and his scholarly antagonists were at one in their convictions about a fundamental "revolution in sentiment" during the early modern era. Today's historians of family and childhood question that notion. In their reinterpretations, Ariès's *Centuries* has become the metonymic signature for the generation of scholars that linked the emergence of the affectionate family with the emergence of a developmental conception of the life process. Pollock refers to the approach as the "modernization paradigm."

Here the new historians of family life would seem to take issue not only with Ariès and his scholarly adversaries of the 1970s but also with the larger Annales project for a new kind of cultural history, whose beginnings might be traced all the way back to Lucien Febvre's appeal to historians in the 1940s to inquire into the unknown history of sentiment, and whose culmination might be identified with the multivolume history of private life published in the 1980s under Ariès's editorial direction. The new historians of family challenge the notion that changes in the organization of emotional life may be measured in centuries rather than eons, so deeply are human emotions grounded in what is constant in human nature. Whereas most historians would be quite willing to concede the historical emergence of the reality of changing psychological needs in the political sphere (as in rising expectations for individual liberty and personal opportunity), these historians remain reluctant to acknowledge its counterpart in the cultural one (the search for a new kind of intimacy tied to private identity and personal fulfillment). Family affection is presented as the bedrock of human relations since time immemorial. While conceding some indexes of changing modes of familial affection, they maintain that these sentiments are too deeply embedded in the human condition to stray very far from timeless norms. The Cambridge historian Eamon Duffy, reviewing the recent literature, draws a further conclusion. He presents Ariès as an early apostle of the notion of constructed identity that so mesmerized historians during the 1980s. "If Ariès was right," he observes, "then human nature itself was entirely in our own hands, a construct, not a given."[27] So the essentialism of a younger generation of cultural historians would displace the constructivism of the older one in what has become a fascinating debate about the extent to which human nature itself is subject to demonstrable historical change.

It was the issue about which the young Ariès had puzzled during the Vichy years, and it was one to which he would return in late life.[28] In his attempt to make sense of demographic trends among French families in the modern era, he had turned to mutable cultural factors to challenge the biological determinism espoused by Vichyite educators. His first interest in "mentalities" had been situated on that boundary between the biological and the cultural, and his intuition was to emphasize the latter as a route to understanding the vicissitudes in birth rates among the French across the ages. In the cultural sphere, he concluded, people in the early modern era did come to believe that they could exercise some measure of control over the techniques of life, and so had recourse to the Malthusian practices that reshaped the emotional lives of their families.

Thus Ariès's proposition about a "revolution in sentiment" during the early modern era, with its implications about a "collective mentality" that changes over a middle range of historical time—centuries rather than millennia—continues to inspire controversy.[29] Whatever the merits of the Ariès thesis, two propositions seem incontrovertible as a preface to my consideration of its place in his life's work. The first concerns his contribution to the new cultural history. *Centuries of Childhood* had an enormous impact on subsequent scholarly inquiry into this topic. For much of the 1970s, it was a working model for historians.[30] As the book that ignited interest in the field of childhood and family history, it not only served as a point of departure for scholarship on childhood and family life, but also paved the royal road into the broader field of the history of private life.

The second concerns Ariès's authorship. Critics continue to focus on *Centuries* rather than on the ensemble of Ariès's work. It is the book to which his identity remains tied, and those who have viewed Ariès's contribution as historian skeptically invoke it as the defining moment of his authorship. For example, in a recent review of a compendium of Ariès's political journalism edited and published thirteen years after his death, the French historian Emmanuel Le Roy Ladurie used the occasion to reduce Ariès's accomplishment to a misguided thesis about attitudes toward children in medieval France.[31] Yet the topic of family was only an example of the cultural trend that Ariès discerned. In keeping with the developmental conception he advanced, he himself was a scholar who developed throughout his life. *Centuries* was a stage on his life's way. Once he had published it, he turned to new topics in mentalities, and he continued to grow intellectually. His critics may not have been aware of his late-life historical writings on the family, which incorporate a wider inquiry into human sexuality, love and marriage, the crisis of the contemporary nuclear family, and the place of the family within the long-range history of an interconnected yet pluralistic realm of private life. One might place the scholars' comments on *Centuries* within the historiographical context in which it germinated, then flourished, and later inspired a younger generation of scholars to pursue the leads it opened into a wider realm of private life.

The Modesty of the Conception of *Centuries of Childhood*

Ariès did not set out to propose a new paradigm of the history of family life in Old Regime France. In his autobiographical assessment of the place of *Centuries* among the projects of his life, he notes how tentative were its beginnings. He suggests that the conception of *Centuries* was accidental, a product of some intellectual brainstorming that proceeded from his earlier work in demography and historiography, together with insights gained through a newfound interest in iconography in the late 1940s, made possible by the intellectual companionship of his wife Primerose, an art historian by training.

Ariès's first idea was to study historical changes in costume, and he and Primerose began to frequent the Salle des Estampes at the Bibliothèque Nationale, which held a major collection of pictorial images of changing fashions. Eventually he abandoned this project, judging his specialized knowledge of the subject too meager and the technical context too daunting to master. But in the course of his research into this collection of illustrations, he noted how the representation of family and childhood changed over the course of the early modern era. As he traced the portraits of families in the portfolios of images at the Salle des Estampes, he noted that its members over time came to display more individualized features. Parents took on a softer, more humane look in keeping with their responsibility and care. Children moved to the center of visual attention. The medieval family had been cast in a public image that portrayed pride and power. But the image of the modern nuclear family had been recast in a more intimate private setting.[32]

As a source of his thinking about the social life of families, Ariès mentions the influence of Fernand Braudel's magisterial study of the culture of the Mediterranean world in the early modern era.[33] It confirmed his ideas about the sociability of traditional society. The family of old France was a sociable unit. It had become centered on its own private concerns, even though it drew in a larger community. Children, who lived on the margins of this family and who received no more attention than maiden aunts or domestic servants, gradually found a more significant place in its affections. Images of the early modern era especially fascinated Ariès because in them he saw the family in transition, presiding over a private world in which children were receiving greater attention than ever before.

Ariès's idea about family affection also harked back to the project in demography on which he had worked during his Vichy days and published shortly thereafter as *Histoire des populations françaises*—his thesis about the secret compact of spouses to practice contraception in the privacy of their sexual relations. That secret involved several "modern" notions: concern for self in the pursuit of happiness; concern for each other in a more loving relationship; greater solicitude for those children that they chose to bear; a need for a more private household in which such attitudes could find expression. Did not these changes in sentiment, he hypothesized, converge upon a new role for the family as a unit of affection? Such intertwined secrets are a deep source of his inspiration to write *Centuries*. Here he made the leap from his early work on the rise of contraception to his more specific interest in the rise of family affection.[34]

There was also a quarrel lingering from the war years that piqued his interest. Conservative church spokesmen continued to voice the Vichyite lament about the decline of the family in the face of modern secularizing trends. But Ariès from his research was convinced that family life in the modern era had been strengthened by the trends he discerned. The modern family was a loving one. In his autobiography he notes that his original intention had been to entitle his book "L'Enfant et le sentiment de famille."[35] One might say that the conception of *Centuries* was all about a changing cultural attitude toward the relationship between sexual love and procreation. The love bond underpinning the revolution of sentiment in the early modern era involved not only love of parents for their children, but also love of spouses for each other. The hidden revolution in contraceptive practices among married couples began with their rising expectations for themselves. Their intentions were modern in that they were based on techniques calculated to master the unruly sexual urges of the human body. Here a private "sentiment" that can only be construed as modern had come into existence to complement the public "reason of state" conventionally invoked to explain the rise of "modern" culture.[36]

I might make one final point about the conception of *Centuries*. Ariès had formulated his thesis quite clearly by the mid-1950s, as two articles published in 1956 reveal. We might consider them as pilot studies for the book that he had in mind, and in some ways he laid out the scheme for his project more explicitly there.[37] More sharply than in *Centuries,* he distinguished three stages of changing attitudes toward family life: medieval, traditional, modern. In these articles, Ariès was clearly most interested in the traditional family of Old Regime France. In this family he found a sociable extended community. He distinguishes it not only from the medieval family loosely organized as a clan but also from the closely bound modern family of the eighteenth and nineteenth centuries, which came to cherish its intimacy and privacy. If the era of the Old Regime witnessed a "revolution" in sentiment, it proceeded *à la longue durée* as a remodeling of tradition over centuries, one barely perceptible to those who were caught up in its ways. Parents became more solicitous of the future of their children from the sixteenth century. But only gradually did children gravitate to the center of a family's attention. A fourth stage, that of the postmodern family of the late twentieth century, is beyond the scope of *Centuries,* but nonetheless a topic to which Ariès would turn in his late-life writings.

Centuries Comes of Age: Mentalities as an Alternative to Psychohistory

Ariès was an unsuspecting psychologist. As a demographer who turned to cultural issues, he ended by explaining them in psychological terms. In this his ideas resonated with the psychological turn in historical inquiry by the 1960s, especially in the United States. There psychological issues seemed urgent to historians. In his presidential address at the annual meeting of the America Historical Association in 1958, William Langer identified historical psychology as the "next assignment" to which historians should direct their scholarly attention.[38] Most of this work, especially in the United States, centered on applications of Freudian psychoanalysis to historical problems. Dubbed "psychohistory," the approach inspired a number of biographies that employed Freudian psychoanalytic technique.[39] But Freud's own interest in history concerned a remote past deep in human origins, too reductionist and deterministic for most historians to countenance. It implied a psychoanalytic approach that struck many as doctrinaire. David Stannard's critique, *Shrinking History* (1980), articulated well the historians' concerns.[40]

One might say that Ariès shared these suspicions of Freud as a carryover from his days in the Action Française. Freud, he later remarked, was a product of his times, and the invention of psychoanalysis reflected the needs of a society that had come to value individual privacy and the cultivation of the self and suffered the strains of doing so. Even in the present age, he argued, psychoanalysis had few applications in collective psychology. He proposed as an alternative a psychology of mentalities, construed as habits of mind that need no hermetic decoding. At the same time, he provided a historical context for the rise of ego-psychology with its rhetoric about lifelong psychological growth that appealed so to the psychoanalytic community during the 1960s. More broadly, ego-psychology was attuned to the romantic sentiments of the counterculture among youth in that era. The central theorist of this revised psychoanalytic approach was Erik Erikson, lionized for his *Young Man Luther* (1958), a psychological study of the transforming adolescent identity crisis of the religious reformer Martin Luther that had prepared the way for his achievements as a young adult.[41] Erikson posed Luther's dilemma as one of coming to terms with his ego-ideal—his self-consciousness about the integrity and direction of his moral intentions. This book, like *Centuries,* spoke to the issue of childhood and youth as developmental stages in life, a preoccupation not only of historians but also of American society at large during the 1960s.

In a way, Ariès devised a historical model of changing attitudes toward the process of coming of age that paralleled Erikson's formulation of an ontogeny of personal growth, and one might contend that Ariès played for the history of mentalities the role that Erikson played for psychohistory.[42] The question that rendered Ariès's work so important in such a comparison was this: could ego-psychology propose a new approach to history without explaining the historically changing understanding of the ego-ideal? Or, to put the question more specifically in terms of Erikson's classic work, could young man Luther have experienced an "identity crisis" in the early sixteenth century of the sort with which psychologists were concerned in the late twentieth century? Erikson's study, while original and useful, was weak on historical context. He treated Luther as if he possessed twentieth-century sensibilities. Ariès, by contrast, in his appreciation of the centuries that had been required for the development of today's more complex ego-ideal, gave a more convincing explanation of the historical circumstances in which a "modern" crisis of coming of age might have emerged. The history of mentalities, one might say, provided a context in which to understand the birth of conceptions today identified with ego-psychology. It addressed basic attitudes toward expectations of life as they have been remolded in recent centuries, not in the eons of time that Freud had allotted for their formulation.[43]

At the time, Ariès received the approbation of historians sympathetic to

Freud who could see the expanding possibilities of Ariès's approach. Peter Gay was among the first of these reviewers.[44] Saul Friedländer also cited the history of mentalities as a promising approach to collective psychology.[45] In terms of the historiographical interests of the 1960s, Ariès was a persuasive spokesman for a nonpsychoanalytic psychology, which soon swept historians up into a broader interest in a cultural history better attuned to the attitudes and sensibilities of ordinary people. If the concept of "mentalities" ultimately proved unsatisfying to professional historians, the field of study it identified enjoyed a decade of highly productive scholarship. Thanks to *Centuries,* the history of childhood and family grew dramatically. By the end of the 1970s, a number of book-length historical studies of family and childhood had appeared, notably those by Edward Shorter and Christopher Lasch, both of whom explored psychological themes.[46] Ongoing scholarship found outlets in three new learned journals devoted to historical psychology, one of which referred to itself as the *Journal of the History of Childhood,* another as *The Journal of Family History.*[47]

The meaning of Ariès's *Centuries of Childhood* for his generation was captured well by Neil Postman in *The Disappearance of Childhood,* published in 1982. A discerning critic of contemporary social and cultural trends, he was struck by the timing and the popularity of Ariès's book. He recognized that while Ariès's book dealt with the family in old France, its primary meaning lay in the remaking of the family for the modern age. Postman had a particular interest in the social impact of changing technologies of communication, and thus emphasized the relationship between the rise of the modern conception of childhood and the rise of print culture. More and more children were learning to read, and so were becoming more precociously self-aware. But Postman was observing the cultural effects of the print revolution from the vantage point of the media revolution of his own day. Among its effects was an analogous change in the sentiments of family life. Here he was especially astute in his observation that Ariès's book appeared at a time when the parent-child relationship as it had been understood through the modern age was visibly and precipitously changing. Ariès wrote of the invention of a modern notion of childhood, Postman observed, just as it was beginning to lose its meaning for the generation of parents who assumed their role during the 1960s. Ariès's book, he suggested, might appear to convey nostalgia for the passing of the traditional family of the seventeenth century. But in fact it incited nostalgia for the modern family that was disappearing for the readers he addressed. It was not just the indexes of the contemporary family in crisis that bothered them—the rising divorce rate and the rising percentage of single-parent households—but also the changing nature of child-rearing. In a dawning age of media, Postman observed, children were exposed at an early age to adult secrets into which they had formerly been initiated only gradually. In the modern age, children had been permitted the time and space to use their curiosity and imagination to explore their own world, with its own language, games, and play. But with the pervasive presence of television in contemporary culture, children at a tender age were brutally exposed to the realities of adulthood, while adults were encouraged by the same medium to indulge in childlike fantasies of their lives and responsibilities. If traditional society had witnessed the passing of the child as little adult, the present one was witnessing the arrival of the adult as persistent child. In this overlapping of the worlds of the "adultified" child and the "childified" adult, the boundary between them blurred. In the process, childhood as a separate estate in life was beginning to disappear, as evinced in the dramatically escalating participation of children in the vices, passions, and crimes of adults. Childhood had been invented in the Renaissance as a cultural construct of social patterning that would contribute to the making of modern culture. Now it was being crowded out in the remaking of the image of the child to suit the needs of a media-driven culture.[48]

Postman addressed what he perceived to be a contemporary cultural crisis, and not everyone might agree with his diagnosis. But his poignant references to Ariès's work as the stimulus for his own provide insight into the broad power of Ariès's appeal to the generation that came of age in the era 1960–80. Without suggesting any change in the profound psychology of basic and timeless parental affection for children, Postman pointed to a dramatic change in contemporary social patterning that altered the expression of human affection, much as had the revolution in sentiment that Ariès attributed to the families of the seventeenth century.[49] Ariès's book held meaning for his generation because he was able to place their urgent worries about parenting in historical perspective and so to help them to come to terms with a revolution in their own sentiments. Without being preachy, *Centuries* was a book that considered the changing social values with which the parent-child relationship has been invested in recent centuries, and so permitted his generation to reflect more fully upon their own. Ariès claimed to write of the past in light of present dilemmas. His enormous popularity and influence upon the public of his day may be attributed in some measure to his insight in identifying a problem that was of such pressing concern to his contemporaries, and in some measure to his talent in setting forth a panoramic perspective on changing patterns of child-rearing that made sense to them. In terms of its crafting, *Centuries* may have been Ariès's least accomplished book. But as it was read by Postman, so it was by many others—as a book to think with. How else can we account for the power of its appeal in the launching of the scholarly history of childhood, a field one might argue Ariès invented? Hundreds of books and articles followed its appearance, whereas very few had appeared before.[50] The disturbing indexes of the disappearance of childhood noted by Postman have remained, indeed they have multiplied. But at the turn of the twenty-first century, they have lost their urgency for today's historians of childhood, who appear to have forgotten the conditions under which Ariès marked out the field of inquiry they now tend in such cultivated furrows.

Legacy: "Private Life" as *Centuries*' Child

Ariès did not stand still with the publication of *Centuries*. Beyond an ongoing exploration of issues concerning the contemporary family, he turned to a new project on the history of attitudes toward death and mourning. Here he received a more favorable French reception. He became a much-sought participant in the discussion of historical topics of the day. After joining the faculty of the Ecole des Hautes Etudes in 1978, he began to take his research interests in broader directions. His essay on "mentalities" for an Annales-directed summary volume on the new history marked out the terrain of his own project within the broad territory of cultural history. It provided a segue to his collegial project on the history of private life, which incorporated the topic of family into a more comprehensive study of the historically emerging divide between public and private life. His reconsideration of family issues also inspired him to undertake historical research on his own family, a project regrettably never realized before his death. Ariès's major legacy among French historians was not *Centuries,* but his history of private life project, published after his death as *Histoire de la vie privée* (1986). It was one he sketched, then parceled out among contributors. It was an ambitious synthesis of some twenty years of research in mentalities. Younger scholars identified with the Annales school took the measure of his importance. Roger Chartier, by then a distinguished historian himself, helped to bring Ariès's project on private life to fruition. He also edited and republished *Le Temps de l'Histoire* (1986), then *Les Traditions sociales dans les pays de France* together with several of Ariès's lesser-known essays (1993).[51] He compared him with other independent-minded historians of the day, notably Norbert Elias, and he underscored his passionate devotion to the study of the past as his distinguishing trait.[52] Michel Foucault remembered him for a quirky originality (not unlike his own).[53]

It is ironical that at the time American scholars, once enthusiastic about his work, began expressing skepticism about its merits, his previously re-served French colleagues came to acknowledge its originality by considering it in a larger context and by drawing him into their own scholarly projects. Viewed from the European side of the Atlantic, Ariès's legacy as historian is broader and more fluid than his American critics may have imagined. His history of the family was eventually incorporated into a broader in-terpretation of the history of private life, which in fact did serve as the guiding paradigm for this synthesis of a generation of work in the history of mentalities. Ariès's own work as a historian remained innovative; his late-life projects tended in new directions, though continuing to draw on the seminal ideas of his youth. In this respect, his *Histoire des populations françaises* is a better place than *Centuries* to look for the deep sources of his scholarship considered in its ensemble.

In light of their focus on *Centuries,* Ariès's critics have been predisposed to view the value of his accomplishment in light of a model of entropy— their expectation that interest in his work would eventually wear down. But such a judgment does not account for the insight he brought to his new avenues of research, or the cumulative influence of his ideas. One might better liken the corpus of his historical work to that of an hourglass, with *Centuries* as the narrowing center through which so many grains of scholarly energy flowed. *Centuries* marked Ariès's passage from demogra-phy to mentalities. What began as a problem in historical demography during the era of Vichyite defeatism of the early 1940s he transformed into one of historical psychology during the early 1960s, an era sanguine about the human potential for personal growth, and by the 1980s into a pano-ramic interpretation of the history of mores across the expanse of Western civilization. Through *Centuries,* Ariès brought the topic of families out of the erudite discussion of demographers into the public discourse of popular concern about the crisis of the contemporary family, and more broadly, about changing social mores in the transition from a modern culture shaped by bourgeois values to the mass culture of the present age. In terms of his own personal growth, therefore, it is his most important book. It marked a point of mid-life renewal in which he found a positive way to re-vision the world from which he came and to detach it from its associ-ation with the tired traditionalism of the Action Française or, worse, the stigma of its association with the shame of Vichy. The image of the traditional family tainted by Vichyite propaganda was redeployed in a different context, to be appreciated for what it revealed about the nature and the needs of the contemporary family. Was not the Old Regime family, he proposed, the source of the modern world of privacy that contemporary society has come to value so?

Finally, to take the measure of Ariès the historian obliges us as well to revisit his youthful aspiration to be a man of letters in the old-fashioned sense, a man of worldly tastes based on refined personal convictions. Like such classic French authors as Montesquieu, Michelet, Tocqueville, and Taine, Ariès may be appreciated not only for his particular contribution to historical knowledge but also for the depth of his insight into the human predicament in his times. It is such an appeal that may keep readers returning to Ariès, whatever the new historical finds about family and childhood. As the America historiographer Hayden White has pointed out, if historians were judged simply for their contributions to an accumulating body of knowledge, then each generation of historians would eclipse its predecessor.[54] But like philosophers, writers, and artists, historians too can have an enduring appeal for the quality of their writing or the depth of their insight into the nature of the human condition. Ariès's was not simply a contribution to scholarship but a personalized portrait of the past with its particular grace, appeal, and defining characteristics. He put a long tradition of child-rearing, tacitly modeled and remodeled across the ages, into historical perspective. In the originality of this perspective, *Centuries of Childhood* is a book that inspires reflection, and it is no surprise that it should have stimulated so much discussion of the topic for so long.[55] As a historian willing to address a topic of such vital concern to his contemporaries, Ariès helps us to understand the way in which the historian in the postmodern world might take on the mantle once worn by the "public intellectual," a social type that has largely disappeared. His reinvention of the model, and its success, may suggest the recent turn of French historians, and some of their American counterparts, to the vogue of *égo-histoire*.

7

Of Death and Destiny

The Ariès/Vovelle Debate about
the History of Mourning

History as a Remedy for an Inability to Mourn

IN THE 1960s Ariès embarked on a massive project of coming to terms with the second major topic he had blocked out in his historical studies in the late 1940s—that of Western attitudes toward death and mourning.[1] Like his study of the family, the source of his project reverts to the Vichy years. The death of his brother Jacques in one of the last campaigns of the war, he confided in friends, had been a major factor in his initial interest in past practices of mourning loved ones.[2] Though he sketched some ideas on the "techniques of death" in his book on historical demography in the late 1940s, his primary interest then was in practices for keeping death at bay—better diet, hygiene, and health through advances in medicine.[3] For the larger project that he took up during the 1960s, he redirected his attention to changing attitudes toward death's inevitability—that is, toward changing practices of mourning across the ages. By then, he was well into middle age, and personal encounters with his own mortality may have been more on his mind. During the late 1950s, he had contracted tuberculosis and spent several months in a sanatorium in the Pyrenées. The death of his mother, Yvonne, in 1964 also affected him deeply.

But there were broader factors that influenced his decision to turn to this topic as well. It is telling that he characterized the popular stance on death in the contemporary age as "forbidden" (*la mort interdite*), as if to convey an inability to mourn that had afflicted his entire generation. One might argue that at some level Ariès was trying to come to terms with losses that he identified with the Vichy years—the demise of his old-fashioned royalist world, mired in the moral compromises of the Vichy regime with the Third Reich. Now in the early 1960s, he may at last have been prepared to place his personal reckoning with his experience of those years in historical perspective. To work through his personal memories of all of his losses, both private and public, he set out to historicize the practice of mourning in the Western tradition.

Ariès's memories of the Vichy era, of course, were intimately tied to the generalized collective mourning attending the fall of France, most of it self-defeating. Such mourning drew heavily on a fatalism readily expressed by right-wing intellectuals at the time. For many of them, France's rapid military collapse stemmed not only from the inadequate statesmanship of the leaders of the Third Republic, but also and more poignantly from the moral decadence of the modern era, and even from the biological degeneration of the French people. A poignant argument was offered by Ariès's mentor, Daniel Halévy, in his memoir on the fall, *Trois Epreuves* (1941); his assessment is learned and discerning, but typical of the resignation with which he accepted its conditions.[4]

Ariès admits to having initially shared these sentiments.[5] But the Vichy experiment had gone awry, and his first reaction in the postwar years was to forget that experience and to strike out in new directions. He retained his affection for the mores of old France, but sought to minimize his sense of loss by placing his memory of that now vanishing world in a modern perspective. In his postwar journey from royalist apologist to critical historian, he voiced his preference for some balance between continuity and change, between the inertial power of the wisdom of the past and the practical appeal of innovation in the present. Still, over time he sensed the need to come to terms with the Vichy years. Whatever his feelings about the misguided efforts of Vichy's leaders to resuscitate a politics born in old France, he wanted to rescue something authentic in that heritage, which he judged not merely a venerable culture but also a vital resource for social renewal.[6] There is thus a paradox at the heart of his project. On the one hand his investigation of past practices of mourning was deeply personal. On the other, it considered in the broadest possible way the collective loss of connection in the contemporary age with ancient traditions of mourning.

It is also worth noting that Ariès's historical inquiry into attitudes toward mourning coincided with his troubled reckoning with the Algerian crisis, which for him and his companions on the right resuscitated so many memories of the unresolved issues of the Vichy years. As he explained in a newspaper article in *La Nation française* in 1961, his painful choices during the Algerian crisis recalled the anxieties involved in like choices during the Vichy era.[7] Similar sentiments appear in his private correspondence with the historian Pierre Vidal-Naquet in 1964. Vidal-Naquet was a man of the

left, and they had had no previous association. But in an impulsive moment, Ariès wrote to him to express his sense of solidarity in their public
opposition to atrocities committed in the name of France during the war
in Algeria. Vidal-Naquet was touched by the gesture. He noted his appreciation of Ariès's article in *La Nation française* about the inhumane practices of the French army in its treatment of Algerian prisoners of war.[8]
Their subsequent correspondence during the 1970s always harked back to
this initial exchange, in which Ariès appears also to have made references
to atrocities that had affected him personally during the Vichy era, notably
the death of Yvonne Picard, the sister of his friend Gilbert, in a Nazi death
camp.[9]

Centuries of Mourning

After a decade of research, Ariès sketched a summary of his findings in his
Western Attitudes toward Death (1974), first presented as a series of lectures
at Johns Hopkins University in Baltimore in April 1973.[10] He divided this
history of attitudes toward death and mourning into four stages, each
easing imperceptibly into the next. In its underlying conception, it was a
study of the way in which a tradition is modified while conveying an
impression of timelessness. This impression is reinforced, he contended,
by the fact that these stages function synchronically as well as diachroni-
cally. Each stage is a model, and each model endures into the following
ages, so that they coexist in the present even if the earlier models tend to
be overshadowed by the more recent ones. As he characterized it, his
scheme plays out "like the tiles of a roof" in a descent from the grieving
practices of the Middle Ages, conceived as a golden age of mourning,
toward the denial of death and the inability to mourn in the contemporary age.

The Tamed Death of the High Middle Ages (la Mort Apprivoisée). Ariès
depicts death as an intrusive presence in a world socialized to accept it as
integral to life at virtually any age. He alludes to the "promiscuity of the
living and the dead," symbolized by the burial of the dead in churches and
churchyards frequented every day by the living. Death was always sad, but
mourning was easy because death was readily accepted by the living and
the dying as a destiny collectively shared.[11]

One's Own Death in the Age of the Renaissance (la Mort de Soi). Ariès notes
a newfound anxiety over "one's own" death beginning in the fifteenth
century. It marks the rising importance of the notion of an individual

destiny played out in life and so postponing the final reckoning with death. The effect was to project death into the future, and thereby to diffuse its anticipation throughout life. Just as children were trained to prepare for adulthood, so adults were obliged to prepare for the passage from life to death, still seen as the ultimate test that would determine their eternal destinies. Life as lived now was reconceived in light of life as it would be lived in its final hours, which lent a disquieting intensity to meditation on it. Mourning was becoming more difficult.

The Death of the Other in the Romantic Age (la Mort de Toi). Here Ariès notes the privatization of death and the interiorization of mourning by the late eighteenth century. The more intense rites of mourning in this era, Ariès claims, reflected the new intimacy of private life with its deepening of personal affections. Accepting the death of loved ones became more painful, and so required commemorative props. The age of "thy death," therefore, was also one of more elaborate funerals and commemorative grave statuary. Still, death, alternately conceived as erotic and morbid, had become exotic, and so was kept at a greater distance. Cemeteries were relocated at a remove from center cities as parks conducive to grieving over loved ones from time to time. Mourning was being segregated.

Forbidden Death in the Contemporary Age (la Mort Interdite). Thus Ariès characterizes the plight of atomized individuals in present-day mass society. Death has been banished from life reconceived in terms of short-run earthly satisfactions. Its contemplation has become intolerable, as death is perceived to be an embarrassing intrusion into otherwise happy lives. The dying often meet their fate alone, tethered to medical rigs in impersonal hospitals, in poignant contrast to the medieval tableau of tamed death at home in the presence of one's family. Mourning has become impossible.[12]

Considered in its ensemble, Ariès's interpretation of historically chang-ing attitudes toward death is intimately tied to his conception of changing attitudes toward human destiny. He plots the disintegration of the harmony of life and death in the face of the disappearance of the naïve confidence of medieval man in an otherworldly salvation. It was a process in which the acceptance of death was first postponed in the act of preparing for it, then deflected by identifying it with other people or larger causes, and finally banished altogether by denying it any place in public discussion of social life. As human aspirations for life became individuated and in time domesticated, the imagined confrontation with death became more anon-ymous and less predictable, and therefore a destiny more difficult to accept.

Rising expectations about life's possibilities, Ariès suggests, were accompanied by rising anxieties about coming to terms with death's realities.

The moral of Ariès's story is that mourning is not simply about coming to terms with losses and endings. The interesting turn in his interpretation concerns the invention of personal mourning in the modern era, which intensified its meaning and inspired a need for personal commemoration. His history, therefore, is also about the compensations and continuities of the traditions into which losses are received. In studying mourning as a mentalities problem, he explained, we note changing attitudes and practices. These are never unambiguous, for change involves trade-offs, not simple progress or decline. History teaches us the wisdom of looking for these negotiations in mores close to life as it is experienced in its most elemental forms—in the way ordinary people face life and death in practical, not abstract terms. The modern doctrine of linear progress, Ariès charged, is an illusion, and today we pay a price for it in our inability to come to terms with our own personal demise. The more we ask of life, the more difficult it becomes to accept its losses and endings. The destiny to which we have aspired in the modern age implies an impossible perfection. The destiny at which we have arrived, therefore, is an inability to mourn a past that can never meet our expectations.[13]

Ariès's assessment of the trend toward "forbidden death" might be regarded as a particularly pessimistic prognosis of the human condition in the present age. But his perspective on the contemporary inability to mourn does presage the enormous interest in the topic sparked by Henry Rousso's book on the "Vichy syndrome" some fifteen years thereafter.[14] Rousso's interpretation deals explicitly with the unhappy memories of the war years, whereas in Ariès's work they are implicit only. Indeed, it would be apt to say that Ariès's perspective on mourning reflects his suspicion of happy endings under any circumstances. This aspect of his view of the human condition was drawn out in his running debate during the 1970s with the Marxist historian Michel Vovelle, whose work provided a counterpoint to his own.

Michel Vovelle and Mourning the Demise of the Revolutionary Tradition

It is interesting that Michel Vovelle (1933–) should have become Ariès's scholarly rival. Vovelle too aspired to write a comprehensive history of mourning in the Western world. But he came out of a left-wing political tradition that was reckoning with its own losses. Whereas Ariès was a royalist, Vovelle was a Jacobin, with intellectual commitments to a Marxist vision of history and at least a nominal attachment to the Communist party. Some twenty years Ariès's junior, Vovelle came of age in the postwar era. He was touched by the Vichy experience to the degree that he was caught up in the idealism of the postwar communism that was a response to it. Like other youths with sympathies for the left, he was taken with the heroism of the party in the Resistance. Vovelle and his political companions were of the first generation to read the young Marx, whose struggle for liberation from bourgeois oppression lent meaning to their own against Nazism and other tyrannies.[15]

In contrast with Ariès's erratic career as a student, Vovelle's story was one of ongoing academic success. He graduated from the Ecole Normale Supérieure at St. Cloud, then went on for doctoral work with the celebrated economic historian Ernest Labrousse at the Sorbonne. Labrousse was the key figure in directing the research of the aspiring left-wing historians who came of age in the 1950s, and of integrating them into the work of the great tradition of historical writing about the French Revolution, from Jean Jaurès via Albert Mathiez and Georges Lefebvre to Albert Soboul. This history was not doctrinaire but rather appreciative of Marxism for the insights it permitted into the goals of the popular revolution, considered against the backdrop of the boom and bust of preindustrial economic cycles. Labrousse was famous for his thesis about the conjuncture between economic privation and political discontent as the source of the radical "revolution from below" in 1789 and beyond. His work and his mentoring shaped the conceptions of many of the best historians of this generation, Vovelle among them.[16]

Vovelle approached Labrousse with a proposal to study the Paris Commune of 1871. But Labrousse redirected his protégé to a study of the social structure of the city of Chartres in the late eighteenth century, through which, he opined, he might contribute a passage to the "grand fresco of social history" being painted according to his mentor's design. Such was Labrousse's authority that Vovelle dutifully complied. But he was savvy enough to see that the historiography of the French Revolution had grown sterile in continually revisiting a well-worn thesis about the social foundations of "the revolution from below." In his later writings about the Revolution, he continued to invoke the plot line given in the Jacobin/ Marxist interpretation of modern French history.[17] In looking for avenues for new research, however, he turned to cultural history as an unexplored domain. His political allegiances had been shaken by the Soviet repression of the popular uprising in Hungary in 1956, and he had become interested in obstacles to change in the struggle to create the good society. Mentalities, which he construed as habits of mind tenaciously resistant to innovation, was a topic that promised to shed light on this neglected aspect of modern history.[18]

Vovelle's crossing from social to cultural history was not uncommon among his generation of left-wing historians. Even Labrousse gave his approval by baptizing mentalities a "third level" of sophistication in quantitative research. Vovelle himself explained it as a search for a more complex dialectic of history, one that integrated the multiple dimensions of the past. Cultural issues, he cautioned, must be considered in relation to the social tensions and economic processes in which they are grounded. In this his methodological thinking was close to that of the Marxist philosophers Lucien Goldmann and Louis Althusser, both of whom he admired.[19]

But in turning to mentalities, Vovelle, like Ariès, had a particular past to mourn, and it lent poignancy to the history of mourning on which he was soon to embark, and eventually to his exchange with Ariès over its interpretation. While not declining as visibly as the royalist tradition, the revolutionary one was losing its practical appeal, and Vovelle was trying to come to terms with that. By the late 1960s, a younger generation of left-wing historians wanted to address contemporary issues in new ways, rather than reaffirm past visions of the future. As an ideological beacon out of the past for guiding contemporary politics toward unrealized goals, the French Revolution was growing dim. Of what value was it for a society that no longer believed in the Communist revolution, they asked? Or for one that sensed the waning appeal of its proposed destiny for modern history generally?

In seeking answers to these questions, many of these historians on the left engaged in the same kind of soul-searching as had Ariès a generation earlier concerning the nature of their political commitments and its relationship to the history they would write. Like Ariès, they too found an intellectual refuge in cultural history. Most would repudiate their ideological past in doing so.[20] Vovelle was an exception. He retained his affection for the Jacobin vision of a *sans-culottes* democracy and for the rationalist rigor of Marxist analysis practiced by its great left-wing historians.[21] There was in his convictions an element of loyalty to the revolutionary tradition as well. In a rare autobiographical aside, he noted that he, a child of school teachers and a descendant of humble artisans, had been permitted to take advantage of his opportunities for upward social mobility. But he did not want to lose sight of the egalitarian ideal of the popular culture that was his heritage. That is why he may have identified to some degree with Joseph

Sec, of whom he wrote a biographical study.[22] As he explained, "Here was a man who rose on the basis of talent yet never denied his origins. He remained a good Jacobin, uncorrupted by his social ascent."[23] Maintaining a buoyant optimism about a Marxist historiography that most of his colleagues had abandoned, he confidently endeavored to reconcile the old social with the new cultural history.[24]

Vovelle on the History of Death and Mourning

Vovelle first developed his argument on the history of death and mourning in regional studies of Provence.[25] But he also published *Mourir autrefois* (1974), a précis of his broader argument analogous to Ariès's *Essais sur l'histoire de la mort*, written at about the same time.[26] His Marxist vision of history is implicit in his argument, as he identifies changes in attitudes toward mourning with rational consciousness-raising across the span of Western civilization. Coming to terms with death in Western society over the long run, he contended, has been a matter of demythologizing it, of ridding it of the illusions of the sacred in which it had been enshrouded.

Rather than devoting his primary attention to plotting the long-range patterns of commonly held attitudes, however, Vovelle focused on transitional periods of crisis in which tensions over opposing attitudes toward death presented themselves. Here he held fast to Labrousse's model of showing the breakdown of long-term structures in short-term crises of conjuncture. It is in these decisive moments of recognition, he explained, that the historical meaning of long-term social conflict is revealed. In its way, Vovelle's account of these crises over the representation of death signified the struggles and triumph of the bourgeoisie over the aristocracy in the passage from traditional to modern society. Still, none of this is stated directly. In this history, class conflict is no longer boldly delineated in the way it had been in classic Marxist historiography. In Vovelle's rendering, the Marxist terminology of social struggle passes into tacit understanding, as he directs our attention to the cultural contexts of consciousness-raising. The task, he argued, is to grasp the dialectic of cultural conflict for what it reveals about a long-range historical process. In dying as in living, he concluded, our destiny lies in a dialectical process of becoming conscious of our predicament and of addressing it in a rational way. To understand the dialectic of changing attitudes toward death and mourning, the historian must integrate three perspectives: death as measured (*la mort subie*), in which he includes quantitative data of wills and testaments; death as perceived (*la mort vécu*), by which he means eye-witness accounts; and death as discourse (*discours sur la mort*), the edifying essays of theologians and other intellectuals. Disparate sources, they nonetheless enable the historian to plot a navigational fix on the crises that reveal the meaning of long-range change.[27]

While broadly conceived, Vovelle's history of mourning tended to privilege the boundary between the Baroque culture of the seventeenth century and the Enlightened one of the eighteenth century as a crucial divide. It was a time of rupture between old attitudes in which death was seen in a morbid way as the ultimate punishment for our sins, and new ones in which it came to be accepted as a natural phenomenon. Baroque attitudes, he explained, were an exaggerated expression of a religious mentality in its passionate death throes. Like the supernova of a dying star, the Baroque death ritual was intensely emotional and given to brilliant display.[28] Enlightenment attitudes, by contrast, evinced a decorum and acceptance of death as part of the natural order. Proof of this change in sensibility, he contended, is to be found in waning references to hellfire and damnation in the learned discourse of theologians, and more tellingly in the wills and testimonies of ordinary people. Even purgatory faded into oblivion.[29] Quiet meditation replaced pomp and circumstance in the protocols of mourning during this era.

At the same time, Vovelle maintained, this is not a simple tale of traversing a great divide between the religious traditions of the Old Regime and the secular ones of the modern age. The passage presupposes a more complex dialectic in that each of these traditions has its own inner tensions. Within Baroque culture, for example, there are opposing viewpoints about the merits of ostentatious display versus austere simplicity in commemorative rituals. Correspondingly, on the Enlightenment side one notes tensions between deists and materialists, the former preferring to link grieving to rarefied conceptions of immortality, the latter wishing to dismiss such abstractions altogether. Such tensions have their historical antecedents in the conflict between clericalists and humanists at the end of the Middle Ages. The discord in that era turned on efforts to purge Christian mourning of its pagan vestiges of belief in the miraculous. Resistance to that change produced an exaggerated anxiety about death, evinced in macabre descriptions of its realities. In the modern age the Romantic obsession with death recalls the grotesque depictions of the late Middle Ages and reveals new forms of resistance to the larger trend. The neo-Romantic mourning of the late nineteenth century is an even fainter echo of this same process.[30]

Vovelle's interpretation suggests an oscillation between periods of acceptance and periods of anxiety over death. But his history converges on the central drama of demythologizing death in the eighteenth century, an emblem of the social crisis of the aristocracy that culminated in the French Revolution. The tensions attending these changing attitudes toward death linger into the modern era, confirming the difficulties of the hard-won struggle of the bourgeoisie to overcome remaining resistances to the general trend toward a rational acceptance of the natural order.[31]

The Ariès/Vovelle Debate as a Rendezvous with Destiny

Like Ariès, Vovelle was loyal to a political tradition whose fortunes were waning, and he tried to integrate his respect for it into his understanding of changing interpretations of its meaning. Vovelle's rejection of Soboul's doctrinaire Marxism as a conceptual framework for understanding the Revolution, therefore, is analogous to Ariès's rejection of Maurras's stance for understanding royalism.[32] Vovelle and Ariès's encounter was not only about scholarship but also about the fortunes of the political left and right in the present age. Their debate evoked the enduring substance of a political quarrel that on its surface had lost its force but that in its cultural depths laid claim to opposing conceptions of human destiny. The debate lasted nearly a decade, from a conference at Strasbourg in 1974 to one at Saint-Maximin in 1981, shortly before Ariès's own death. They published conference proceedings of their exchange along the way.[33] Ariès's big book, *L'Homme devant la mort,* appeared in 1977, Vovelle's *La Mort et l'Occident* in 1983, and their final texts were based upon revisions undertaken in light of this exchange. Relying heavily on wills and testaments, sensitive to the uses of iconography as historical evidence, their empirical findings were not that far apart, and they plotted the long-range changes in attitudes toward mourning in much the same way. They differed rather in their respective interpretations of the human destiny such a history revealed.[34]

In these culminating studies, the broad outlines of their respective theses remained largely intact. But their debate highlighted three issues on which they made some reassessments:

The Question of Historical Periodization. Vovelle was puzzled by Ariès's indifference to Baroque death rituals and to their implications for understanding Christianity as a factor in attitudes toward death and mourning. For Vovelle, the age of the Baroque had been the crucial moment of his history, for it signified a rising anxiety over the loosening authority of Christianity as a cultural force in the modern world. Hence its rites and rituals, especially those attending mourning, became more emotion-laden and exaggerated.[35] Ariès had not paid particular attention to the period, or for that matter the religious issue it raised, in his 1974 study because he did not see this era as decisive in the longer-range transition from a focus on the self ("one's own death") to one on the other ("thy death"). For him, the crisis was not about an old-time religion but a newborn individualism. More important, he claimed, was the effort dating from the Renaissance to diffuse personal awareness of death across life. As affection among family members was deepened and the obligation to grieve for loved ones passed into tacit understanding, some formal aspects of mourning lost their raison d'être and were abandoned. It was not a matter of giving up traditional ways of mourning but rather of incorporating them into the private sphere, where they retained their intensity. For Ariès, the techniques of life and death continued to go hand in hand. In "thy death," mourning displayed the affection and intimacy characteristic of romantic love.[36]

The Question of Mentalities. Vovelle also accused Ariès of having taken the history of mentalities in a new direction, one that severed its "ideological" links to social and economic realities. He argued that mentalities, as originally conceived by Lucien Febvre and renewed by Robert Mandrou and even by his own mentor Ernest Labrousse, put the accent on forces that retard change. For Vovelle, mentalities are the habits of mind that bear the inertial power of the past. As such, they are the counterpoint to ideologies in the dialectical equation, for they operate in constant tension with the innovative ideas that inspire creative change. Their interaction reveals the nature of social tensions at play. Ariès, Vovelle charged, was spiritualizing the history of mentalities, recasting it in such a way that it acquired an autonomy divorced from social and economic realities. In light of this, he revisited more critically Ariès's working notion of a "collective unconscious," which he now construed as a disembodied spiritualism, impossible to locate and a temptation to mystification.[37]

For Ariès, the notion of a "collective unconscious" constitutes a realm of tacit understanding whose subtleties he had not analyzed closely before. Now he was obliged to wrestle with the substance of the term, for it was crucial to his thesis. At their last formal encounter, that at the conference at Saint-Maximin, Ariès acknowledged the quasi-religious significance he had invested in the term. But he contended that his early usage of it had in fact been quite concrete, an attempt to get at the visceral realities of life that had inspired the revolution in attitudes about birth control in the seventeenth century. In the intervening discussion of death, he observed, this source of his notion may have been obscured and easily misconstrued as disembodied fantasies of the sort that Vovelle had identified with the morbidity of the late Middle Ages and the spiritualism of the Romantic era. As a concession to Vovelle, he now sought to divest the term of spiritualist connotations by renaming it the "collective non-conscious," which he characterized as the living memory that sustains evolving traditions. It embodies popular wisdom that has been integrated into the common sense of life experience.[38]

The Question of Destiny. Ariès had a question to pose to Vovelle as well, one that went to the heart of what he believed to be the Marxists' need for happy endings. In a critique of the manuscript of Vovelle's soon-to-be-published book, he noted the inconclusiveness of Vovelle's findings in terms of the larger issue of history's patterns. Ironically, he suggested, there is no moral to Vovelle's story, of the sort the Marxist vision of history had originally anticipated. The denouement that the social and cultural crisis of the eighteenth century supposedly foretold remains not only unrealized but unrecognized. Rather the historical pattern that emerges in Vovelle's history is one of crescendo/decrescendo, culminating in Enlightenment secularization of attitudes toward death, then playing out in struggles of diminishing intensity into the present age. Implicitly, Ariès was chiding Vovelle for having bracketed the Marxist vision of destiny. Vovelle's history, he suggested, for all the crises of attitudes it highlights, points not toward some ultimate crisis of the sort that Marx had prophesied but only to the remodeling of ongoing social tensions in the modern age. While Vovelle insisted on the generative role of conflict in historical change, the Marxist notion of a culminating crisis is rendered problematic in his account of tensions of dwindling importance in the approach to the present.[39]

In his book published in the following year, Vovelle stopped short of a full-scale reply. But he did reaffirm his faith in the spirit in which he had embarked on the project some twenty years before: the prospect of a better future through consciousness-raising. "Our investment in death," he reflected, "is not so much derived from our hope for life as it is from our hope for well-being [*bonheur*], which is more complex and saturated with meaning." In breaking the silence that has surrounded the topic of death for nearly a century, he noted, we historians in the late twentieth century may not have fully deciphered its meaning. But we have at least become aware of the way it is rooted "in the depths [*l'épaisseur*] of time."[40]

As for Ariès, he had couched his question in light of his own reassessment of the relationship between death and destiny in the modern age. A few years before, he had written an article on pattern and meaning in the civilizing process, in which he denied that civilizations rise and fall. All our causes are transient, he asserted, and they change with circumstances. In the modern age we may have the sense that we can shape our private lives with more assurance that ever before. But ultimately we cannot control our destiny, whose historical meaning is not to be found in demonstrated progress but rather in ongoing reconfigurations of the human quest for fulfillment. Death is a reality. But the destiny it implies is a human imagining, conceived in light of the faith we hold in the future. Its pursuit may have become more self-conscious. But it is conducted with the acceptance of our limits and our place within our living traditions. In this respect, our reference point is not the future but the present.[41]

So culminated the respectful, even friendly, debate that Ariès and Vovelle had conducted. They were linked at least in their fidelity to their respective traditions, for each remained true to the spirit of his youthful ideological allegiance, while transposing his convictions to the more erudite plane of the history of mentalities. As cultural historians, they carried on what had been the more visibly political quarrels of their ideological predecessors. That it should have been conducted so politely suggests that the traditions they honored were dying. In their exchange they mourned the passing of the revolutionary tradition over which royalists and republicans had struggled since the eighteenth century. In that sense, their dialogue about death was a requiem for the modern age that was passing. In their modest expectations for the future, they gave expression to what some philosophers would soon characterize as the end of a regime of historical time.[42] From this perspective, the Ariès/Vovelle debate on death and mourning in the 1970s prefigured a wider one about the destiny of France as a nation in the 1980s.[43]

Tombs without Sepulchers: From Mourning to Memory

Ariès died in 1984. In the same year Vovelle was named to the famous chair in the history of the French Revolution at the Sorbonne. Soon thereafter he was chosen to coordinate the preparations for the bicentennial of that event. It was a prestigious job, but it turned out to be a troubled one.[44] Almost immediately, he was obliged to confront the historians' waning enthusiasm for this commemorative enterprise, and a problematizing of the meaning of the revolutionary tradition that it had inspired. The assault on the Revolution as heritage came from within the academy, indeed from one of its own historians. I am referring to François Furet, whose revisionist argument subverted the justification of a celebration modeled on that of the centennial, staged as an apotheosis of the revolutionary tradition.[45] Furet, too, had been trained in the Jacobin/Marxist tradition of historiography, though he had since repudiated it. His critique, therefore, was all the more vehement. He captured the historians' attention with his provocative claim that the French Revolution as a model for political inspiration had outlived its usefulness. He argued that the notion of destiny had been an invention of the Jacobins, enshrined by historians sympathetic to its egalitarian vision.[46] Playfully, he raised the question of whether the Revolution should be celebrated at all, for it had lost its commemorative role as a guide for present-day action.[47]

The quarrel about the staging of the bicentennial thus stimulated a new debate about the meaning of the heritage of the French Revolution. For the first time in a hundred years, the Revolution was again an object of historiographical contention. Vovelle's planning for the bicentennial, therefore, was conducted under this shadow, for Furet had challenged its supposed role as an emblem of a shared national identity. Under the circumstances, Vovelle's words did not carry the incontrovertible authority of the sort once exercised by his eminent predecessors, and he soon found himself managing a quarrelsome politics of splintering factional identities. No longer was the Revolution an event to be mourned. Once a touchstone of moral intention for the nation, it had become the prey of the culture wars of present politics.[48]

The issue about destiny raised in the Ariès/Vovelle debate was thus transposed into a different historiographical context. The focus, however, remained the philosophical issue about historical time first raised by Ariès in *Le Temps de l'Histoire* some thirty years before: specifically, the dissolution of a way of understanding history as moving toward a denouement. It was in that work that he had first called for a reconceptualizing of historical time in order to focus on the present, not the future, and so to pay greater attention to differences between past and present.[49] Vovelle may have continued to judge the meaning of history in light of his commitment to the revolutionary tradition. But he, too, had abandoned any simple sense of a sustained direction in historical change of the sort in which his illustrious predecessors had believed.[50] History might continue to proceed through the dialectical resolution of conflicts, he maintained, but for those of the present he clearly had diminished expectations.

Focusing on the present age, moreover, carried important implications for understanding the relationship between history and memory or, as Ariès had put it, history (the past interpreted) and History (the past remembered). As collective identity reverted to places of memory, the grand narrative whose construction Ariès had plotted in *Le Temps* unraveled into multiple story lines located at sites without temporal, conceptual, or logical connections. As the grand narrative dissolved, history was reconceived spatially as a congeries of topical problems. In an interesting coincidence, 1984, the year of Ariès's death, also marked the appearance of the first volume of Pierre Nora's *Lieux de mémoire*, an ambitious collaborative study of the French national identity. It signified a historical stance on mourning in a larger, collective sense, a mourning of national rather than personal identities of the sort about which Ariès and Vovelle had written. Proceeding genealogically from the present, this inquiry reframed the past spatially around discrete sites of memory whose numbers multiplied in the deepening recessional into the past. So conceived, French history had no beginning or end. In such circumstances, Nora queried, how might mourning, in the modern age so closely tied to notions of destiny, henceforth be understood?[51]

In pioneering this line of inquiry into mourning, Ariès, too, had been obliged early on to establish a critical distance from his personal experience. But he did carry with him a personal perspective, of which he gave careful readers a glimpse in a passage buried within the text of his culminating study, *L'Homme devant la mort*. The passage concerns the death of his mother, thinly disguised as the legend of the death of Mélisande, a mythological queen.[52] She accepted her death with such modesty that her passing was barely perceived by the loved ones who attended her.[53] Her son was distraught that he had not had time to say good-bye adequately. But he later came to see that such modesty in the face of death is a virtue. Mélisande's death was testimony of the natural dignity of the dying, in keeping with the diminished conception of destiny in the present age.[54]

This image of the modest death of the mother also tells us something of the modest perspective on mourning at which the son had arrived in the course of his life and work. In the Middle Ages, he observed, "death was the awareness by each person of a Destiny" to which he surrendered without qualms. He acknowledged that in our technological culture it is no longer possible "to regain the naïve confidence in Destiny that had for so long been shown by simple men when dying."[55] Today, he concluded, "death must simply become the discreet but dignified passing of a gentle person from a caring society that is not torn, nor even upset by the idea of a biological transition without significance, without pain or suffering, and ultimately without fear."[56] Ironically, it was a position on death in the modern world not that far removed from that espoused by Vovelle.

In taking on the topic of mourning, Ariès was justifying his own minimalist historical perspective on the way in which destiny may be conceived in our times. In doing so, he showed us how the spectrum of permissible mourning contracted over time while the need remained essentially the same. His encounter with Vovelle brought out the conflicts that punctuated this history and revealed how mourning in its many styles has been our constant way of reconciling ourselves to time's passages.

8

The Sacred and the Profane

Lifelong Commitments

The Profane Needs of Religious Faith

IN HIS AUTOBIOGRAPHY, the historian Raoul Girardet tells of his last encounter with his old friend Philippe Ariès, about a month before he died. They had lunch together in Paris, animated by the quips and banter in which they often engaged. They had been friends since their days at the Sorbonne together, then as earnest young royalists writing and speaking in behalf of the Action Française. In those days, they often gathered at the apartment of the Girardet family in the heart of the Latin Quarter, where Raoul's mother lavished maternal affection on their band of friends. During the war and long thereafter, they had worked together on literary and journalistic projects identified with a dying royalist cause. Though they had been at odds over the fate of Algeria during the early 1960s, their friendship remained solid and sure. Now in the throes of a terminal illness, Philippe was on his way back to Toulouse, where he had taken up residence with his wife shortly before her death the previous summer. After lunch, Raoul accompanied him to the bus stop, and offered his best wishes until they should meet again. Philippe knew otherwise. "We shall not see one another again," he replied simply. "I am preparing to die and for that matter I am at peace. But I find it truly a shame that you do not believe in God."[1]

Just what Ariès meant by belief in God is one of the secrets he took with him to the grave. Almost as elusive were the convictions that inspired his conception of regionalism. In this chapter, I consider these two basic commitments of faith that guided him throughout his life. One was sacred—a conception of religious understanding that sanctioned hope for the future in the memory of a transcendent past; the other profane—a conception of community that favored local identities. The former concerned his awe in the face of the mysteries of the human predicament, the latter his belief in personal loyalty as a foundation of the good society. Both notions evince his underlying respect for *fidélité* to basic commitments through life's varied fortunes.

Some of Ariès's ideas about religious faith surfaced in the long interview with Michel Winock in 1980, which served as the basis of his autobiography. Winock eventually placed this discussion in an appendix, sensing that such issues suffused his experiences and could not be limited to particular episodes in his life.[2] Here I expand on the replies that Winock drew forth from Ariès in the course of their interview. His recollections were those of an old man, and they have sources in his youth that he may have understood differently back then. I proceed retrogressively toward those roots— from his late-life reflections on the meaning of religion and politics to his youthful dilemmas about them. One notes an essential continuity in his commitments, even though he formulates his views differently over time.

Ariès had never expressed much interest in theology. Yet he held profoundly religious views of life and history, and it is impossible to take the measure of his work as a historian without giving them some consideration. Not that he was disposed to discuss his own religious faith openly. In the Winock interview, he noted his "difficulty in speaking of that which is closest to my heart." As he explained, his was a "*fidélité cachée*" in his pursuit of truths that exist in a "secret garden beyond our understanding."[3]

This mystifying image notwithstanding, Ariès was no mystic, nor had he a particular desire to be mysterious about his religious views. Skillfully, Winock queried him about his formal religious beliefs. We learn from the interview that Ariès was profoundly Catholic in a modest, even unassuming way. He accepted Christianity as a religion of revelation and the Nicene creed as the covenant of its articles of faith. For him, the Resurrection of Jesus was a necessary precondition of Christian faith, and he made few concessions to symbolic compromise. Though he regarded Pope John XXIII as a saintly figure, he had misgivings about the liturgical reforms ushered in by Vatican II. He was especially disappointed by the abandonment of the Latin rite in favor of the vernacular in the Christian Mass. A Latinist himself, he believed that the French translation never adequately conveyed the profound meaning of the liturgy, and in his later years he found some consolation in listening to the Latin Mass broadcast on the France Culture radio station.[4] Winock's focus on Ariès's profession of faith might lead one to believe that he was devout in a conventional way. Personally, Ariès preferred to treat religion in terms of practice rather than theory. To put it more concretely, piety, not theology, was his route toward religious understanding. He was curious about the mores of popular religion, just as he was about other aspects of everyday life. As he explained, he sought to comprehend the meaning of the "external signs" of religion rather than the internal ones of religious awakening.[5]

In this respect, Ariès expressed considerable interest in, and one might say sympathy for, popular religious devotions. He was willing to accord wide latitude to the popular religious imagination that blurred the boundary between orthodox belief and popular legend. He was especially sensitive to the syncretism of the present age. In the mixing of many cultures, he explained, the tightly knit fabric of particular religious traditions was unraveling. In the absence of coherence of belief, strands of religious meaning were often found in the practices of everyday life, and even in hidden thoughts that an individual might be reluctant to share. He marveled, for example, at the intense mourning for the popular singer Edith Piaf at the time of her death in 1963, when thousands followed her cortège to the Père Lachaise cemetery. For Ariès, such an outpouring of popular sentiment suggested a recrudescence of pagan religious views in this devotion to a contemporary folk heroine who touched the deep feelings of so many with the compelling resonance of her voice. Religion today, Ariès speculated, is more "social than sacred," and we must look for unsuspected religious meanings in the mores of popular culture.[6]

As a counterpoint to his sympathy for popular religious devotions, Ariès maintained a suspicion of the clergy for the same reason that he looked askance at politicians. Both represented hierarchies of power in large organizations. His major concern about present-day religion was his sense that the church as an ecclesiastical organization had lost touch with the religious sentiments of the people. He was particularly critical of progressive clergymen in their posturing in favor of liberation theology and fashionable social causes. But he was equally dismissive of traditionalist reactionaries, who threatened to create a schismatic church of old believers.[7] Ariès had a few allies among the clergy. In the early 1970s, he became friendly with Serge Bonnet, a social historian and Dominican priest whose *Prières secrètes des français d'aujourd'hui* struck a responsive chord with his own feelings about popular piety. He recounts the story of his attendance at a clerical colloquy with Bonnet in which various prelates decried the decline among the laity in the use of sacramentals such as holy water. Ariès rose to chide them for their blindness to their own role in devaluing these simple accoutrements of religious piety. Though he met with astonished silence, he took some pride in his intervention. His point was that the clergy in their misguided attempts to comply with modish fashion often imposed their "progressive" views upon a laity that had little sympathy for them.[8]

During the 1970s Ariès was heartened by the newfound scholarly interest in the historical anthropology of popular religious devotions. He had long felt the inadequacy of scholarly approaches to the history of Christianity in France. Historians concentrated too narrowly on ecclesiastical policy and clerical politics, and neglected the significance of the religious practices and mentalities of the laity. As early as the 1950s, he had discovered the writings of the sociologist Gabriel Le Bras, who was among the first scholars to address such issues, and he may later have been influenced by Alphonse Dupront and Jean Delumeau, historians with the anthropologist's sensitivity to the workings of myth and ritual.[9]

Drawing on this new research on religious mentalities, Ariès conveyed his views on popular piety in its relationship to clerical doctrine in a carefully crafted essay, originally composed for a talk he had been invited to give to Michel Vovelle's seminar at the University of Aix-en-Provence in 1973. At the time, he was working on his history of attitudes toward death, and the structure of the scheme he devised to explain the historical relationship between popular piety and clerical theology provides an interesting parallel with that which he had employed to interpret historically changing attitudes toward death.[10]

To illustrate his argument, he presented a graphic scheme of the changing relationship between clergy and laity on issues of popular piety. He identified alternating phases in the opening and closing of their rapport across the history of Western culture. The Middle Ages, for example, was a time of open accommodation between popular piety and clerical orthodoxy. This mutual understanding was revived once more in the Romantic nineteenth century. The alternate phase, one of opposition between elitist theology and popular belief, applied to the Reformation (Catholic and Protestant) of the sixteenth and seventeenth centuries, echoed in the reforms of Vatican II in the mid-twentieth. Ariès contended that before the recent interest in mentalities historians tended to adopt the reformers' viewpoint. In other words, they took clerical orthodoxy as their standard, and so construed popular religious devotions as deviations from it. But who is to judge what is authentically religious, he queried? One is not obliged to look at religion from today's clerical perspective, which bespeaks an elitism that ignores popular mentalities. With this criticism in mind, he plotted the historical variations in the clergy/laity relationship along Christianity's way in this fashion:

The Late Middle Ages (Fourteenth and Fifteenth Centuries). In the late Middle Ages, he noted, there was little distinction between the views of the hierarchy and those of the people. Pagan and Christian ideas were inter-mingled in an archaic religious culture, out of which gradually emerged on the margins of society a tiny elite of doctrinaire Christians. This cultural milieu favored a sociability of religious understanding, for it tolerated a wide spectrum of religious belief. In the absence of explicit doctrinal teach-ings in what was a culture still embedded in orality, he pointed out, or-dinary people held wildly diverse, imaginative, and eccentric religious views. Christianity as conceived in the popular mind, he suggested, might be characterized as a para-religion, for it catered in an atavistic way to rituals of blood lust and sexual excess. Freely incorporating irrational su-perstition into its habits of belief, the popular religion of the day was often closer to paganism than to Christianity. A more orthodox Christianity practiced by a cultural elite struggled to gain a foothold in this milieu. But its influence was limited, since the prevailing popular sentiments of the age militated against doctrinaire religious elitism.

The Age of Reform (Sixteenth and Seventeenth Centuries). The Reformation was crucial in introducing a distinction between the theology of the clergy and the religious devotions of the people. Whether Catholic or Protestant, it marked the triumph of clerical theology, which penetrated popular mil-ieux more intrusively than ever before. As a stance on religious piety, it was harsh, dour, rigorously moralistic, and intimidating in its emphasis on sinfulness and its condign punishment. Here Ariès's interpretation is quite similar to that of Carlo Ginzburg, whose *The Cheese and the Worms* (1976) enjoyed enormous success internationally as a history of religious mental-ities.[11] Both contend that the theological controversies of the Reformation took place within a learned culture apart from the popular religious milieu and concerned esoteric differences over doctrine that affected very little the attitudes of ordinary people, whose religious views continued to mix pagan and Christian belief in the unrefined idiom of oral culture.

The Modern Era (Eighteenth and Especially Nineteenth Centuries). By the nineteenth century, Ariès argued, French society was no longer exclusively a community of Christian believers. An emerging secular society stood apart from the old world of Christian religious belief and challenged it in the name of the new science and its technological applications. In light of this trend, Ariès explained, historians had long contended that the church in the modern world had failed to adapt to the changing social realities of an industrializing society, and so succumbed to a corresponding process of "de-christianization," notably among the working class. The corollary was that the reforms of the Vatican II Council provided the only remedy for a church that would otherwise slide into obsolescence.

Ariès took issue with this view. It presupposed that Vatican II was the only redoubt for a church that wished to maintain its place in the contemporary world. Basing his observations on the religious sociology of Gabriel Le Bras, he challenged the notion that Christianity should be interpreted in light of its orthodoxy alone. Popular religious devotions survived in the nineteenth century, he contended; indeed they took on new life. They differed from those of the Middle Ages in that they were saturated with Christian imagery and articles of belief. Medieval paganism had largely disappeared, as belief in the miraculous receded into obscurity over the course of the eighteenth century. The popular Christianity of the nineteenth century was closer to the official view, but tended to stress practice over doctrine, and so maintained a vitality despite the apparent trend toward secularization in the society as a whole. In many ways, Ariès proposed, this was the golden age of religious piety. It was a time of expanding popular religious devotions, scrupulous confessions and frequent communions, feast days full of pageantry, and pilgrimages to venerated sites, such as Lourdes and Rocamadour. Popular religious devotions took on a new intensity in dramatizing rites of passage: marriage, baptism, first communion, burial, and memorial commemoration of the dead. Ariès's point was that in this popular milieu, religious practice took decided precedence over theology for the ordinary believer. In this context, Ariès noted the emergence of what he characterized as "seasonal believers." They were "practicing Catholics" who participated in religious rites but were otherwise indifferent to belief in any conventional theological sense. Seasonal belief, Ariès argued, was especially important because it permitted a rapprochement between official Catholic teaching and popular folklore. The nineteenth century, therefore, was a time when clergy and laity found themselves in easy harmony about the social side of religious practice. Recognizing the value of accommodating seasonal believers, the clergy displayed a new tolerance for popular piety. They cast a benign eye upon the ritual excesses of penitential confraternities. They gave their blessing to the new cult of commemorative monuments for the dead. If they judged popular religious practice unorthodox, they nonetheless accepted it as an authentic expression of an essential faith. Overall, Ariès's sense was that nineteenth-century Catholicism received worse press among historians than it deserved. Once again, one notes his idealization of the nineteenth century for its popular mores, blending old-fashioned ways with modern needs. The heyday of the modern family was also one of harmony between religious faith and popular piety.

The Present Age (Twentieth Century). The present age, by contrast, was again one in which the relations between clergy and laity were subject to reserve and suspicion. Despite sharp political disagreements within their own ranks, the clergy reasserted their demand for doctrinal orthodoxy. Once again seasonal Christians were treated as people of lukewarm faith in need of moral reinforcement. The clergy quarreled among themselves over doctrine in a way reminiscent of the Reformation, elitist discourse that hardly mattered to ordinary people. So, Ariès contended, the church threatened to lose its pastoral role, notably for those seasonal Christians who a century before had been its most important constituency.[12]

Though presented as a scholarly article, Ariès's essay extrapolates on history's value as a route toward a more profound religious understanding. He wanted especially to rehabilitate scholarly understanding of seasonal Christians with whom, one suspects, he identified personally. In larger terms, he wanted to show that Christianity was a dynamic faith, whose nature was as likely to be found in its common practices and its habits of popular belief as in its learned theology. He cautioned against passing judgment on the quality of religious faith among ordinary people or of searching for some imaginary model of a pure Christianity. For him, the key to religion—and the reason why it would not recede into the oblivion to which modern secularists wished to consign it—was the practical way it served the social need for consoling remedies for the travails of everyday life. In the history of popular piety, he argued, one could see how shared commitments were sustained over the course of the ongoing transformations of historical experience. Situated on the boundary between the known and the unknown, religion in popular practice eased the doubts of ordinary people and assuaged their dilemmas about their everyday problems. As social realities changed, so too did the tenor of religious expression. But the longing for spiritual consolation endured. The sacred, he believed, might be discovered in the midst of profane need, and he used the occasion to reiterate his profession of faith in the co-mingling of historical and religious understanding. "A man who considers religious things," he commented, "has the right to seek to understand the Divine, the relations between man and God, from the vantage point of history as well as that of metaphysics or theology." The historian has the privilege of being able to grasp synoptically noncontemporaneous ideas and to place them in a context in which their similarities and differences may be more meaning-fully appreciated. So the historian approaches what is ultimately an "in-accessible transcendence."[13]

Despite his late-life focus on historical issues of piety, Ariès had not always been reluctant to affirm a more theological profession of faith when it suited his particular needs at a turning point in his life. In younger days, just after the war, when he was seeking to explain his passionate interest in the past, he had written openly about his views on the relationship between religious faith and historical understanding. His essay "A Child Discovers History," composed in 1946 and published in 1954 as the lead chapter of Le Temps de l'Histoire, provides an autobiographical reflection on the naïve beliefs of his childhood, when his faith in God and curiosity about History intermingled. As a child, he allowed, "I imagined a link between the God of the catechism and the past of the historian." That historical world was a place of "friendship, tenderness, nostalgia," nurtured by the legends of a family that delighted in idealized images of old France as a golden age. This past that had enveloped him as a child remained near and familiar. His childhood conception of the past was not really history, he conceded, but only a "poetical transfiguration of History."[14] In late adolescence, as he became more critically aware of the mythical nature of this conception of the past, he felt the painful loss that demythologizing implied, and so sought to take possession of his past once more in what was still a naïve and parochial conception of history. He began to think of History as a "lost Eden" that he was determined to recapture. He recalls his efforts while a student at the lycée to reduce history to events that fit easily into a scheme defined by the genealogical succession of the kings of old France. The project seemed possible because he still felt embraced by that world, surrounded as he was by family and friends who hailed from the same milieu. Among them he continued to feel this royalist history's inspiration, even as he began to acquire intellectual sophistication as a student at the Sorbonne.[15]

The war years abruptly wrested Ariès from such lyrical illusions. He recognized that the history in which he had believed prior to 1940 was only an "oasis" apart from the History with which he found himself con-fronted after the war.[16] The History that had transported him into the realities of the present against his will was to be measured on a scale beyond any he had previously imagined. Its presence was invasive, and it made him aware of a past of such vast scope and relentless force that he might never hope to decipher its meaning completely. History became "elemental, unyielding, inimical."[17] In this way, his sentiments of religious harmony were displaced by those of religious awe in the face of History reconceived on this grand scale. From a religious standpoint, he felt humbled by its power, and a sense of his own limitations in the face of it. History therefore remained for Ariès the place where religious understanding resides, though its significance for him had changed. One fathoms history not in accepting a comforting grand narrative, he concluded, but in paying attention to disruptive existential moments that reveal a past of unsuspected interest. The living testimonies of witnesses to the past, more than the conventional narratives of history textbooks, are a better source for discovering its secrets.[18] Sensitivity to personal memoirs of lived experience, he explained, can serve as points of entry into a wider, more complex, often alien world. For that matter, he wondered if his own experiences did not epitomize the points of entry he had been seeking. Had he not encountered History in the disruption of his life under Vichy, and had it not inspired him to seek an understanding of the past apart from the reductionist narrative of once beloved royalist historians? Not that his childhood impressions of the past were without meaning. The child's vision may not adequately represent the past, he conceded. But it does convey his intuition of something "infinitely desirable" in the past, with its intimations of life's joy (*douceur de vie*) and well-being (*bonheur*), and so suggests that historical inquiry in its deepest promptings has a religious quality in which even the aging savant, "in his vision of the ages gathered together, setting aside his objectivity, experiences a saintly joy: something quite close to grace."[19]

It is significant that Ariès wrote this essay in the immediate aftermath of the war. He sensed a precipitous break with his past, and he was trying to make sense of it. He recognized that his views before the war had been naïvely held. What he had gained through the painful experiences of the war years was a more critical perspective on the world of his childhood. His question was how he might remain faithful to commitments formed within the tenderness of that nurturing environment now carried over into a world that was new and strange. History was to be his consolation for the disruption of his youthful innocence. He believed that he was embarking on a journey of historical research to grasp through the analysis of evidence a reflective understanding of what he had once held as lyrical myth. There could be no return to the past as he had imagined it as a wide-eyed child. Nor would he ever again resort to theological statement in his historical writings. But he did at the time wish to reestablish the continuity between his present life and his youthful convictions through his rededication to history. So he presented with candor the ingenuous views he held as a child as the source of his inspiration to become a historian. In this sense, *Le Temps de l'Histoire* was written as living testimony of his much-loved childhood. One might argue that it provides a clue to his following interest in the historical sources of family affection, a connection of which he himself may never have been fully aware.

The Sacred Sources of Profane Commitment

Winock also pressed Ariès about his present political views. Here Ariès was once again elliptical in his reply. He said that as he had grown older his understanding of the political had merged with that of the social, and it was an ideal of community rather than a regime of power that had come to serve as the basis of his political thinking. As he put it, "Today, a larger conception, at once historical, ethnological, and philosophical, is more useful and necessary than political action, at least that is the conviction at which I have arrived after a journey that in its beginnings was admittedly oriented toward politics."[20] Ariès was alluding to his past as a journalist for the royalist cause. By the time of the Winock interview, he had long since abandoned any interest in party politics. As a traditionalist, he explained, his political position had been crowded out of the right-wing lexicon with the coming of the Fifth Republic. Neither a Gaullist nor a nationalist, he found little of interest in contemporary right-wing politics. What he wanted politically, he told Winock, was only a public awareness of the enduring presence of the traditions that embody France's heritage.[21]

Ariès's self-characterization as an "anarchist of the right" served as a covering emblem for his old-fashioned views. His principal political target was the big state, "which expands its nebulous network of actions, regulations, surveillances, and punishments." As he noted, his anarchism was "not resignation, but rather a displacement of goal, a change in strategy."[22] As in his stance on religion, much of the meaning he had once found in politics had since been absorbed into his critical perspective as a historian. In this respect, he voiced his concern about the erosion of particular traditions in the homogenization of contemporary mass culture. "The great contemporary phenomenon," he explained to Winock, "indeed appears to me to be the dissolution of society, of its ancient structures, the loosening of its brakes and its controls, the obliteration of oral custom that regulated human relations in the community, among individuals, the State and the Sacred."[23] He was equally outspoken about environmental degradation. Attuned to current arguments about the need for limits to economic growth, he identified the environmental interests of idealistic young ecologists with the regional interests of his own youth.[24]

It is interesting to probe the deep sources of Ariès's late-life formulation of his social ideals, for they reveal a parallel with those that underpin his religious views. Throughout his life, he held fast to an ideal of personalism as the sacred wellspring of human relations. The ideal emerged out of the affectionate ties of his extended family and served as the basis of lifelong friendships formed in his days as a university student. It contained the germ of his vision of community as a network of personal connections. I have made reference to Ariès's "personalism" at several points in this book. He never specifically used the term, but his insistence on the value of personal rapport in social relationships as these reached toward a larger conception of community invites comparison with others who openly espoused "personalism" in the philosophical discussions of the 1930s and 1940s, notably left-wing Catholics who gathered around the journal *L'Esprit* under the editorial direction of Emmanuel Mounier. Mounier was only a decade older than Ariès, and a review of his intellectual formation reveals some surprising correspondences with Ariès's own. Both were serious about Catholicism, both valued their studies at the University of Grenoble with the philosopher Jacques Chevalier, and both attended the Sorbonne. Both were critical of higher education in France, and both pursued their lives as scholars in what might be characterized as serious intellectual journalism apart from the university. During the Vichy years, both were affiliated with the écoles des cadres and had some hope for the social values such an education might promote.[25]

Still, they moved in very different intellectual circles and approached politics from opposing perspectives. Mounier was a philosopher by temperament, directly engaged in the contest among the rival ideologies of the day; Ariès was by disposition a historian, more concerned even in the militancy of his youth to trace present problems to their sources in dilemmas inherited from the past. Mounier's thought tended toward analytical discrimination among abstract concepts, and his quest was to provide the philosophical groundwork for the appreciation of spirituality in contemporary culture. He stood at the center of a coterie of prominent Catholic intellectuals and sympathizers with progressive leanings. They were looking for some "third way" between left and right, between what they regarded as a bankrupt liberalism and a despotic authoritarianism, and so were intrigued by the possibilities of a benevolent French fascism.[26] Ariès thought more concretely about the way ideas emanate from and develop within historical contexts, and his primary concern was to identify them. Mounier emphasized the urgency of moving beyond the failed ideologies of the contemporary age. Ariès sought in the needs of the present the rediscovery of the enduring values of the traditions of the past. Deeply immersed in the activities of the Action Française, he remained unequivocally loyal to the traditionalist politics of royalism. In his public stance on religious issues, Mounier presented himself as an activist in behalf of Catholicism committed to social reform; Ariès cast himself more as a reflective observer and was dismissive of the progressive projects of left-wing Catholics.

Such differences of politics, intellectual milieux, and critical methods notwithstanding, there is an interesting affinity between them in their shared belief in the revelation of the sacred in personal relations. Mounier stressed the irreducibility of the spiritual integrity of the individual; Ariès emphasized the spiritual aspect of personal connections.[27] One might also argue that over the course of his life, Ariès moved toward Mounier's political position. Breaking with his sectarian affiliation with the Action Française in the mid-1960s, he evinced surprising sympathy for the students' protest against conditions in the universities in the "revolution" of 1968, and afterward for the young left engaged in the ecology movement. He noted correspondences between the environmentalism of the younger generation of the left now and his own regionalism of the right then. In this respect, his use of the term "anarchism" is telling because he disassociates the concept from that of disorder and connects it instead to political decentralization, just as had Mounier in an essay on anarchism and personalism some years before.[28] As an "anarchist of the right," Ariès had come to see politics more as orientation than as program, which had been Mounier's posture from the outset.

As a young journalist writing for *L'Etudiant français*, the student organ of the Action Française during the late 1930s, Ariès had first professed his faith in royalism and regionalism in a programmatic way. In his mind at the time, the two notions were closely intertwined. Royalism was his more prominent theme in light of the political crisis then raging in Europe because of Nazi aggression. France, he warned, was in danger of losing its way in this turmoil, as had the nations of central Europe. Recently returned from a trip to Austria and shaken by the *Anschluss*, he wrote an article in which he lamented the fall of the Hapsburg empire, whose rulers he praised for their long and effective role as arbiters among the diverse elements of a loosely federated middle-European kingdom.[29] Ariès believed in the symbolic value of kingship. A king is a tangible figure, he explained, well suited to personify a nation of varied constituencies. His role transcends the routine confrontations and negotiations of modern political life, for he represents the continuity of the nation with traditions emanating from the deep recesses of its past.[30] A modern king, he believed, might still reign as a benevolent arbiter among a nation's regional communities.[31] Such optimism about royalism explains his enthusiastic participation in the royalist-sponsored Action Française. From his perspective, the Action Française was the best vehicle for the defense of the traditional world in which he sensed himself so securely rooted.[32]

With the coming of the Vichy era, Ariès's regionalism took precedence over his royalism, as he sought to identify intermediate communities that might contribute to France's rehabilitation by fostering the values he admired most in traditional society: personalism, sociability, civic-mindedness, and respect for the mores of popular culture.[33] The ancient *pays* of France seemed to him places for promoting such a conception. He explained that he himself, scion of an old-fashioned Bordeaux family, had been born into one of those vanishing settings in the early twentieth century.[34] His teachers at the Sorbonne, several of whom were especially attuned to the importance of regional history and geography, encouraged his interest in the diversity of France's regional cultures.[35] As he noted, "My path to regional history is easily understood: the *pays*, a geographical milieu at once limited and thick, is the natural extension of the family unit; it cannot be distinguished from it. The network of childhood memories, of family alliances, of genealogies, of family papers, of oral traditions, opened naturally on the village, the *pays*, the province."[36]

Ariès published two major essays during the Vichy era. One concerned regionalism, the other royalism. The former, *Les Traditions sociales dans les pays de France,* published in 1943, is now well known, thanks to its republication in a 1993 anthology of Ariès's shorter writings edited by Roger Chartier. The latter, "Le Journal de l'Estoile: Pour le règne de Henri III," published in 1944, is more obscure, though both originally appeared in the same editorial series, Les Cahiers de la Restauration française, a venture launched by Ariès and a few of his old friends from the Sorbonne.[37] They had supported Vichy in its beginnings in 1940, but by 1943 had grown disillusioned with the inability of its leaders to take seriously the traditionalist vision of society. Vichy had succumbed to opportunism in its humiliating subservience to the Third Reich. In launching this series of historical and literary studies, therefore, Ariès and his friends found some intellectual consolation. In their editorial preface to books published in the series, they noted their shared commitment to the "intellectual and mental restoration" of their nation. But France was an occupied and partitioned nation in a world at war. The authors had to be cautious about the political expression of patriotic sentiment. They wrote of what were ostensibly politically neutral historical subjects. But they had long thought of themselves as a secret political brotherhood, and it is not far-fetched to contend that they sought to convey an indirect message that kindred intellectual spirits and learned sympathizers could readily discern.

Ariès's book on the traditions of the ancient regions of France provides insight into his initial sympathy for the Vichy regime. He was then looking for a principle of decentralization that might serve as an alternative to the republican-inspired, centralized nation-state. The *pays*, he argued, provided an ideal of community that was large enough to transcend the networks of extended families, yet small enough to maintain personal rapport in social relationships. The social traditions of the geographically and culturally diverse *pays* had once given rural people a deep sense of communal identity. Concrete and practical, their time-honored customs, mores, and folklore carried with them the authority of the past, even though they were continually being adapted to serve present needs. Conveying the presence of a past that had emerged from immemorial beginnings, their cultures provided an uninterrupted continuum between past and future.[38]

Much of Ariès's text is devoted to inventorying the geographical, economic, and cultural differences among several of the regions of old France: Normandy, Brittany, Champagne, Burgundy, the Languedoc, and the Ile de France. Here he drew upon the scholarship in regional geography that had proliferated in the 1930s and then acquired particular relevance under the political conditions of Vichy.[39] He analyzed the varying ways in which urbanization had penetrated the different regions of France, with attention to the integration of such changes into their local economies and traditional cultures. With an eye to the success of practical solutions in the past, he argued that even the proliferating "zones" of industrialization might be integrated into the framework of the ancient *pays*.[40] The challenge, he contended, was to envision a new kind of regionalism, sensitive to the historical diversity of the ancient *pays*, that might blend the new urban culture into preexisting rural ways.

In their ensemble, Ariès suggested, these regional entities provided a prototype for a federalist alternative to the homogenizing and centralizing nation-state. Federalism as a political option had been suppressed since the founding of the First Republic in 1792, and its possibilities further obscured by the rationalizing tendencies of modern administrative organization. He extolled the role that the notables, the landed gentry with deep historical roots in the *pays*, had played in local governance before their power had been eclipsed by a prefectoral administration and a legislative system imposed by the central government. The administrative redesign of France into departments during the French Revolution may have obscured the political identity of the *pays*, he suggested. But their social traditions continued to thrive, and Vichy, whatever the unfortunate conditions of its emergence, provided an opportunity for resuscitating them as a foundation of a restored French nation.[41]

Ariès's 1944 essay on royalism was a review of a recently published critical edition of the journal of Pierre de L'Estoile, a late sixteenth-century noble of the robe, who offered personal testimony of everyday life in the era of crisis that culminated in the assassination of Henri III in 1588. Herein Ariès's political meaning is once more thinly veiled. The late sixteenth century was a time when France was weak and vulnerable, torn by civil wars of religion and a prey to outside influences. By implication, France in his own time was again dealing with a civil war, this time over the modern secular religions of ideology, and under the shadow of meddling foreign powers.[42]

Ariès admired L'Estoile's chronicle for its keen observation of daily life in that troubled era, especially for its evocation of the untoward passions that intruded into its midst. He notes L'Estoile's depiction of vagabondage, famine, pestilence, dearth, and incessant warfare as incitements to the hysterical fanaticism and prevailing psychological insecurity.[43] Here he presages themes that he and others would later address under the guise of the history of mentalities. He notes the memoir's value as testimony of the times, given the scarce evidence available for gaining access to this hidden historical realm of popular mores. L'Estoile was well-born, wealthy, and intellectually sophisticated. Yet he was able to see across the cultural divide and to comment on the humble lives of ordinary people.[44]

Ariès suggested a parallel between L'Estoile's predicament and his own. Amidst the passion of this time of crisis, he explained, when the vicissitudes of life were dramatized in assassinations, massacres, religious pogroms, and devastating epidemics, L'Estoile maintained his dispassion, prudence, and foresight, searching for practical remedies by which France might overcome decades of religious discord and warfare by trusting in an arbiter king who appealed to all of the constituencies of the realm. In his reasoned approach to problems of the day, L'Estoile was a harbinger of a new political culture.[45]

L'Estoile, a conservative professional, yet practical and open to new solutions for present problems, signaled an approach to reconciliation with which Ariès could identify. Both were aspiring cultural historians. Both developed the capacity to view the crisis-ridden worlds to which they belonged from a critical distance. Both sensed that they lived in times of epochal change. Both sought to judge their circumstances in terms of long-range trends. Both sought to preserve the old order by accommodating change. In Ariès's cryptic review, L'Estoile epitomized the kind of intellectual leadership France would need in the aftermath of the Second World War.

Of course this was not to be. The purge following the Liberation of France unleashed passions of its own. Vichy leaders were officially tried and condemned, while some supporters of the Vichy regime were punished in random acts of vigilante justice. The merits of regionalism and royalism were lost in the reprisals against Vichy's apologists.[46] The ferocity of the purge drove Ariès back into royalist journalism.[47] But his commitment to the old royalist cause was half-hearted because his own views had been so thoroughly altered by what he construed to be the magnitude of historical change underway. In *Le Temps de l'Histoire,* he wrote not at all of the war itself and little of its politics. His focus was on the crisis of culture that the war had revealed. The war signaled the demise of the traditional communities of the *pays* of France to which he had been so personally attached.[48] In the deluge of History, regional culture as a saving shore appeared to have been swallowed up, and Ariès went in search of another refuge for the traditions of old France. In the end, it led him to the historical study of the family as the modern repository of ancient traditions.

Ariès was nonetheless pleased late in life to report that his prophecy of the death of regionalism had been much exaggerated. His youthful commitment to regionalism had been reanimated during the 1970s by the emergence of the ecology movement among a younger generation of political idealists. He tried to put his early ideas about regionalism in historical perspective in an essay that he published in 1979. With the critical distance of nearly forty years, he observed that the regionalism with which he had once identified was a nineteenth-century phenomenon, not something older.[49] The point is worth lingering over, for it helps us to understand Ariès's sense of his own place in the modern era. His vision of the good society during the Vichy years was grounded in what he perceived to be the golden age of provincial culture, which had flourished in the easy rapport it permitted between the old France and the new. By the early twentieth century, political attachments to old France were beginning to wane, as royalist politicians fought a valiant but losing battle to maintain their role in public life. The new France, born of the Enlightenment and institutionalized in the French Revolution, had streamlined public institutions along more efficient lines, in keeping with its expectation that centralized government was the engine of rational progress.[50] In its republican guise, it came to supplant royalist power well before century's end. But if old France was losing its role in the public sphere, its culture remained vibrant in the private one, and in fact experienced renewal in the aftermath of the revolutionary era. The nineteenth century witnessed a renaissance in regional arts and artisan industries, the revival of folklore, the reawakening of popular religious devotions, and the reassertion of the autonomy of the family, made manifest in its lavish weddings and grandiose funerals.

Regionalism in the popular memory of the traditions of the *pays* of old France remained alive through the nineteenth century, Ariès claimed, because of the persistent power of oral tradition in a culture increasingly influenced by literacy. In addressing the reading public, the press professed to be the medium of progress, but its capacity to mold social mores was still limited. Thus Ariès opined that French culture in the nineteenth century epitomized an ideal balance between orality and literacy, and so regional traditions remained a sustaining element of popular conceptions of the good life in French society.[51] The influence of regional culture, he noted, began to erode only in the early twentieth century. Though it had weathered the rise of print literacy, it had been unable to survive the onslaught of the new audiovisual media, whose influences had now intruded into the inner recesses of family and communal life.[52]

Ariès also reaffirmed the royalist faith of his youth in an essay he published in 1980 on popular nostalgia for kings in the contemporary age. Here he took up once more the interpretation he had first voiced during the 1930s. Royalism, he wrote, was no longer a politics but only a sentiment. It appealed to people like himself who felt themselves drifting to the margins of a mass political culture with which they could not identify. Like the ecologically informed proponents of the counterculture, royalists in the present age were quirky in the causes they supported, anarchistic in their protest, modest in their expectations, and nostalgic for a world they had lost. In the practical spirit of their forbear L'Estoile, they called for limits to industrial growth and a prudent policy of environmental planning. They were skeptical of present-day politics with its short-run solutions. The popularity of the sentimental memory of a royal family long since deposed, Ariès maintained, revealed a profound popular attachment to the ways of old France, and suggested why the ancient chateaux of kings and their courtiers remained the most frequented places of tourism in France.[53]

What is more, Ariès believed, the image of the king, once the symbol of centralized political authority, had come to serve this regional conception of society in comforting ways. A king might no longer hold sway as a sovereign political ruler invested with sacred power. But he could exercise a different appeal in a profane and more familiar image as a father king and family man. The image resonated well with the renewed respect for the modern family as a social unit in the nineteenth century.[54] Even into the twentieth century, regional popular culture and royalism coexisted in the popular imagination. The blend of royalism and regionalism to which Ariès all his life was committed was based on a principle of equilibrium. He favored social identities on a human scale in communities that were less intimate than families, yet more personable than nation-states. Regional identities, he believed, harmonize social relations in the balances they establish and the sociability they promote. Regionalism reconciled the social mores of the old France and the new, the private and the public sphere, the family and the state.

In closing I might revisit the last conversation of Philippe Ariès and Raoul Girardet, the episode with which I began this chapter. It is poignant that in the last days of his life Ariès should have offered intimations of his faith commitments to an old friend from his prewar days, someone to whom he was close before the debacle of the war and the breakup of the harmony he had felt in that vanishing milieu. Friendship was the deep source of his ideas about sociability, and he treasured his commitment to his old friends through the vicissitudes of life.[55] Friendship was the way he confirmed his lingering attachments to an old-fashioned world, and it is interesting in light of this to look at one of his rare late-life observations on the subject, interjected into an essay he contributed to a collaborative study on the history of sexuality in 1982. Therein he surmised that friendship had declined in importance in the present age, displaced by family ties in the private sphere and contractual relationships in the public one. His faith in friendship issued from the informal sociability of the traditional society to which he sensed he had belonged while a student in Paris in the 1930s. In such a society, he observed, friendship "acted as a lubricant in many service relationships that are today governed by contracts. Social life was organized around personal ties, dependence, patronage, mutual help." Friendship for Ariès stood at the innermost center of concentric circles of personal relationships that reverberated outward, like ripples from a stone's throw into placid waters, to "clients, fellow citizens, clan members, one's own circle. One lived amidst a web of sentiment, at once diffuse and sometimes marginal, which was only partially determined by birth and circumstances, and which was catalyzed by chance and haphazard encounters."[56]

In his recollections, Ariès thought of the friendships of university days as a bridge across the divide of Vichy to the consoling shore of his enchanted childhood. Again, it testifies to the central role that Vichy played in his personal and intellectual maturation. The Vichy years obliged him to recontextualize his commitments within a wider world. He acknowledged the limits and the naïveté of his prewar understanding. But he saw his task as a historian as one of figuring out a new way to maintain his connection with the traditions of old France by reflecting on them from a critical distance. His work as a historian was dedicated to that task and was in some moral sense an act of expiation for the way Vichy had vitiated his "royalist" vision of harmony among sociable communities. From a historical perspective, he recognized that his conception of the regionalism of the ancient *pays* was a vision of the good society lost in time. The sociability of old France had passed with its traditions. But the need it had once fulfilled endured and would find new forms of expression, as it had in the mores of the modern family, and more recently in the regionalism associated with the ecology movement. That was the point about his faith in his profane calling as historian which he wanted to make in his interview with Winock and which comes across softly in the impromptu observations of his late-life writings.

9

Late-Life Historical
Reflections on the Family in
Contemporary Culture

The "Indissoluble Marriage" of Primerose and Philippe Ariès

PRIMEROSE ARIÈS died in Toulouse late in the summer of 1983, leaving Philippe, her husband of thirty-six years, alone.[1] Their intimacy as a couple was legendary among their acquaintances. They had been friends since adolescence, hailing from families among the provincial bourgeoisie that prided themselves in their enduring attachment to the royalist politics and traditional culture of old France. Affianced in what might be construed as an arranged marriage, they had some difficult beginnings to their life together. But over time they drew closer. They traveled together extensively, initially in connection with Philippe's work as director of the commercial documentation center, later and more often with that of his historical research.[2] Their closest bond was their shared love of learning. Recently they had collaborated on a last scholarly project, preparation of a book of hauntingly beautiful images of death as it had been represented across the ages.[3] Primerose was an art historian, and her influence upon her husband is most visible here. Philippe dedicated the book to her, for she "enabled me to see what I might otherwise have passed by without noticing. On every page, [this book] awakens memories of our life together."[4]

The Ariès had only recently moved to Toulouse, Primerose's natal home, after she had been diagnosed as terminally ill with cancer. She had wanted to return there to die. Their friend François Leger recalls the "moral, physical, and intellectual suffering" they experienced during their last days together, though their care for one another provided much consolation.[5] In the months following her death, Philippe mentioned to a close friend his intuition about the imminence of his own and his acceptance of it.[6] "It was the love of his wife that enabled him to make that leap [of faith],"

Leger remarked in an obituary he wrote shortly after Ariès's death. "He survived the following few weeks only in the hope of finding her once more, in reliving spiritually their shared existence, deciphering the spiritual meaning [*le code de l'âme*] of each of the events that had marked it, discovering there a new meaning and a new value."[7] Ariès had in his last years come to think of his marriage to Primerose as akin to that of Philemon and Baucis, the mythological couple who having grown inseparable in old age beseeched the gods to permit them to pass into eternity together. In his later writings, he refers to the legend as a metaphor for "indissoluble marriage," the romantic ideal of marital fidelity in the bourgeois culture of the nineteenth century. It was a closing gesture of identification with a vanishing world whose destiny he had come to associate with his own.[8]

As I have noted, Ariès's destiny among historians has been to be remembered for his signal role forty years ago in launching scholarly work in the history of the family. His *L'Enfant et la vie familiale sous l'Ancien Régime*, published in 1960 and better-known in its English translation as *Centuries of Childhood*, set the stage for new scholarship on the subject, which grew rapidly from the late 1960s.[9] Largely overlooked is his return to that history in his later years, this time to consider it in light of the crisis of the contemporary family. These late-life historical reflections were especially sensitive to the new social realities of the late twentieth century. While continuing to use his earlier work on the "modern" family as a frame of reference, he went in search of a more adequate interpretation of its present problems. He pursued his inquiry along three paths: the crisis of the contemporary family, with particular attention to adolescence; the changing relationship between love and marriage across the ages; and the historical emergence of the separation between public and private life as the key to understanding long-range changes in the dynamics of the modern family. More directly than in his earlier work, these writings express his critique of contemporary culture, and highlight once more his appreciation of the small communities of old France as examples of alternative ways in which the good society might be conceived.[10] Here I assess the meaning of these late-life writings that broadened his interpretation of the topic which had first made him famous: the family considered in long-range historical perspective.

One must take into account the changing context in which Ariès carried on his work as he grew older. Most students of contemporary French historiography still regard him as an "isolated pioneer," conducting his research apart, influencing others to the degree that he inspired interests that they explored independently.[11] That may have been true of his early life. But his last years—roughly 1975 to 1984—were conspicuous for his participation in a dynamic network of scholarly associations. From 1977 to 1982, he taught a seminar at the Ecole des Hautes Etudes en Sciences Sociales and was intensively engaged in a variety of collaborative ventures that explored new realms of the genre of history that he had helped define, the history of mentalities.[12] At the time he took up this appointment, he retired from his position as director of the documentation center of the Institut de Recherches sur les Fruits et Agrumes, where he had worked since 1943.[13] Henceforth he was no longer the "Sunday historian" to whom he self-deprecatingly referred in his autobiography. Freed of administrative responsibilities, he wrote prolifically in his later years.[14]

One notes the scholarly recognition Ariès was belatedly accorded among professional historians, particularly those identified with the Annales movement. With their rising interest in his work during the 1970s, he moved from the margins to the center of the historiographical stage. *Centuries of Childhood* had by then gained considerable notice and sold well throughout the Western world. Whereas his early writings had been brought out by minor publishing houses and were for the most part ignored in the professional reviews, the most important were republished by the prestigious Editions du Seuil in the early 1970s. His major project of the late 1960s and 1970s, a study of attitudes toward death and mourning, involved him in a running debate with some of France's leading historians. By the late 1970s, his role as a pioneer in the new cultural history was being heralded in France and abroad. He was invited to lecture at universities throughout North America and Europe.

Though suggestive of his deepening insight into the predicament of the contemporary family, Ariès's last project remained unfinished. It consisted of a series of articles and lectures that pointed toward a comprehensive study that he would not have time to complete. Sick with colon cancer, he sensed that his days were numbered. Though he had once preferred to work independently, he came to understand this last scholarly inquiry as a collaborative venture in which he would pass on his project to his colleagues. By then the term "collective mentalities," so closely associated with his particular scholarship, was being discarded in favor of "private life," which gave a more capacious meaning to the new cultural history. As a faculty member at the Ecole des Hautes Etudes, he encouraged others to join him in the task of synthesizing the many strands of research in this field over the previous two decades. The multivolume *Histoire de la vie privée* (1985–87), which bears his name as coeditor, was the culmination of this effort.[15]

Reflections on the Changing Nature of the Contemporary Family

Ariès's reputation was made in America. During the late 1960s and early 1970s, he found an appreciative audience there that would bring him to intellectual prominence. *Centuries of Childhood* had a tonic effect on American scholarship. Practitioners identified with the "helping professions"— psychiatrists, psychologists, and social workers—were the first to be intrigued by his work.[16] Ariès spoke to their worries about the socialization of their children by providing a historical perspective on a present-day culture in which the family was visibly changing.[17] The professional historians soon followed. They were drawn to the vistas he had opened into a new cultural history apart from the socioeconomic history that had dominated historiographical fashion after the Second World War. Noteworthy was Ariès's friendship with Orest Ranum, an America historian of early modern France at Johns Hopkins University, who invited him there to deliver his first lecture series in America. Ariès took the opportunity to present an overview of his current work on attitudes toward death in Western culture across the ages. Delivered in the spring 1973, his lectures were published the following year by the press of that university.[18] Ranum also helped him win a fellowship at the Woodrow Wilson Center for Scholars in Washington, D.C., where he continued research and writing on this project, and he facilitated his introduction into North American academic circles.[19] Leading scholars of family life among them, such as Edward Shorter, a professor at the University of Toronto, took a particular interest in his work.[20] The American reception of Ariès's writings, together with his journeys to America, was crucial to his rising prestige as a historian internationally, and, ironically, eventually in France.

In retrospect, it is easy to see the appeal of Ariès's thesis on the long-term rise of the modern nuclear family, for it provided a frame of reference for considering the crisis of childhood and family in the contemporary age. In *Centuries of Childhood* he noted a balance between continuity and change in the mores of the family emerging in early modern Europe.[21] From the sixteenth to the early twentieth century, the family adapted to the modern world by maintaining open channels between the increasingly divergent needs of public and private life. On the one hand, it fostered individual initiative among children as a preparation for the responsibilities to which they would be called as adults in the public sphere. On the other, it preserved the communal mores of traditional society in the intimacy of its private life. The modern family taught respect for traditional ways by fostering the personal loyalties and sociable habits on which traditional culture had once thrived. It was a crossroads between two worlds, easing movement between them by encouraging independence without rending the fabric of social custom. Ariès deeply regretted the disappearance of the small communities that had sustained the traditional society of old France—corporate guilds, fraternal and religious societies. But he found in the modern family some solace, for it reconstituted in miniature the network of old-fashioned sociability that was fast disappearing in the public sphere. In his view, the family as a social unit in modern culture had taken on a newfound importance in its obligations to society at large. If it was a sanctuary of privacy in a world of impersonal public transactions, it remained connected to that world and in some measure tempered its antisocial tendencies.[22]

In the mid-1970s, however, Ariès reconsidered this model of the modern family in order to grasp more adequately its current dilemmas. The family in the present age faced challenging new problems with which it struggled to cope: permissive parents, alienated adolescents, wives restless under their domestic burdens, accelerating instances of domestic turmoil, rising divorce rates, and media publicity about child abuse. Ariès sought to uncover the historical sources of this emerging crisis so as to identify the interplay of forces pulling families apart. Such a project led him to put his accent upon the differences between the family today and the "modern" one on which his original thesis had focused.[23] Though he never consolidated his reinterpretation in a book-length study, his inquiry, distilled from his numerous articles and essays on the topic during the 1970s and early 1980s, draws out his explanation of why a nuclear family that treasured its privacy was paradoxically loosening its bonds, and how an emerging mass culture was taking advantage of its vulnerability to undermine its autonomy. Ariès looked at the crisis of the contemporary family from two perspectives:

The Contemporary Family as a "Prison of Love." For Ariès, the present-day family was beating a deeper retreat from society at large. Hitherto a refuge from a public world with which it maintained vital connections, the family now betrayed signs of having become a "prison of love."[24] By this he meant that the family was turning inward upon its own pursuits and pleasures. In the affluence of postwar society, it came to covet material possessions in an open-ended way. Kitchen conveniences, television sets, new cars, country homes—these were but the most conspicuous forms of consumerism in which it indulged.[25] The effect was to trivialize the socializing role the family had formerly provided for its children. The modern family, he recalled, had set itself a high pedagogical mission. Parents lavished attention upon their children to prepare them for productive lives as mature adults.[26] The contemporary family, by contrast, "dethroned" the child from this privileged position in its midst, as parents reappropriated that place for themselves. Children, the pride of the "modern" family, came to be viewed by contemporary parents with mixed feelings, in their most reluctant moments as inconvenient burdens on their own journeys toward wider personal horizons. This reconfiguration of the dynamics of family life to favor personal needs over social obligations tended to weaken family solidarity. Some parents were less mindful than had been their own about how best to advance the interests of their children. In a poignant way, Ariès noted, the private retreat from the obligations of child-rearing paralleled the public retreat from involvement in civic affairs. The contemporary family thus jeopardized the mediating role it had previously played between private and public life.[27]

For Ariès, adolescence was the breaking point at which the crisis of the family presented itself.[28] From a historical perspective, he explained, adolescence was a comparatively recent refinement in the modern psychological delineation of the life cycle. Psychologists recognized it as a developmental "stage of life" only toward the turn of the twentieth century.[29] Wedged between childhood and youth, adolescence filled a social need to punctuate further the lengthening process of a child's psychological growth. Originally adolescence was viewed as but one stage along life's way, a bridge between the child's dependence upon the family and the young adult's independence in the world at large. Today's delay in the integration of adolescents into that world, Ariès argued, had the ironical effect of expanding the place of this stage in the life cycle, with baneful consequences.[30] As parents became more self-involved, so too did their children. Adolescents were in crisis for want of the sense of purpose that family life had previously inculcated. What had enabled families to thrive in the modern age, he maintained, had been the balance they established between training for independence and respect for social tradition. But in the present age, adolescents were given less parental direction, while family traditions were more and more ignored. A lengthening process of formal schooling assumed some of these burdens, but it could not compensate for the weakening bonds of family solidarity and may in some measure have contributed to their dissolution. Increasingly adolescents socialized exclusively among themselves. It was as if they were orphaned from their own families, as their more visible expressions of alienation seemed to attest.[31]

The Family Adrift in a Mass Culture. Having abandoned its public role, Ariès argued, the family became vulnerable to the policies of the expanding welfare state.[32] If the state dispensed greater largesse among its citizens than ever before, it also began to set standards for the private sphere that the modern family had cherished as its own. The "policing" function of the state, which hitherto had dealt with peripheral delinquencies, came to influence conventional family life.[33]

At the same time, Ariès did not wish to lay undue emphasis upon the state's responsibility for the declining social role of the family.[34] He preferred to consider the state as part of the larger culture of "planning, organization, and calculation" that was working its inexorable influence upon contemporary social mores and reshaping family life in the process.[35] The new mass culture undercut the sociability that had once gathered people together in small, personable groups. Here the media had become an insidious influence, propagating banal, conformist stereotypes of the good life. The imperative to create a more rational and efficient social order also had the effect of segmenting time into ever more discrete units, creating an illusion of its quickening pace, and leaving less of it for the informal socializing that had once been the stuff of family life.[36]

This new mass culture, Ariès concluded, eroded the already diminishing authority that parents exercised within the fragile networks of the contemporary nuclear family. In the new mix of permissive parents and self-indulgent children, the family was losing its role as the principal agency for the socialization of the young and was becoming instead an object of public scrutiny and benign management.[37] Some adolescents came to view the family not as a haven from public authority but as an instrument of it. The student revolts of the late 1960s, Ariès contended, were at a profound level a reaction against a society driven by the imperatives of its technology. So too was the movement for women's liberation, which struggled to create opportunities outside the home for women hitherto denied them. Both sought to liberate the family from its role as a "prison of love" within an emerging consumerist culture that promoted meretricious personal satisfactions while neglecting genuine social needs.[38]

Toward a History of Love inside and outside Marriage

The crisis of the contemporary family was also one of contemporary marriage. In a second strand of research, Ariès inquired into why the ideal of "indissoluble marriage" had become so difficult to uphold. The conventional view extolled it as a timeless conception.[39] Ariès, by contrast, wanted to show that "indissoluble marriage," whose origins stem from the Middle Ages, was reinvented in the Romantic era.[40] Life-long marriage had been easier to accept in earlier times when life spans were less predictable and generally shorter. Traditional marriage had been based on practical considerations of wealth and social advancement. Erotic love in marriage was among the least important of these, a matter of good fortune in a culture that tolerated extramarital liaisons more openly. "Indissoluble marriage" in the modern era, by contrast, was a more fragile alliance, founded on a precarious balance between the need for family solidarity and the desire for romantic love. As marriage as a public act came to be defined by more formal matrimonial codes, marriage as a private act was reconceived around deepening expectations of conjugal intimacy. As a unit of affection the modern family demanded not only parental love of children but also spousal love of each other. For "indissoluble marriage" to reconcile these opposing needs of child-rearing and restless passion, Ariès suggested, romantic love had to be transformed over time into friendship. But with fewer of the supporting props of traditional society and rising expectations about lifelong personal growth, such a maturation was difficult to attain. Marriage more frequently than ever before ended in divorce.[41]

In his investigation of the history of love in marriage, Ariès brought together several of his interests: sexuality, marital fidelity, friendship, and the widening divide between public and private life. He played out his ideas in a seminar with students and colleagues at the Ecole des Hautes Etudes in 1979-80.[42] This collegial venture was published as a special issue of the journal *Communications* in 1982, then as *Sexualités occidentales* in 1982.[43] Ariès's own contributions to this volume were modest, and his inquiry into this topic was even more provisional than had been that on the changing dynamics of family life. Still, he sketched a pattern of changing attitudes about marriage across the ages that provides an intriguing parallel with the model he had earlier devised for his study of the history of attitudes toward death and mourning. Therein he had plotted four stages in the evolving conception of its meaning.[44] In his scheme for the history of marriage the same pattern is discernable, and the historical parallel might be diagrammed this way:

Personal Responsibility in "Tamed Death"/Private Marriage Vows (High Middle Ages). In Ariès's tableau of death in the High Middle Ages, the moribund person on his death bed presided over his own demise in the presence and with the blessing of his local community. Correspondingly, the betrothed in their marriage bed spoke their own vows of commitment in the same kind of setting: surrounded by friends and family. Marriage rituals were private contracts; they were sanctioned and supported by local communities. Because of the harsh conditions that cut short so many lives, long-term marriages were rare, and so lifelong marital commitment seldom presented itself as a troubling issue. Traditional marriage privileged the prestige of family connections, and medieval culture was little interested in whether erotic love was to be found inside or outside marriage.[45]

Public Accountability in "One's Own Death"/Ceremonial Marriage (Late Middle Ages). For Ariès, the emerging preoccupation with one's own death reflected the influence of public accountability in the late Middle Ages. This attitude was inspired by the growing influence of the church in defining the meaning of death in the public sphere. So conceived, the attitude toward death, previously understood within the context of life, was reconceived in light of a preoccupation with its denouement: the state of the soul at the hour of death.[46] In the popular imagination, the issue was dramatized in a tableau of the heavenly struggle for the soul of the dying person. The matrimonial counterpart to this move toward public accountability was the removal of the wedding ceremony from the home to the door of the church, and later to its interior. In the process, the clergy gained a symbolic role in sanctioning the legitimacy of marriage, while the betrothed lost a measure of autonomy in defining the nature of their own vows. Marriage took on not only a formality but also a fixity it had not known before. Sanctioned by the church, it became irrevocable.[47] Benign as the church's influence might appear to have been, Ariès claimed, its new role signified the beginning of the long-range intrusion of public authority into family life, a glimmer of what would later become recognizable as a transaction across the widening divide between public and private life.[48]

Private Meanings in Demonstrative Grief/Passionate Love (Early Nineteenth Century). Ariès's notion of "thy death" in the modern age reflected the influence of Romanticism, with its intense sentiments of irretrievable loss. Funerals were marked by demonstrative grief, followed by the commemoration of the loved one in monumental statuary, a quest to overcome loss in grandiose remembrance. The counterpart was the introduction of erotic love into the equation of the matrimonial ideal. Hitherto marriage had valued almost exclusively procreation to perpetuate family dynasties. Henceforth undying passion was touted as an essential element of an "indissoluble marriage," while amorous liaisons outside its bonds were judged illicit.[49]

Forbidden Death/Ephemeral Marriage (Mid-twentieth Century). For Ariès, "forbidden death" bespoke an uneasiness about the meaning of death conceived as a mark of human destiny. He presented disquieting images of dying alone in antiseptic hospitals, deprived of the support of family and friends. Death took on the frightening specter of anonymity. As his matrimonial parallel, he offered an equally troubling conception of marriage in the present age. "Indissoluble marriage," with its high expectations for marital fidelity, became more difficult to accept, in part because of the dwindling support of private communities, in part because of rising expectations about personal fulfillment in adulthood. Most important, however, was the context in which the marital ideal was framed. Immersed in a public culture that proffered a romantic image of marriage, the couple was faced with unrealistic expectations of conjugal love that created pressures of their own. Such a culture neglected the more profound foundations of fidelity that only the shared experience of life's challenges over time can provide. Marriage based on fickle passion was likely to founder over the long term.[50]

As one personally taken with the ideal of "indissoluble marriage," Ariès noted that it sometimes worked. Love as commitment over time can grow into a more profound bond in any age, he explained, as the classic tales of the Homeric epics (Ulysses and Penelope) and Greek tragedy (Admetus and Alcestis) attest.[51] But such examples are rare, and especially so today. As a marital ideal for everyone, Ariès had not much hope for the future of indissoluble marriage. He speculated that alternative patterns might emerge in which only some couples would choose formal marriage agreements, and these on a fixed-term basis.[52] His larger point was to show that most of our cultural absolutes are relative to historical circumstances and are modified with surprising rapidity.

Participants in Ariès's seminar also paid considerable attention to the little-studied realm of sexual mores. Herein Ariès returned to the thesis about contraception that he had formulated from his demographic research in the mid-1940s and that had first launched him into the study of the mentalities of families. In seeking to account for declining birth rates in France from the seventeenth century, he had argued that the private decision of married couples to practice birth control was a self-conscious strategy of liberation, calculated to improve the quality of their own lives and those of their children. Such was the hidden "revolution in mores," Ariès contended, that signified the emergence of a modern mentality committed to exercising mastery over natural reproductive processes to which previous generations had simply resigned themselves.[53] In his work during the late 1970s, Ariès expanded on his early insight. In severing the fatalistic connection between sexual activity and procreation, he argued, the married couple renounced the sexual asceticism of traditional society in favor of understanding marital sex as the pursuit of pleasure, a connection previously associated with illicit love. The search for erotic love in marriage, he maintained, reinforced the notion of the family as a unit of affection.[54] It also set the course for acknowledging and liberating peripheral sexual behaviors, notably homosexuality.[55]

Issues concerning the history of sexuality permitted an intellectual exchange between Ariès and Michel Foucault, who was then launching his own investigations of the subject. Though they proceeded by different routes, their research had come to converge in a shared interest in the relationship between sexual practices and techniques for the care of the self.[56] Both addressed the topic with an eye to the modern effort to manage sexuality through an elaboration of its science. Ariès invited Foucault to be a guest lecturer in his seminar and to contribute an essay to its published proceedings.[57] Foucault was a man of the left, trained as a philosopher but making his reputation as a highly original cultural historian. As historians, the two had led parallel lives.[58] Like Ariès, Foucault was drawn late in life to the topic of sexuality as an inner sanctum of privacy. Both were intrigued by the anarchy of sexuality, and, with variations, both identified the project of sexual liberation as an arena where power between the private and the public sphere was negotiated. For Ariès, the advent of birth control signified a revolution in mores in which married couples aspired to take control of their private destinies. For Foucault, sexuality itself was an unmasterable domain, defying the hubris of modern man to locate there his search for truth.[59]

But the intellectual connections between Ariès and Foucault go beyond the topic of sexuality. Both offered a critique of the soft technologies of conformism in the society of the late twentieth century. Both were suspicious of the big state and concerned about the erosion of privacy in the modern world. This was the basis of their shared interest in the public/private tension and privacy as the sphere of the self.[60] Foucault's method of argument is original, whereas that of Ariès is conventional. But each worked from a powerful motivating insight that subtended the topics of historical inquiry that they explored. Their shared interest in the boundary between public and private life is what eventually drew them together. In his work in its ensemble, Ariès's originality was to mark out its historical emergence. Foucault, by contrast, explored the idea of boundary itself in the rhetorical forms that humans invent to block out their cultural worlds.

Roger Chartier and Philippe Ariès, at the conference at Saint-Maximin on
death and mourning, 25 July 1981

A reception at the mairie, Saint-Maximin, 25 July 1981: from the left,
Roger Chartier, Ariès, and Orest Ranum

Primerose and
Philippe

Philippe and
Primerose, at
home in
Maisons-Lafitte,
22 February 1980
(courtesy of
François Leger)

Friends at the fête for the Ariès on the bateau-mouche, François Leger at center, 14 October 1981

Marie-Rose and Philippe at the same fête, 14 October 1981

Ariès delivering a conference paper

Another view of
Ariès at the
same conference

Ariès engaged in
conversation

Portrait of Philippe Ariès by Anne de Brunhoff

Ariès giving an outdoor lecture at the cemetery at Marville (Lorraine), 11 June 1980

Ariès analyzing a mural plaque at the same gathering

A round-table on attitudes toward mourning, 1983: from the left: Ariès, Jean Delumeau, moderator Bernard Pivot, unidentified woman, Michel Vovelle

An Inquiry into the History of Private Life

Private life, the third strand of Ariès's late-life research on the family, proved to be the most elusive. His inquiry into the historical emergence of the distinction between public and private life was the broadest context in which he considered the history of the family. For Ariès, it was the most intriguing topic underpinning the contemporary historiographical interest in mentalities, for it highlighted the historical conditions that were eroding the ideal of sociability in the contemporary world.[61] In his view, the history of mentalities had to consider not only the mores of everyday life but also the cultural evolution through which everyday life came to be understood as a realm apart. When modern historians made the politics of the public sphere their primary subject matter, Ariès explained, they relegated the study of private life to folklorists. With the disappearance of popular tradition in the contemporary age, however, historians were turning at last to this lost world. Certainly there was an element of nostalgia in this new historiography, he conceded, for the sociability identified with traditional society remained an essential human need unsatisfied in the consumer culture.[62] In this respect, Ariès's interpretation of the decline of sociability is paired with his critique of the ideal of progress, which he associated with the techniques of rationalization that produced contemporary mass society. The scope of this ambitious project on the making of private life inspired him to plan an international scholarly conference to explore its dimensions.

The idea for such a conference grew out of an invitation to him from German scholars to visit Berlin for an overall assessment of the significance of his contribution to the new cultural history. Heinz-Dieter Kittsteiner, director of the Wissenschaftskolleg of Berlin, asked Ariès to spend the spring of 1983 as a visiting scholar at that institution.[63] The conference, scheduled for May, was to be the capstone of his sojourn there. More important, it was to be a gathering of leading scholars in the emerging international collaboration in this field. His American friend Ranum was to be in Berlin simultaneously. French scholars were to be invited to join their German colleagues in this conference. For Ariès, it offered an excellent opportunity to confer with potential contributors to his project on the history of private life and to test some of his ideas about it within this wider community of scholars. In its expansive possibilities, this German connection contrasts sharply with the constraining one into which he had been drawn during the Vichy years.

The conference convened in Berlin in May 1983. In reviewing the roster of non-German participants, one notes the presence of Yves and Nicole

Castan, Roger Chartier, Arlette Farge, Michelle Perrot, and Orest Ranum, all of whom would later contribute to the history of private life anthology.[64] The highlight of the conference, however, was the encounter between Ariès and Norbert Elias, who despite the striking affinities of their interpretations of the privatization of social life had established no previous contact or communication. A German Jewish sociologist, Elias had fled Germany in 1939 and had spent much of his life in exile in Britain. His celebrated study of the history of manners, *The Civilizing Process*, first published in Germany in 1939, went unnoticed until the early 1970s, when scholars recognized its importance as a contribution to the history of mentalities.[65] During the war years, he found a teaching post at a polytechnic institute, and over the course of his years in Britain published some conventional sociological studies, disappointing in comparison with the originality of his youthful work in Germany. A contrite Federal Republic sought to make amends for his exile by recognizing the value of his scholarly accomplishment. From 1978 to 1984, he was appointed a fellow of the Center for Interdisciplinary Research at the University of Bielefeld. In his later years, he published a series of more significant books on which he had been working and acquired a certain following throughout western Europe.[66]

As scholars on the margins who eventually found their way to the center of scholarly attention for their contributions to the new cultural history, Ariès and Elias may be said to have led parallel lives. Their explorations of the revolution in sentiment in early modern Europe now set them on a converging course. Elias's *Civilizing Process* traced the emergence of the code of manners in Western civilization as an expression of psychosocial development. As an approach to the public/private divide, his scholarship bears many similarities with Ariès's work.[67] Both noted the compartmentalization of space in the making of modern culture, and both discussed the interrelationship between privacy and the cultivation of emotional sensibilities. But in Berlin, they appear to have established surprisingly little personal rapport. If there were similarities in their interpretation of the emergence of an emotional dimension to private life, Elias was not prepared to acknowledge them. Rather than emphasizing their common ground—the privatization of social life—he criticized Ariès for failing to place his discussion of parent-child relations in *Centuries of Childhood* within an adequate theoretical framework, of the sort that he had developed in his own interpretation of the "civilizing process." "There are an infinite number of details to be gleaned from historical sources," he allowed. "And if we do not see any kind of order, any kind of structure in the many details which we have, we will end in having a certain confusion, a certain multitude of details, but no unity."[68] Here Elias was following up on a criticism he had presented in an earlier essay, in which he had contended that Ariès's romantic nostalgia for traditional society had beclouded his understanding of the psychosocial process at work in the making of modern civilization.[69] He mistakenly assumed that Ariès had misgivings about the revolution in sentiment that had transformed parent-child relations during the early modern era.

Some genuine differences in their interpretations of the nature of long-range historical change became evident from their interchange, notably over the issue of how modern culture had come into being. Elias stressed the continuous evolutionary development of the psychosocial process through which personal emotional sensitivity emerged, indexed in the refinement of a code of manners over several centuries, and culminating in the etiquette governing bourgeois life at the end of the eighteenth century. He likened the process to the crystallization of a supersaturated solution through which its essential structure was revealed.[70] Ariès preferred a more dynamic approach to cultural structures, based on mindsets that were periodically reconfigured. For Ariès, the divide between public and private life emerged slowly, but in a succession of overlapping stages. Within each, the relationship between the public and the private was significantly different.[71] Nor did Ariès posit a culmination to the process, preferring to leave the future open to new configurations.

In this respect, Ariès would seem to plot three historical stages in the long-range decline of sociability: that of medieval traditional, modern bourgeois, and contemporary mass society.[72] He characterized traditional society as a milieu. Therein one did not make a conscious distinction between public and private life. Milieux were sociable. Work and play were intermingled.[73] In an all-too-brief observation in his autobiography, Ariès suggested that secrecy had played a social role prior to the rise of privacy. Thus traditional milieux of sociability, which knew no privacy, did have a place for secrecy, as exemplified in the secret societies of the late eighteenth century.[74]

Bourgeois society was a transitional stage that maintained channels between both worlds. Traditional sociability survived within private spheres, which served as places of memory of this earlier age. In the modern era, Ariès contended, social life came to be divided between home and work. Within these restricted settings, sociability retained a place, while the conviviality of the open middle ground began to disappear. In other words, sociability came to be compartmentalized in both the private and the public sphere. In the former, the home became a place where family members and close friends socialized freely. In the latter, the café played an analogous role. Both provided a respite from the world at large, with the understanding that one would return to it. As places of sociability that permitted prescribed openings between public and private life, the family and the café flourished in the bourgeois culture of the nineteenth century.

Ariès argued that contemporary mass society, with its rational bureaucratization and techniques of efficiency, has less place for sociability. Symptomatic of the change has been the disappearance of open spaces in which people can interrelate informally. In today's cities there are fewer places in which to play. In the late twentieth century, both the home and the café have lost their role as its arenas. Café life, for example, the principal forum for urban sociability in nineteenth-century France, began to disappear from the mid-twentieth century. The decline of public space for socializing thus intensified the preoccupation with private pastimes that diminished social interaction. Such, Ariès contended, are the preconditions of our present-day crisis of culture: the marginalization of conviviality in a mass society that covets consumerism in private life and that ties public life to unrelenting work.[75]

Ariès's presentation at the Berlin conference might be thought of as his valedictory address to his colleagues. It testifies to his reorientation toward collaborative scholarship. His posthumously published lead essay to the third volume of *Une Histoire de la vie privée* sums up his reflections in light of the conference's discussions. Rather than emphasizing the singularity of his own views, he canvasses the topic of privacy in its many possibilities for further research: some personal (soul-searching in solitude, shared experience of friendship, the pursuit of love); others social (the configuration of the interiors of homes, the mores of family life); still others threats to it (the encroachments of the modern state, the sameness of a pervasive mass culture). The family stood at the center of all of these compartmentalizations, the beleaguered bastion of a sociability as vulnerable as it was essential to human relations. In his way, Ariès's last essay on privacy was his bequest of the topic to a new generation of scholars.[76]

The "Tamed Death" of Philippe Ariès

Philippe survived Primerose by less than a year. The circumstances attending the hour of his own death in a hospital ward in Toulouse during the night of 8–9 February 1984 might seem closer to the "forbidden death" of the present age that he abhorred than to the "tamed death" of traditional society that he had idealized. But Ariès's own extended "family" was based more on friendship than kinship, a circle of intellectuals like himself, some longtime companions from his days as a student activist in the Action Française, others associations formed more recently in the historical profession. They paid him homage in reflective ways befitting his role in life.[77] Their obituaries engaged his ideas, and some pursued the meaning of his scholarly work in detail in the learned journals over the following years.[78] The most enduring testimony was that of his colleagues Roger Chartier, Georges Duby, and Paul Veyne, who saw to a successful conclusion the multivolume *Histoire de la vie privée* that he had inaugurated. We might say that their fidelity to his memory was a modern expression of the traditional ideal of presence at the passing of a loved one.[79] This project constitutes the most significant legacy of Ariès's late-life scholarship. Consolidating twenty-five years of research, it marked the culmination of work in the history of mentalities. Just as he had played a leading role in ushering in this genre of history, he would play a corresponding one in leading it into a wider historiographical domain.

Ironically, Ariès, regarded by his colleagues as a traditionalist, may be remembered by future historians as a modernist—an interpreter of the "modern" age on the eve of its passing. For Ariès late in his life recognized the symptoms of a further change in outlook, and in these last writings he sought to shed light on the mentality of the changing world in which he lived. The diminishing role of the family as a moral agency, the proliferation of sexual identities, the emergence of alternative conceptions of the family, and most important, the threat to privacy posed by the managerial imperatives of public authority were the elements of a new kind of culture and a new set of problems. Ariès addressed all of them. His essential insight was that the rise of a need for "privacy" was concomitant with the decline of communal life. In effect, the family retreated into privacy because it could not relate to public life any longer in a meaningful way. In doing so it became vulnerable to the state's encroaching claims on private life and ultimately to the pervasive influence of a conformist mass culture.

Ariès never had a chance to bring to fruition his inquiry into the history of privacy. But he had always been less interested in endings than in the processes of which he was a part. He believed that dynamic change is inherent in the human condition and that what we used to call human nature is continually changing. The study of history, he professed, makes us aware of the historical character of the human predicament by showing us how different is the present from all that has gone before.[80]

This is what Foucault appreciated most about Ariès's work. In an obituary he wrote shortly before his own death, he meditated upon Ariès's intellectual journey. Ariès's youthful conservatism, Foucault explained, was a product of the prewar times in which he came of age. What distinguished Ariès from his *confrères* on the right was his capacity to outgrow a narrow, timeworn politics of cultural elitism to become the master of a panoramic new history of the culture of our everyday lives. It enabled him, Foucault concluded, to relocate his search for the sources of our social values in the rich terrain of collective mentalities, and so permitted him to give us "the unexpected gift of original insight."[81]

CHAPTER

10

A Time in History

Framing Historical Time

IN HIS AUTOBIOGRAPHY, Philippe Ariès tells a charming story of an illuminating moment in his ruminations on the concept of historical time. As with so many of his ideas, it comes intertwined with an account of the personal circumstances that attended his reflections, in this case a tale of the way he and Primerose began to share their lives as a married couple in the late 1940s. In those days, they sometimes made weekend excursions into the Loire valley. It was not that far from Paris, an easy journey on the train. They often took their bicycles with them and explored the byways of this storybook countryside, dotted with the chateaux of old France. On one such journey, they happened upon the chateau at Beauregard, sequestered on a back road south of Blois. On the second floor, they entered a gallery adorned with dozens of portraits of the high and mighty—of lordly kings, imposing generals in battle costume, high prelates in cardinal red, alongside occasional images of solemn women in pious poses. Staring up at this ensemble of distinguished personalities, their eyes were led from portrait to portrait, sequentially aligned around the interior of the rectangular hall according to their chronological place in the rise of the French monarchy from the late Middle Ages through the early seventeenth century.[1]

This gallery of historical portraits, some 363 in all, had been put together by Paul Ardier, a noble of the robe who had purchased the chateau in 1617 as a place for his retirement and who spent the next two decades furnishing it. Along the upper walls, he arranged the portraits of kings and their courtiers, beginning with Philippe VI, who had ascended to the throne in 1328, and concluding with Louis XIII, the then reigning monarch. The space below was given to displays of famous battles across these centuries. Here, Ariès explained, was a "gallery of history," a pictorial representation of the saga of French history in the transition from the medieval to the early modern era (see figure 3).

FIGURE 3. Galerie des Illustres, Chateau de Beauregard (courtesy of Editions Valoire-Estel, Blois, with permission of Mme. du Pavillon, owner of the Chateau)

Learned in the genealogy of the French royal dynasties and the leading figures in their entourage, Philippe was intimately acquainted with the lives of the illustrious personages on view. But what struck him particularly about the gallery was the visual effect of its tableau in the uniform composition of its portraits and the unvarying linear sequence in which they were arranged, each one of the same dimensions, and each one stamped in the same mode of simple, unadorned pictorial representation (save for the portraits of Henri IV and Louis XIII, of the new dynasty of Bourbon kings, who were given a more prominent place apart). In effect, the gallery was a "pedagogical theater" (*exposition pédagogique*), cuing visitors about how to conceptualize the history of France in that era. Ariès also noted the modernity of its tacit assumptions about a linear timeline of French history that proceeded without variation through the royal succession. So conceived, the gallery of history at Beauregard prefigured the national conception of French history that would gain official sanction later in the seventeenth century. Once immersed in such a conception of historical time himself, he was now able to see it from a critical distance as but one among many ways in which historical time might be conceived. This insight became the seminal idea that enabled him to pull together the series of historiographical essays he had been writing since the war about his own discovery of history. As for his reflections on the gallery of historical portraits at Beauregard, these were incorporated into his chapter on seventeenth-century historiography, the last to be composed for *Le Temps de l'Histoire* before it was published in 1954.[2]

In the early 1980s, Ariès turned once more to this historiographical study, and to questions about historical time that he had not addressed in a direct way since its publication twenty-five years before. He was planning to edit and republish this book when death cut his work short. Roger Chartier, his younger colleague at the Ecole des Hautes Etudes, drew together the loose ends of this unfinished project. He reordered the chapters of the text as Ariès had been thinking of rearranging them, conforming to his first plan for the book when he had originally written it.[3] While preparing the new edition in 1986, Chartier had the good fortune to come across a previously unpublished essay in Ariès's private papers, written during his stay in Berlin in 1983 as an intended preface to it.[4] Chartier published it together with some other significant but neglected essays from across Ariès's career in an anthology entitled *Essais de mémoire* in 1993. In this newly discovered essay, Ariès moved back and forth between 1946 and 1983—between his purpose then and his perspective now. It was a meditation on his own time in history, and he sought to show how his current thinking on the present age had taken its beginnings during the war years. He wanted to explain what had been on his mind as he embraced his passionate inquiry into the hidden history of everyday life, and how the interests of historians in the contemporary era had come to confirm his essential insight about the changing nature of their time in history. As in all his work, his focus was on the present but with an eye to its differences from the past.

Ariès explained his purpose this way. *Le Temps de l'Histoire* was intended as a history not of French historical writing, but rather of the changing ways in which French historians had conceived of historical time as they pursued their craft over the centuries. The lines of demarcation with which they framed the past into historical epochs, he suggested, were conceptual props invented to give the past shape and meaning. The most fundamental of these shaping forms, he contended, are derived from notions about time itself. His point was that the epochs that historians have identified are better appreciated for their shared attitudes toward time than for the crucial events that might seem to distinguish them. Ideas of time occupy a place among habits of mind that historians in a given epoch tacitly accept, a "regime of historical time" that is reconceived only when basic attitudes toward life take new directions.[5] In other words, mentalities, more than events, underlie the temporal schemes that historians devise. Much can be learned from appreciating the history of historiography as a record of these changing conceptions of the structure of historical time. The modern age (mid-seventeenth to mid-twentieth century) was one such time in history. So too was the then dawning postwar era since characterized as the post-modern age. For good or ill, he observed, his own fate had been to witness the passage between these temporal epochs.

For Ariès it was a dangerous passage marked by the violent upheaval of the Second World War, but worth the journey in that it permitted him to witness the beginnings of a regime of historical time whose character had yet to be defined and whose history had yet to be written. Historians had long since elaborated the structure of time associated with the modern era in a grand narrative of its salient events. The historians who wrote during the modern epoch of historical time had framed their histories with turning points that seemed to them to augur its future course—*l'histoire événe-mentielle* was the term the scholars used. But how the regime of time in the contemporary age would be plotted as yet only inspired awe, given its immense possibilities. Historians engaged in writing a history of the present age would be called upon to explain its meaning on a global scale. For the moment, the present was noteworthy only for its raw realities, a history known only through the memories of its participants. Because there were not yet histories there were only memoirs, diaries, and eye-witness accounts on which to rely. Here Ariès judged the contemporary historiographical predicament much as he had that of the Middle Ages. These testimonies were places of memory from which a new temporal scheme might eventually be sketched, much as those of the Middle Ages had become the constituent elements of the modern regime of historical time.[6]

Ariès observed that the dawning of this new era had best been portrayed in the epic vision of André Malraux, the romantic novelist, essayist, and adventurer.[7] Malraux likened his experience of history to a torrent that swept up everything in its path. Conventional ideas about history were tossed aloft in the tide of events that engulfed the old order during the Second World War. History's new course could not yet be clearly understood, save only that its destiny would be conceived in more expansive terms than ever before. Still, Ariès hoped to catch glimpses of the historical meaning of this chaotic time of transition in exemplary testimonies of war veterans and other adventurers, whose sagas of the war years he briefly recounted. But the structure of this new regime of time, and the "sense of history" that it embodied, had yet to take form in the midst of their experiences.

Ariès could identify personally with Malraux's depiction of the existential power of the currents of contemporary history, for they had uprooted him as well. He, who had been so happily ensconced in his enchanted royalist garden, had been turned out to deal with the momentous new realities. He acknowledged the appeal of the most manifest political perspective on the new historical epoch in the making. He labeled it "revolutionary history," a broad historiographical movement that blended elements of the new Marxist scholarship on economic substructures with the old moral imperatives of the revolutionary tradition. Its proponents held fast to a vision of history modeled on prophecies enunciated during the French Revolution, a conception of historical time that privileged a transcendent future toward which today's historical actors were determined to hasten at an accelerating pace. Whereas the revolutions of the modern era—the English, French, and Russian—had clear and immediate objectives, the revolutionary imperative of the present age was more open-ended, foretelling only of "an interminable apocalypse." In retrospect, he recognized why Marxism had been able to gain such a wide following at the edge of this new era, particularly among intellectuals. Marxism had come to capture the "sense of history" that was identified with social progress and so became the ideology in which left-wing intellectuals invested their hopes for a better future. As Jean-Paul Sartre rejoiced in his own commitment, "Far from being exhausted, Marxism is still very young. . . . We cannot go beyond it because we have not gone beyond the circumstances that engendered it."[8] While rejecting that proposition in light of his reading of the new realities, Ariès conceded that he should have accorded more weight to Marxism's influence in the postwar era.[9] But "like Ulysses," Ariès reminisced, "I resisted its Sirens' song." In reaction against the intellectuals' promise of the opening of a royal road to revolution in the "rushing river of a grand history," Ariès turned toward "the placid pools of family memory"—what historians had hitherto regarded as the insignificant byways of private life. As he put it, he wondered whether the future of historical inquiry might rather be found on "the utopian shores of my families whose babble could hardly be heard over the [chords of] great planetary organs."[10]

Writing in 1983, Ariès felt that the course of postwar historiography had justified his decision in 1943 to go in search of the secrets of the private lives of ordinary people. His inquiries had opened a hidden world of mentalities that was more congenial to the present-day sense of historical time, one better attuned to private satisfactions than grand designs. Meanwhile, Marxist ideology had betrayed the hopes of revolutionary history. The linear direction of history's course that it prophesied had ended in cruel disappointment, for the Marxian paradise turned out to be only an oppressive Communist state. For that matter, he argued, the liberal vision of the welfare state in the West brought its own disappointments, for it had contributed to the making of a commonplace and homogeneous mass culture that "blotted out the brightly colored pattern [*la bigarrure*] of particular traditions." For Ariès, the end of the modern regime of historical time signaled the end of the identification of historians with a historiography that looked to the liberation of nations and the making of the welfare state as avatars of progress. The fervor for the revolutionary tradition had dissipated. Its goals reified in governmental institutions, the revolutionary movement had permitted its politics to harden into tyranny in the east and authoritarian benevolence in the west.

In the new regime of historical time, Ariès explained, the historians' search for meaning in the past was being redirected toward those on the margins who ignored or resisted the demands for dutiful obedience to the imperatives of modern culture. A history for the present age, he argued, would do better to fix its attention on present needs, not future expectations. Its value is practical, not utopian, for humans thrive in variegated settings far better than they do in conformist ones whatever their promise.

A history for the present age should consider the existential realities of life as it is lived by ordinary people every day. Such a history reveals the differences between present and past realities, and the variety of possible responses to the human predicament. History's sense of time today, therefore, privileges the present, not the future, and its task is to help humankind to recover the lost diversity that historians of the revolutionary tradition had overlooked in their haste to find in the past the makings of some future heaven on earth.

Ariès among the Annalistes

Ariès's meditation on history in his times provides a useful perspective with which to reconsider the Annales movement, the triumphant historiography of the third quarter of the twentieth century. The pioneers of the Annales project, Lucien Febvre and Marc Bloch, liked to present themselves as underdog historians combating a deeply entrenched political history.[11] They revolutionized historical research and writing in the first half of the twentieth century by shifting attention from political to economic, social, and cultural topics, particularly as they were appreciated over long periods of time. In their rise to historiographical prominence from mid-century, they and their students projected a bold and optimistic outlook. They wrote disparagingly of the old-fashioned political history, which they dismissed as timeworn and dull. Theirs was a campaign not to supplement but to displace history as it had been traditionally conceived—narrative history, with its focus on the politics of parties, ideologies, and significant events.[12]

In this ambition, the Annalistes may be said to have succeeded admirably. By the 1970s, the "new history" had become the standard history. By then the oppositional posture of Febvre and Bloch had given way to the magisterial stance of Fernand Braudel, who presided over the historical section of the Ecole des Hautes Etudes. More than a journal, the Annales had become an institution of higher education. More than a method, it had become a historiographical practice. Braudel spoke with confidence of the expanding scope of Annales scholarship, as if its practitioners were still engaged in a new beginning. But "combat," the term Febvre coined to characterize their activities, had by then given way to mastery of a field and an endeavor on which they began to reflect in a self-congratulatory way. The leading Annales historians drafted manuals and encyclopedias that reviewed their methods and summarized their accomplishments.[13] Their historiographers told the saga of their ascent across three generations.[14] There is a way in which Annales historiography fulfilled Malraux's vision. History henceforth would be conceived on a global scale. In this they were well attuned to the managerial style of the contemporary age. Like that of their political counterparts who directed the affairs of the welfare state, their approach was entrepreneurial, collaborative, supremely confident, totalizing in its scope.

It might seem appropriate to portray Ariès as a bit player in this compelling drama, for it is the one to which he is ordinarily assigned by students of the movement. He was, after all, exceedingly grateful for the recognition and respect the younger Annalistes belatedly accorded him. In his later years, he worked closely with some of them. The projects he pursued had stimulating effects upon historical writing in that era, opening windows in the Annaliste mansion that shed light on hidden alcoves. Ariès did not so much add new territory to the Annales terrain as redirect attention to some of its less traveled byways, contributing to the self-reflection and eventually self-doubt that descended upon Annales' historiographical discourse by the 1980s. In fact, there is widespread sentiment today that the Annales adventure is over, at least to the degree that it is no longer a coherent intellectual movement defining new directions of research.[15]

Symptomatic of the changing fortunes of Annales historiography was the turn to the history of mentalities in the 1960s. As I have noted, some scholars attributed the rise of this new cultural history to the growing sophistication of the Annales' research techniques, notably in quantification. In their view, the history of mentalities was Annales historiography at a "third level" of quantitative refinement that its historians, having mastered the first (the political) and the second (the socioeconomic), were at last prepared to address.[16] From a research standpoint, they contended, it was the most difficult to do. Others explained it in light of their growing appreciation of the mores of non-Western cultures. Nor did some Annalistes wish to attribute to mentalities an undue importance in an agenda that maintained the centrality of social and economic research. For Jacques Le Goff, one of the school's most important professors, the "deep song of mentalities" is "most precious to a history that is more interested in the sustaining beat than the fine melody of the music of the past."[17]

But at issue was more than research technique or the Annalistes' research agenda. One might argue rather that the new cultural history took on added importance in light of the changing realities that accompanied the rise of the welfare state during the 1950s and 1960s. A popular culture deeply rooted in tradition was being displaced by a mass culture without profound attachments to the past and open to the appeals of the present. It suited the needs of what came to be called the consumer society, a product of the affluence promoted by the welfare state. It was a society that was increasingly homogenized and hence oriented toward individual satisfactions rather than group loyalties. It signaled the waning role of civic and professional societies that had once played a mediating role between the state and the individual.[18] More pointedly, it evinced the declining power of the family to shape the values of its members. The consumer society fostered a new individualism, but one in which the individual was particularly vulnerable to the appeals of a pervasive and beguiling commercial advertising, as well as to the soft, authoritarian voice of a new cadre of professionals who managed public health and mores. Part of the appeal of the new cultural history was its evocation of images of group and family loyalties that were fast disappearing from public memory. It was intriguing, too, because it spoke to the issue of who possesses the power to shape images of the good life within the context of the emerging mass culture.

It is ironical that the new cultural history was initially perceived to mark a retreat from politics. In fact, it brought politics back into history—not the old politics of parties and ideologies, but a new politics concerned with the management of mass culture. The Annalistes prided themselves on their disdain for political history. But the politics of culture had visibly come to suffuse the historiography of the postwar era from the 1960s, and the Annales movement would feel its effects. The scholarly projects of the Annales epitomized the transition between times in history. In its collaborative, managerial style, the Annales movement took on the cast of other centers of cultural power in contemporary society.

Here Ariès's argument about changing conceptions of historical time in the present age assumed concrete meaning. Ariès did not challenge the methods or teachings of the Annales movement so much as introduce a cultural perspective that had been less visible in the "total" history the Annalistes aspired to write. The issues he raised, the vistas into previously unseen domains of the past he opened, the decisive turn from social to cultural history that he was among the first to popularize, contributed to the reflective turn in French historiography. In subtle ways, it prepared the ground for questioning the totalizing approach of Annales scholars, for whom cultural history was but one more field to conquer. In the end, the role of the Annales movement itself became a subject for soul-searching on the part of historians seeking to come to terms with their memories of the unresolved issues of the war years as these were bequeathed by both the political right and the political left.

The Vichy Syndrome

I have underscored the Vichy years as a turning point in Ariès's coming of age as a historian. His efforts to come to terms with his unresolved memories of those years tends to confirm Henry Rousso's interpretation of "the Vichy syndrome." For Rousso, remembering Vichy is a tale of the return of the repressed—of the unrequited memories of the era of the Second World War. He presents the war years as a seedbed of troubling issues about the French identity that grew untended into the late twentieth century. His is essentially a psychoanalytic interpretation of the inability of the French to come to terms with the unhappy memories of the years in which France suffered military defeat, occupation by Nazi Germany, and some measure of governmental collaboration in the roundup, internment, and deportation of Jews to the death camps of eastern Europe. He uses the Freudian notion of a screen memory as the basis of his explanation. He argues that the defeat, compromises, and even collaboration of the Vichy years were experiences that had been difficult to endure and too painful for the French people to remember in undiluted form. They therefore repressed much of what had happened, a process of forgetting eased by the legend of France during the Second World War fashioned by Charles de Gaulle during the postwar decade. De Gaulle's image of the war years as a time of resistance by the French people in their ensemble— Pétainists, Resistance fighters, the Free French, ordinary people, each in the way they best could—rendered tolerable otherwise intolerable memories. De Gaulle's legend was a screen memory blocking access to historical reality. It postponed a genuine historical reckoning with the Vichy experience at least until de Gaulle's passing, and its discussion excites passions to this day.[19]

This screen memory of the Gaullist legend, Rousso contended, provided the foundation of the politics of national reconciliation on which de Gaulle based his return to power in 1958. It also permitted the emergence of a cluster of other screen memories that came to constitute the Vichy syndrome. The syndrome enabled Vichy sympathizers on the extreme right to minimize the degree of their complicity in resignation to defeat or the fascination of some of them with the romantic, Volkish philosophy out of which Nazism had emerged. Likewise it enabled Communists on the extreme left to exaggerate their role in the Resistance. In simplifying the collective memory of the Vichy experience, the syndrome staved off closer scrutiny of its complexity. For decades it enabled the French to avoid facing directly the shameful, compromising events in which many Vichy leaders had participated, notably the instances of collaboration with the policies of the Third Reich and even complicity in the persecution of Jews.[20]

Certainly the reckoning with French compliance in the Holocaust was slow in coming. Generally, the French were reluctant to address the collaboration of their government in the roundup, internment, and deportation of Jews, until prodded into self-examination by North American scholars in the early 1980s.[21] But as these realities at last came to be exposed, the search for war criminals who had thus far escaped prosecution became a national obsession. The most notorious among them, Paul Touvier, Maurice Papon, and René Bousquet (who was assassinated before standing trial), were brought to justice only in the 1990s.[22]

For Rousso, however, this concerted dragnet to track down and punish high-profile collaborators amidst great publicity narrowly compressed the memory of the Vichy years, leaving intact the broader screen memory underpinning the Vichy syndrome. As he put it, the French continued to remember the past as it was reflected in a "broken mirror" (*miroir brisé*). Their search for particular villains failed to address the deeper tensions between the royalists of the right who had rallied to Vichy and the Jacobins of the left who had opposed them, playing out a rivalry that dated from the French Revolution. The conflict between their opposing conceptions of the national identity, repressed upon the fall of Vichy, continued to haunt the French unconsciously through the Fourth and into the Fifth Republic, resurfacing in major political crises, notably that over the status of Algeria in the early 1960s.[23]

Rousso's interpretation sheds light on the reluctance of Ariès and his royalist friends to openly acknowledge the shame of Vichy. Ariès's attachments to right-wing politics continued long into the postwar era, and in some measure were strengthened by the onset of the Cold War, as his cohort within the Action Française endeavored to reinvent itself one last time. The imbroglio within his circle of friends at the time of the Algerian crisis exemplifies Rousso's interpretation of the way the controversies of the Vichy experience continued to rouse emotions. For Ariès and his aging companions of the royalist campaigns of an earlier era, the crisis invited a return of the repressed. It was a time of terrible discord over issues that dated from the era of the Second World War. The crisis threatened to rend the fabric of Ariès's lifelong friendships. Most of his royalist comrades remained steadfast in their original beliefs and refused to acknowledge Vichy's tainted past. But Ariès made a separate peace. His lingering commitment to royalism is less testimony of his inability to mourn his past, more of his struggle to work through the long, painful process of breaking his direct ties with its politics without sacrificing what he continued to believe was authentic in its heritage. Like a divorce after long years of marriage, his psychological reckoning proceeded as a series of fits and starts, of becoming accustomed to letting go of a way of political life to which he was temperamentally attuned. My point is that Ariès found his way over time toward a solution through which he reinvested his political heritage in cultural history. He did so by probing the deeper culture underpinning the royalist cause, obscured by the political rhetoric of the Action Française. Royalism in Ariès's histories became an affair of traditional popular culture and the basis of his critique of the contemporary mass culture that had come to displace it.

Ariès's Critique of Contemporary Culture

As a historian, Ariès may have returned to the culture of old France. But he did so to address the problems of contemporary culture. He underscored the political importance of popular traditions as countervailing forces at the local and regional level to the claims of the omnicompetent state to shape and manage public culture and even to intrude into hitherto autonomous realms of private life. His thesis about the dynamics of popular culture taught that basic attitudes toward everyday life are the stuff of wisdom ("common sense" as it had been understood in traditional society). The values they affirm do not disappear, but rather are continually reworked as they are carried forward in living popular traditions.

In this respect, the family was for Ariès an ancient political force sustaining such traditions. It was the prototype for the array of social, religious, and fraternal societies that give form and vitality to social intercourse. Therein, he maintained, the traditions of old France remain alive and well. Cultural history, he taught, enables us to comprehend the evolution and modification of collective mentalities embodied in such traditions. These are attitudes close to life in its most visceral expression, lodged at the threshold between instinct and conscious thought. These mentalities operate beneath the high culture of formal politics and are better indexes of the political and social values of ordinary people.[24] Such values evolve, he argued, but always in response to perceived needs close to life as it is actually lived every day.

Ariès's quest to identify mentalities as the sinew of living tradition was the inspiration behind his early research in demography and then the book that made his reputation as a historian, *L'Enfant et la vie familiale sous l'Ancien Régime*. In the latter he evoked a powerful image not only of the traditional family, but also of the ways in which that family had over time grown smaller, more intimate, more attentive to children, and ultimately more removed from public life in its search for a more fulfilling private one. In tracing changing attitudes toward the family as indexes of the rise of modern social life, he offered a subtle criticism of the modern mentality in the name of the apology he had once offered for an idealized image of what the Vichy regime might have been. In highlighting the differences between the social attachments in traditional society and the pursuit of individual autonomy in its modern counterpart, he provided a perspective on the virtues of a public culture that had been lost—one that valued personal loyalty, informal social interchange, public space in which to play, the unpaid dedication to civic responsibility, the advantages of a decentralized political culture. The sense of his work, and one might conjecture its long-range importance, may be understood as an apostrophe to his fellow citizens about the inherent shortcomings of an omnicompetent state and the psychological deprivations of a mass culture.

Ariès was addressing in a poignant way what he perceived to be the temptations that were leading contemporary society into its crisis of culture. A selfish individualism, a veneration of new technologies, and an indulgence in the appetites of consumerism together disposed his contemporaries to take too lightly the civic virtues that had once provided old France with its social glue: filial piety, personal loyalty, and respect for social custom. This was the secret world of mentalities—of tacit assumptions about social life so deeply embedded in popular tradition that they did not need to be stated openly. These were the qualities of a sociability that he believed was eroding in contemporary public life. Not that it had completely disappeared. Rather it was nested in family and fraternal societies, a newly constituted world of privacy.

Herein lies Ariès's appeal—in his highly original interpretation of the historical rise of privacy as an element of modern life to compensate for what had been expunged from public life. In his history of mentalities, he highlighted basic social needs that he believed would continue to ensure a place for old-fashioned values in new social settings. While mourning their loss in public life, he showed the secret of their survival in private spheres. That is why his study of childhood and family elicited such interest. The family, the repository of traditional values in the modern world, was under assault to a degree that he conceded only in his last years. Still, he showed his readers the direction of cultural change in France at the dawn of the modern era. In his work, the old folklore of the Action Française reappeared in the guise of a new history of popular culture.

The Waning Fortunes of Marxist Historiography

The story of Ariès's contribution to historiography opens on a larger saga of his rendezvous with the left in the new cultural history. That encounter provides insight not only into his *agon* with his intellectual adversaries but also into the ambiguous relationship between Annales and Marxist historiography.[25] Generally the Annalistes maintained a cordial rapport with leading historians of the revolutionary tradition with Marxist sympathies, such as Albert Soboul and Ernest Labrousse. In some measure, the Annalistes sidestepped the issue of the Marxist vision of history by taking refuge in methodological formulations, thus bracketing the philosophical issue of their sense of history within a more technical definition of the historian's task. Some spoke of a "serial history" that would eliminate all sense of ends or expectation from historical interpretation.[26] They promised to acquaint their students with a different context for studying the past, one based on deep structures of human experience that would render the issues raised by the revolutionary tradition obsolete. Yet the influence of the left-wing tradition of the historiography of the French Revolution, with its strong sense of the direction of history's course, lingered on, confronting a younger generation with a dilemma about how it should view the future.

My point is that the Marxist vision of history remained a perspective with which a younger generation of Annalistes was still coming to terms. I have alluded to many of the Annaliste historians who had flirted with Marxism in their youth. In the years following the Second World War, Marxism had enjoyed a certain renaissance among university students, drawn to the Communist party by the idealized image of its role in the Resistance. They believed that the party was the only remaining vehicle for fulfilling the destiny of the French Revolutionary tradition in the postwar world. Some of these students would become leading historians by the 1970s, and they spoke of their circle of friends in the Communist party of the postwar years in much the way Ariès had spoken of his in the Action Française in the years before the war.[27]

Most of the young intellectuals who had rallied to the Communist party so enthusiastically in the late 1940s left it after the Soviet repression in Hungary in 1956. By then they had come to realize that the Soviet Union was not a workers' paradise but a police state that enforced its will by consigning dissidents to the gulags of Siberia. The party that had nurtured a memory of its heroic role in the Resistance turned out to be a dogmatic, anti-intellectual sect.[28] Those intellectuals who wished to retain a Marxist identity often turned to cultural issues, notably to that of alienation, ironically inspired by their repulsion at the party in which they themselves had once served.

I have noted the reconsideration of his youthful enthusiasm for communism by Emmanuel Le Roy Ladurie, possibly the most widely read and appreciated among the cultural historians of the Annales school. He repudiated his Communist youth to become the most popular historian of mentalities of the 1970s. His structuralist microhistories, notably *Montaillou*, a study of everyday attitudes about life in a medieval village, made him famous in the way *L'Enfant et la vie familiale* had Ariès a decade earlier. Ladurie, we might say, found his way toward a history that explored the values of old France without identifying with them to the degree that Ariès had. In his autobiographical memoir, *Paris-Montpellier*, Ladurie revisited his youthful involvement in the Communist party with the bemused detachment of middle age. He retained a sympathy for the socialist cause to which he had gravitated in the 1960s. As for abandoning his Communist attachments, he had few regrets.[29]

Still, Marxism continued to exercise a particular influence on the historiography of the French Revolution tradition through the 1960s. For many intellectuals, history was Marxism's last refuge in France, and one might argue that in French historiography, at least, Marxism enjoyed an Indian summer. Over the course of the twentieth century, Marxism had significantly shaped a tradition of historical writing about the revolutionary cause, from Jean Jaurès via Albert Mathiez and Georges Lefebvre to Albert Soboul.[30] This history was not doctrinaire but rather appreciative of Marxism for the insights it permitted into the goals of the popular revolution against the backdrop of the boom and bust of preindustrial cycles. Ernest Labrousse, a professor at the Sorbonne, was the key figure in directing this research for aspiring historians during the 1950s. He was famous for his thesis about the conjuncture between economic privation and political discontent as the source of the radical "revolution from below" in 1789 and beyond. His work and his mentoring would inspire the generation of historians of the Revolution that came of age during the 1950s—Maurice Agulhon, Michelle Perrot, Annie Kriegel, Madeleine Rebérioux, and Michel Vovelle, to mention some of the best known.[31] This left-wing, Marxist-inspired historiography had an influence that endured into the 1970s, especially in academic circles.

Still it was a history with diminishing appeal to a society that sensed that it had already arrived, as the student-inspired uprising of 1968 tended to confirm. This younger generation of left-wing students wanted to address the issues of the contemporary world in terms of present need, not timeworn prophecies of what the future holds. The most influential among them in challenging the Marxist interpretation of the French Revolutionary tradition was François Furet, president of the Ecole des Hautes Etudes and one of the most prominent Annales scholars of the 1970s. Like Ladurie, he had been a young Communist militant who later abandoned the party—if with more nostalgia for its youthful comradeship.[32] Furet is famous for having pronounced the "end" of the French Revolution as its objectives had been pursued in the revolutionary tradition in the modern age. He explained the Revolution in terms of the consolidation of state power (as had Alexis de Tocqueville before him) and Jacobinism, not as the ideology of a party but rather as a new way of talking about politics that came to pervade nineteenth-century French political discourse generally.[33] While abandoning political activism, Furet arrived at a position sympathetic to old-fashioned liberalism. Suspicious not only of Marxism but also of deterministic theories of history generally, he became a champion of liberalism, with its commitment to personal autonomy and its claims for individual initiative and inalienable rights. In this reorientation, he hoped to resuscitate the liberal interpretation of the Revolution, dormant since the nineteenth century.[34] With Furet, political issues returned to the center of the historiographical stage, but this time in the postmodern guise of such topics as the invention of a new political discourse, the appeal of the revolutionary imagination, and the reconstruction of the national identity. In his later writings, he denounced the effects of communism, the heir of the Jacobin revolutionary tradition, on the politics of the twentieth century.[35]

Others, however, were reluctant to abandon their ties to the revolutionary tradition. I have paid particular attention to the route chosen by Michel Vovelle, who eventually succeeded Soboul in the chair for the history of the French Revolution at the Sorbonne in 1984. Rather than repudiating his left-wing heritage, he tried to reconcile it with the new cultural history.[36] He claimed that his turn to this kind of history followed the natural evolution from social to cultural issues proposed by Labrousse.[37] His traditionalism of the left, therefore, was a counterpoint to Ariès's traditionalism of the right, and it is not altogether surprising that they should have found their way into dialogue. Their encounter provides the most poignant illustration of the convergence of the old left and right in the politics of the new cultural history, and hence of the way old ideological issues now reappeared in a new cultural guise. During the 1970s they wrote works that paralleled one another in their explanations of the long-range evolution of attitudes toward the role of mourning in popular culture. Ariès identified

that process with the habits of mind derived from the collective unconscious of popular traditions. Vovelle identified it with a more rational
consciousness-raising that he believed was implicit in evolving popular attitudes toward death. In that sense, each remained true to his youthful
ideological allegiance while transposing his convictions to the loftier plane
of cultural history.[38]

The Ariès/Vovelle debate, ultimately one over the meaning of historical
change, revealed political differences that could not be reconciled by their
common commitment to Annales methodology. In a way theirs was one
of the last significant debates between two fading ideologies that were being
absorbed into the new cultural history. It was a commemoration of an old
ideological quarrel rather than a reaffirmation of the ideology each had
once championed. In this respect, their debate provides insight into why
commemoration, in its theory as in its practice, took on such urgency in
the late twentieth century. With more tenuous commitments to the political traditions that dominated the modern age, commemoration has since
become a technique for marking their passing.

The Time of Memory in French Historiography

Ariès did not live to witness the memory phenomenon in French historiography. By coincidence, he died on the eve of its emergence. I am referring
particularly to the French national memory project, *Les Lieux de mémoire*,
edited by Pierre Nora during the mid-1980s. Nora was a senior editor at
the prestigious Gallimard publishing house in Paris as well as a member
of the faculty at the Ecole des Hautes Etudes. A collaborative venture of
some fifty noted historians, this study might be said to mark the commemorative end of modern French history. As a meditation on the historical role of memory in the making of the French identity, *Les Lieux de
mémoire* is probably the most important historiographical work of the
1980s. It showcased the many possible perspectives on the past passed over
in favor of the particular agenda of the writers of modern French history.[39]

Les Lieux de mémoire may not have been composed with the bicentennial of the French Revolution in mind. But one effect of publishing this
work on the eve of its celebration was to underscore the degree to which
the revolutionary tradition, in which so many of the ideas about the history
of modern France had been conceived, had lost the force of its earlier
appeal. Nora's approach to the memory/history problem proceeded from
the proposition that living memory is the ground of history. The memory
of the French Revolution had inspired many of its greatest historians, and

their histories themselves became vehicles for the perpetuation of the tradition. With its waning, Nora suggested, histories that had once inspired passion for the event had now become commemorative monuments to its passing. The task of writing the history of France's national memory, he proposed, had become "archaeological"—to inventory the commemorative ruins of the French collective memory in the myriad of forms in which it had been elaborated along the way.

So for the inheritors of Annales historiography, history had dissolved into a plethora of memorial forms. Nora's method was deconstructive. He journeyed back from the present rather than forward out of the past, as in the genealogical branching of a family tree: from the places of memory around which the image of Republican France had been enshrined in the late nineteenth century; to the deep structures out of which the identity of old France had congealed in the Middle Ages. Proceeding backward in this way, Nora's history of memory's representations revealed the diversity of and the discontinuities within the making of the French national identity. It showed not how firm but how unstable, not only how deep but also how varied were the sources of the French identity, and how since the Middle Ages historians have used their histories to commemorate the past as they wanted it to be remembered. In doing so, the national memory project dramatized not only the crisis of the French national identity, but also a historiographical one about how best to conceptualize the temporal structure of French history.

Here some of Ariès's ideas about time resurfaced to make their claim upon this new approach to history, for in many ways *Les Lieux de mémoire* was a requiem for the passing of the modern regime of historical time. From a historiographical perspective, the national memory project was a studied reflection on the breakup of the grand narrative. In redirecting attention from events to memories—the past as it was imagined—Nora and his colleagues had shown how memory is the vehicle for creating the illusion of the presence of the past. As Ariès had prophesied, the dissolution of the modern regime of historical time enabled historians to see how memory had influenced earlier generations of historians in the construction and reconstruction of their understanding of the French identity.[40] It is worth noting that Nora's project marked a descent into particularity of the sort that Ariès considered essential for the vitality of culture. There is not one France, but many ways of imagining the French identity. In memory, the past discards timelines to focus on the present in which identity is always constructed. It meant that French history would be reconceived in light of its many realms of memory. In this study and in the numerous studies of commemoration that thenceforth used it as a model, the grand narrative was parceled out into discrete micro-narratives, each located at a different site of memory. As the timelines of the past dissolved into a myriad of places in this present-minded model for the study of history, the predictable sequence once plotted between past and future was rendered problematic and unpredictable.[41]

Et in Arcadia Ego-Histoire

Nora's project was a preface to the enormous interest in public memory in our times. By the 1990s, French historians were preoccupied with collective memory in a way they had been with collective mentalities during the 1960s and 1970s. The attempt to write a history of a past obscured by memory's distortions took historians to a deeper meditation on the implications of their abandonment of the grand narrative of ideological struggle in favor of a new cultural one that sought to sort out the layered structures of collective identity. One might say that all the soul-searching about cultural history as a refuge from politics had rendered the historians more self-conscious about the politics of how and why they wrote history at all. Historiography itself began to receive an unprecedented attention, as historians devoted more time to writing the intellectual history of their predecessors, and even of themselves.

Taking their cue from Ariès's autobiographical memoir, the leading historians of France wrote books and essays in which they offered personal insights into their formation as historians.[42] The confessional style of these authors might be construed as compensation for the anonymity of the cultural history they had been writing. Even though they downplayed the importance of the life stories of history's principal actors in their scholarship, they nonetheless directed attention to their own lives as storytellers. So was born *égo-histoire* for the 1980s.[43] The term might best be translated as "my history," given the individualized vision of history each sought to convey. Among its practitioners, personal mnemonic schemes displaced the common grand narrative in which their predecessors had once located their historical studies. In *égo-histoire* history became an art of memory, located in the places of personal origins and formation in which each author found his own voice. As an autobiographical genre for our times, it revealed how the identification of individual historians with particular historiographical traditions had broken down. In its personalizing of the historian's identity, the genre was ironically at odds with the Annales imperative of collaboration. Historians stressed their personal differences and distinctiveness, the Annalistes notable among them.

What did this historiographical phenomenon mean? The immediate assessments of these autobiographical essays were inconclusive.[44] But in that Ariès's own provided a prototype for the genre, it is worth noting another of his essays on an adjoining topic: the matter of what it means to write one's memoirs.[45] He briefly sketched the history of men of letters who since the Renaissance had done so. He noted a transition from memoirs that record one's exploits to those that record one's thoughts. Among men of letters, the trend was toward a desire to be remembered for the refinement of one's way of thinking. The memoir became an art of writing disguised as an art of memory. The issue was not how well shall I remember my life but rather how can I shape the way you will remember me? The modern memoir, Ariès explained, signified a personalizing of one's sense of destiny. It was not enough to be remembered for one's participation in a cause or, for the historian, one's contribution to a historiographical tradition. Beyond particular exploits or accomplishments, the memorialist sought to immortalize the power of his own capacity for reflection and so to leave for posterity a memento of that which he cherished most in life. As a historian, Ariès seems to have had much the same goal.

In making some larger assessment of Ariès's life, the judgment of the historian Raoul Girardet is a good place to conclude. In his own venture into *égo-histoire*, he offered this comment on his lifelong friend: "I . . . lived too close for too long to Philippe Ariès to have ignored what was, over a period of more than forty years, the slow journey of a genial spirit toward total possession of himself. His was a mind always in motion, open to the end toward all appeals and all the possibilities that I was able to see, without denying anything of his essential loyalties, deprived little by little of his first attachments [*gangues*], to expand and renew, in a way to reconstruct himself all the way to his definitive affirmation of the full autonomy that he assumed. Time did not in his case work its effects in a single sense of completion or confirmation; his was a work progressively built whose orientation and even whose gifts could not have been clearly foreseen at the outset."[46]

What was that sense of the journey to which Girardet alluded? Ariès may have been preoccupied with the question himself in his last days, though he cast his meditation in terms of his thoughts on history itself. In his work as a historian, Ariès wanted to show the relationship between continuity and change in historical understanding. This disillusioned royalist, perplexed about how to reconcile his need for continuity with his royalist past with his appreciation of the new world he had entered after the Second World War, reconsidered his conception of historical time, and thereby discovered a key not only to a deeper understanding of the old France he loved but also of the new one in which he made his own public life as both archivist and historian.[47] In an impromptu interview, he was asked to consider the question of how civilizations decline and die. True to his contrary way, Ariès disputed the proposition. Civilizations do not rise and fall, he answered. There is a thread of continuity in civilized life that extends back to the cities of the Near East in antiquity. But the traditions through which the creative endeavor of civilization is carried on are constantly being modified. The changes are imperceptible, since we live within traditions that tend to blur our sense of sequential time. But historians can help us to see the direction of such panoramic change over long periods of time. The understanding of change is the essence of history, and history itself the ground of the human condition.[48]

Philippe Ariès was a man on the margins—provocative, insightful, endearing to many. He taught only briefly, invented no new method, and invited no particular following. In his aspirations to become a historian, he knew major personal disappointments. But he courageously persevered in his quest and, in his way, raised fundamental questions about what historians are looking for in the past. His deepest faith was that history is our most fertile field in our search for the meaning of the human predicament. Like Georges Lefebvre on the left, Ariès on the right is likely to be remembered as a historian not for his politics but for his profound interest in humanity. That is why in the long run he is likely to stand out among the French historians in France's golden age of historiography. As the French continue their search for identity, the perspective on the past presented by Ariès remains a provocative and appealing portrait of social mores in France across the ages, in keeping with the vitality of its popular culture. Something of his stature was suggested in a comparison with Fernand Braudel offered by Pierre Nora. He wondered how posterity would compare Braudel, the man at the center of the profession, who wanted to group historians in a grand movement in which individual participants would slip into the anonymity of teamwork, with Ariès, the man on the margins, who held fast to his particular originality and inspired his colleagues to do the same.[49] Much depends, I suspect, on what one is looking for. French historiography, like French politics, has thrived on its oppositional character, which has provided openings not only for criticism but for creativity, even and one might say especially in an age so susceptible to the appeal of conformism and so amenable to public scrutiny of our private lives. In his cultural histories, Ariès showed a route for rescuing the right from the ignominy with which it had lived since the Second World War, and he did so by showing the authenticity of a conservative perspective on the human condition for the present age that was deeper in its hidden promptings than all of its visible failures. In the process he probed his own personal depths, and so came to show us in his life's work not only his panoramic perspective on a previously unseen past but also his insight into the relationship between what is constant and what is changing in the human condition.

Chapter 1

1. The term "singular history" was coined by André Burguière as a title for an interview with Ariès that drew out the connection between his political views and his historical research. André Burguière, "La Singulière Histoire de Philippe Ariès," *Le Nouvel Observateur,* 20 February 1978, 80 ff.

2. Once synonymous with the new cultural history, "mentalities" is now more often construed as a stage in its development, a historiography identified with a particular time in history. On mentalities in French scholarship, see Lynn Hunt, ed., *The New Cultural History* (Berkeley, Calif.,1989), and Patrick Hutton, "Mentalities, History of," *Encyclopedia of Historians and Historical Writing,* ed. Kelly Boyd (London, 1999), 800–803.

3. Philippe Ariès's essay "L'Histoire des mentalités" in *La Nouvelle Histoire,* ed. Jacques Le Goff, Roger Chartier, and Jacques Revel (Paris, 1978), 402–23, offers a good overview of his perspective on the field. I trace the evolution of his understanding of the term in chapter 5.

4. Ariès's discusses his purposes in writing *Le Temps de l'Histoire* in an essay written in 1983 as an intended preface for a proposed revised edition. After Ariès's death, his colleague Roger Chartier found the essay among his papers and published it posthumously as "Le Temps de l'Histoire," in Philippe Ariès, *Essais de mémoire,* ed. Roger Chartier (Paris, 1993), 45–67.

5. See David Harlan, "Intellectual History and the Return of Literature," *American Historical Review* 94 (1989), 581–609, and idem, *The Degradation of American History* (Chicago, 1997), 3–31.

6. Norman Cantor, *The American Century* (New York, 1997), 423–24, points out how the political right never succeeded in expiating its complicity in the Collaboration and so has been unable to recover a viable political role.

7. Useful historiographical studies that reconsider the relationship between Ariès and Annales historiography include: Hervé Coutau-Bégarie, *Le Phénomène nouvelle histoire* (Paris, 1989), 162, 350–53; François Dosse, *L'Histoire en miettes* (Paris, 1987), 201–4; and Gérard Noiriel, *Sur la "crise" de l'histoire* (Paris, 1996), 298–300.

8. On the right in the intellectual life of the 1930s, see Michel Winock, *Le Siècle des intellectuels,* rev. ed. (Paris, 1999), 226–37, 405–13, 592; Raoul Girardet, "L'Héritage de l'Action Française" (1957), in *Révoltes de l'esprit: Les Revues des années trente,* ed. Pierre Andreu (Paris, 1991), 149–74; and Pierre Nora, "Les Deux Apogées de l'Action Française," *Annales ESC* 19 (1964), 127–41.

9. The newspaper articles in question here, all in *L'Etudiant français*, are: Philippe Ariès, "Un Aspect de la pensée de Charles Maurras," 25 November 1936, 1; "L''Enseignement de Maurras," 10–25 December 1936, 2; "Avec Maurras: sceptique ou dogmatique?" 10 March 1937, 2; and "Charles Maurras et la tradition littéraire," 10 and 25 June 1938, 1.The later work referred to: idem, *Un Historien du dimanche,* ed. Michel Winock (Paris, 1980), 58, 68; and idem, "Le Thème de la mort dans 'Le Chemin de Paradis' de Maurras," *Essais sur l'histoire de la mort en Occident du moyen âge à nos jours* (Paris, 1975), 115–22. See also François Leger, *Une Jeunesse réactionnaire* (Paris, 1993), 113.

10. Philippe Ariès, "La Ressemblance" (1980), in *Essais de mémoire*, 59–67.

11. Philippe Ariès, *Le Temps de l'Histoire* (Monaco, 1954), 26.

12. On Ariès's views about Bainville, see William R. Keylor, *Jacques Bainville and the Renaissance of Royalist History in Twentieth-Century France* (Baton Rouge, 1979), 214–18.

13. Ariès, "La Ressemblance," 63–64; François Leger, "Philippe Ariès: L'Histoire d'un historien," *Revue universelle des faits et des idées* 65 (1986), 65.

14. In *Le Temps de l'Histoire*, 268–72, Ariès distinguishes the historians of the Académie Française from the university historians in the late nineteenth and early twentieth centuries, noting the broad erudition of the former as opposed to the specialization of the latter.

15. Daniel Halévy, *Visites aux paysans du centre (1907–1934)* (Paris, 1935). On Halévy, see Sébastien Laurent, "Halévy (Daniel))," in *Dictionnaire des intellectuels français*, ed. Jacques Julliard and Michel Winock (Paris, 1996), 580–82.

16. Philippe Ariès, "Le Secret" (1978), in *Essais de mémoire*, 29–30; idem, "Daniel Halévy," *La Nation française*, 7 February 1962, 1, 11.

17. *Histoire d'une histoire* (Paris, 1939), 8–9, 80–102. In his tribute to Halévy, "*Histoire d'une histoire*: Laissez l'ordre rentrer en vous," *La Nation française*, 21 February 1962, 20, 23, Ariès alluded to this work.

18. Philippe Ariès, "La Terre promise," *L'Etudiant français*, 10 January 1938, 3.

19. Ariès, *Le Temps de l'Histoire*, 34–43.

20. Philippe Ariès, "Réflexions sur la Contre-Révolution (III): La Fronde Vendéenne," *L'Etudiant français*, 25 February 1938, 1–2.

21. Ariès, *Historien du dimanche*, 119.

22. Marc Bloch, *Apologie pour l'histoire, ou métier d'historien* (1941), 5th ed. (Paris, 1964), 1–16; Ariès, "La Ressemblance," 64–67. On privileging the present in historical interpretation (with particular reference to Ariès), see François Hartog, "Time, History, and the Writing of History: The *Order* of Time," *KVHAA Konferenser* 37 (1996), 106–8.

23. Ariès wrote a review of Braudel's work in *La Table ronde* no. 26 (February 1950), 147–52.

24. Ariès did not meet Braudel personally until 1976, when their paths crossed in Washington, D.C. Some polite correspondence followed. Ariès, *Historien du dimanche*, 133–34; Arch. Ariès, Braudel to Ariès, 25 June 1980.

25. Philippe Ariès, *Le Présent quotidien*, ed. Jeannine Verdès-Leroux (Paris, 1997) contains the complete run of Ariès's articles from *La Nation français*, together with a useful introduction.

26. Lucien Febvre, "La Sensibilité et l'Histoire: Comment reconstituer la vie affective d'autrefois," *Annales d'histoire sociale* 3 (1941), 5–20.

27. William H. Schneider, *Quality and Quantity* (Cambridge, U.K., 1990), 208–29.

28. On the place of La Chapelle in the Vichy educational plan, see Wilfred D. Halls, *Les Jeunes et la politique de Vichy* (Paris, 1988), 317–21. On eugenics in the curriculum of the Ecole des Cadres at La Chapelle-en-Serval, Archives Nationales, F17 13367 (jeunesse et sports), dossier "Ecole des cadres."

29. Alain Drouard, *Une Inconnue des sciences sociales: La Fondation Alexis Carrel, 1941–45* (Paris, 1992), 271–78. See also Philippe Ariès, "Pourquoi la démographie française n'est pas restée malthusienne," *La Nation française,* 16 December 1959, 9.

30. Ariès, *Le Temps de l'Histoire,* 22–24, 300–311. See also his "Le Temps de l'Histoire" (1983), in *Essais de mémoire,* 45–58.

31. Ariès, *Le Temps de l'Histoire,* 45–59, 140–53, 160–71.

32. Ibid., 26–33, 271–72.

33. On the survival of traditions at the margins of social life (and on the interpretation of tradition generally), see David Gross, *The Past in Ruins* (Amherst, Mass., 1992), 122–24.

34. Philippe Ariès, "Familles du demi-siècle," *Renouveau des idées sur la famille* (Paris, 1954), 162–70; idem, "La Famille d'Ancien Régime," *Revue des travaux de l'académie des sciences morales et politiques* 109 (4th series, 1956), 46–55.

Chapter 2

1. This biographical sketch is based on Ariès's autobiographies and his published interviews noted below, supplemented by my personal interviews with his family (Marie-Rose Ariès), friends (Philippe Brissaud, Jean Bruel, Raoul Girardet, François Leger, Gilbert Picard), and colleagues (Nicole Castan, Yves Castan, Roger Chartier, Natalie Davis, Arlette Farge, Jean-Louis Flandrin, Pierre Nora, Orest Ranum, and Jacques Revel).

2. Erik Erikson, *Childhood and Society,* 2d ed. (New York, 1963), 247–74.

3. See David Hunt, *Parents and Children in History* (New York, 1970), 11–51.

4. Philippe's younger brother Jacques, a career army officer, died in one of the last campaigns of the Second World War; his youngest brother Georges became an engineer and died comparatively young in 1971 at age 48. His youngest sibling, Marie-Rose, who alone survived him, pursued a career as a ballet teacher.

5. Philippe Ariès, "Saint-Pierre ou la douceur de vivre?" in *Catastrophe à la Martinique,* ed. Philippe Ariès, Charles Daney, and Emile Berlé (Paris, 1981), 11–24.

6. Philippe Ariès, *Un Historien du dimanche,* ed. Michel Winock (Paris, 1980), 47. Philippe appears to have used his time to familiarize himself with the regional culture of le Vexin Normand, and reports his findings in his first book, *Les Traditions sociales dans les pays de France* (Paris, 1943), 27–38. His concern late in life about the crisis of adolescence in contemporary society may take its origins from his own rebellious youth.

7. Ariès, *Historien du dimanche,* 28, 30–36, 48.

8. John Hellman, *Emmanuel Mounier and the New Catholic Left, 1930–1950* (Toronto, 1981), 12–13.

9. On Ariès's university years, see the memoirs by François Leger, *Une Jeunesse*

réactionnaire (Paris, 1993), 96–123; and by Raoul Girardet, *Singulièrement libre: Entretiens,* ed. Pierre Assouline (Paris, 1990), 37–43, 125. In my interview with him (21 August 1997), Jean Bruel recalled the high quality of the intellectual debates in which Ariès and Leger engaged in the Latin Quarter in the late 1930s.

10. In his *Le Temps de l'Histoire* (Monaco, 1954), 43–44, Ariès alludes to this experience in a way that suggests it may have been earlier than and separate from his role as an instructor at the Ecole des Cadres at La Chapelle-en-Serval.

11. Ariès, *Historien du dimanche,* 79–81.

12. The Institut des Fruits et Agrumes Coloniaux (IFAC), after the war renamed the Institut de Recherches sur les Fruits et Agrumes (IRFA). Archives de l'Ecole des Hautes Etudes, Archives Ariès (hereafter Arch. Ariès), curriculum vitae of Philippe Ariès, 1978.

13. From 1950 until 1975, Ariès edited the collection "Civilisation d'hier et d'aujourd'hui," and with Robert Mandrou the collection "Civilisation et mentalités." He edited books by Raoul Girardet, Victor Tapié, Louis Chevalier, Robert Mandrou, Yves Castan, and most significant, Michel Foucault's first major work, *Histoire de la folie à l'âge classique.* Arch. Ariès, curriculum vitae of Ariès.

14. The IRFA became part of an expanding group of agencies, le Groupement d'Etudes et de Recherches pour le Développement de l'Agriculture Tropicale (GERDAT), supervised by the Ministère de la Coopération. This consortium became a principal agency of the French government for providing technical assistance in agriculture to developing nations around the world. Arch. Ariès, dossier "Ariès Philippe, directeur d'études cumulant," biographical profile, 1978.

15. Geneviève Hartman, "Philippe Ariès, le documentaliste," *Fruits* 39/3 (1984): 211–14.

16. M. G. Bodart, *Philippe Ariès, un documentaliste pas comme les autres,* (Montpellier, 1994).

17. Interview with Jacques Revel, January 1996 (Paris).

18. Ariès had made a prior trip to the United States in 1965 and had visited the University of California at Berkeley, but in connection with his work as an archivist, not as a historian. He recalls it as a disappointing experience. He thought of his second visit in 1973 to lecture at Johns Hopkins as the symbolic beginning of his welcome to America. Ariès, *Historien du dimanche,* 126–27, 177–78.

19. For Ariès's observations on American culture, see his interview with Armand Fabvre, "Il y a une infinité d'amériques . . . ," *Royaliste* no. 330 (22 January–4 February 1981): 6–7. He found American secondary schools deplorable but greatly admired the universities. He noted the "extraordinary mediocrity" of American television.

20. Philippe Ariès, "Mentalités," in *La Nouvelle Histoire,* ed. Jacques Le Goff et al. (Paris, 1978), 402–23.

21. Arch. Ariès, cartons "Correspondance."

22. Philippe had suffered earlier serious ailments. In the late 1950s, he contracted tuberculosis and retreated for ten months to a sanitorium in Pau (Basses-Pyrenées) to convalesce.

23. Philippe Ariès, *Images de l'homme devant la mort* (Paris, 1983).

24. Interview with Orest Ranum, 28–29 May 2001 (Le Panat, Aveyron); manuscript memoir by Ranum from his personal papers.

25. François Leger, "La Mort de l'historien de la mort," *Aspects de la France,* 16 (February 1984): 13.

26. Ariès, *Historien du dimanche*, 122–23.

27. Even late in life, he thought the term apt, though it never appealed to other historians. Philippe Ariès, "Le Temps de l'Histoire" (1983), in *Essais de mémoire* (Paris, 1993), 48.

28. Ariès, *Le Temps de l'Histoire*, 23.

29. Ariès, *Historien du dimanche*, 43–45, 66.

30. Ariès, *Le Temps de l'Histoire*, 20–21. He notes that he posted the genealogy as a chart on his bedroom wall.

31. "Entretien avec Philippe Ariès," *La Nouvelle Action Française* no. 144 (30 January 1974): 6–7.

32. Philippe Ariès, *La Nation française*: "Le Mendiant napolitain," 12 October 1955, 3; "La Vie quotidienne du présent," 26 October 1955, 4–5.

33. Among Ariès's late-life writings on urban sociability, see esp. "La Famille en ville" (1978), in *Essais de mémoire*, 259–69; "The Family and the City in the Old World and the New," in *Changing Images of the Family*, ed. Virginia Tufte and Barbara Myerhoff (New Haven, Conn., 1979), 29–41; and "L'Enfant et la rue, de la ville à l'anti-ville," *URBI* 2 (1979): 3–14. Here Ariès draws on the research of respected colleagues at the Ecole des Hautes Etudes, notably Arlette Farge.

34. Interview with Nicole and Yves Castan, 30 May 2001 (Toulouse).

35. Philippe Ariès, "Les Commissaires-Examinateurs au Châtelet de Paris au XVIe siècle," diplôme d'études supérieures, Université de Paris (Sorbonne), 1936.

36. Ariès, *Historien du dimanche*, 63. See also, "Entretien avec Philippe Ariès," *La Nouvelle Action Française* no. 144 (30 January 1974): 6.

37. Interviews with François and Margueritte Leger, 23 February 1996 (Paris); Orest and Patricia Ranum, 28 May 2001 (Le Panat); Nicole and Yves Castan, 30 May 2001 (Toulouse).

38. Philippe Ariès, "La Terre promise," *L'Etudiant français*, 10 January 1938, 3.

39. Of Teilhard's theory of human evolution toward a "point omega" of cosmic spiritual consciousness, Ariès remarked, "I prefer the alpha and the omega of each individual destiny, of each personal fable, the eternal return of birth and death: a matter of observation rather than doctrine." Philippe Ariès, "Pour une meilleure intelligence entre catholiques," *La Nation française*, 17 October 1962, 1, 14.

40. Ariès, *Le Temps de l'Histoire*, 22–24.

41. Among Ariès's many interviews, see esp. "Confessions d'un anarchiste de droite," *Contrepoint* no. 16 (1974): 87–99, and "La Singulière Histoire de Philippe Ariès," interview by André Burguière, *Le Nouvel Observateur*, 20 February 1978, 80 ff.

42. See the review by Christian Melchior-Bonnet in *Historia* no. 405 (August 1980): 2, 4, 8.

43. Arch. Ariès, cartons "Correspondance," within them, letters to Ariès from Maurice Agulhon, Jean-Paul Angelelli, Jean Ariès, Pierre de Beco, François Bédarida, Fernand Braudel, François Crouzet, Robert Darnton, Georges Duby, François Furet, Marie-Elisabeth d'Harcourt, Joseph Isaac, René Izac, Philippe Levillain, Jean-Marie Mayeur, Albert Nicol, Panat de d'Adhémar, Gilbert Picard, Antoine Prost, Madeleine Rebérioux, René Remond, Dominique Schnapper, Lawrence Stone, Jean Tulard, and Pierre Vidal-Naquet.

44. On Rousseau's appeal to his readers, see Robert Darnton, *The Great Cat Massacre and Other Episodes in French Cultural History* (New York, 1984), 230–34.

45. Pierre Nora, *Essais d'égo histoire* (Paris, 1987), 6. See also Jeremy Popkin, "Ego-histoire and Beyond: Contemporary French Historian-Autobiographers," *French Historical Studies* 19 (1996): 1139–67, and "Historians on the Autobiographical Frontier," *America Historical Review* 104 (1999): 725–48.

46. On the significance of *égo-histoire*, see Eric Vigne, ed., "Autour d'égo histoire," *Le Débat* no. 49 (March–April 1988): 122–40, and Michael Kammen, *In the Past Lane* (New York, 1997), 3–71.

Chapter 3

1. Philippe Ariès, *Un Historien du dimanche*, ed. Michel Winock (Paris, 1980), 78.

2. On Ariès's relationship to Annales historiography, see Pierre Chaunu, "Le Parcours solitaire," *Histoire, économie et société* 3/1 (1984): 3–5, and Hervé Coutau-Bégarie, *Le Phénomène nouvelle histoire*, 2d ed. (Paris, 1989), 11–12, 160–62, 166–67, 350–52.

3. Philippe Ariès, "Le Secret" (1978), in *Essais de mémoire*, ed. Roger Chartier (Paris, 1993), 32.

4. Ariès, *Historien du dimanche*, 77–78.

5. Archives Nationales (hereafter AN), F17 13366 (Jeunesse et sports), report 10 May 1944.

6. AN, 2 AG 440 CC3 (Archives du cabinet civil), dossier "Reforme de la jeunesse," program for youth, revised 2 April 1942.

7. Ariès, *Historien du dimanche*, 79–82.

8. AN, 2 AG 654 (Archives; documents), dossier "Jeunesse," report 17 April 1941.

9. AN, 2 AG 440 CC3, dossier CC 3A "Documentation préparatoire à l'établissement de la Charte des jeunes travailleurs"; F 17 13367 (Jeunesse et sports, 1942–44), dossier "Ecole des cadres," report 10 May 1944.

10. Recent studies of the Ecole des Cadres Supérieurs d'Uriage include Bernard Comte, *Une Utopie combattante: L'Ecole des cadres d'Uriage, 1940–1942* (Paris, 1991); Antoine Delestre, *Uriage, une communauté et une école dans la tourmente, 1940–1945* (Nancy, 1989); and John Hellman, *The Knight-Monks of Vichy France: Uriage, 1940–45* (Montreal, 1993).

11. Comte, *Une Utopie combattante*, 295; Hellman, *The Knight-Monks of Vichy France*, 139, 164.

12. AN, 2 AG 497 CC 79 (Jeunesse, famille, santé), dossier "Jeunesse," document "Jeunes du Maréchal"; F 17 14178 (Affaires disciplinaires, les Jeunes du Maréchal), document "Jeunes du Maréchal, organisation nationale."

13. On Jacques Bousquet, see AN, F 17 13366 (jeunesse et sports), dossier "Jeunes du Maréchal"; F 17 13377 (Etablissements d'enseignement, 1941–43), dossier "rapports octobre–novembre 1941"; F 17 14178, memorandum 11 October 1941; Wilfred D. Halls, *Les Jeunes et la politique de Vichy*, trans. Jean Sénémaud (1981; Paris, 1988), 317–21; and Claude Singer, *Vichy, l'université et les juifs* (Paris, 1992), 35, 94, 99. He is not to be confused with his more notorious namesake, René Bousquet, secretary general of the police at the Vichy Ministry of the Interior.

14. Ariès, *Historien du dimanche*, 79.

15. AN, F 17 13353 (Correspondance divers), dossier "Neidinger et Bousquet, jeunesse, avril–mai 1942."

16. AN, 2 AG 570 CC 175 (Education nationale et jeunesse), letter from Courtot to Lamirand, 18 July 1942; 2 AG 496 CC78 (Education nationale), report 12 August 1942.

17. The Ecole Nationale des Cadres Supérieurs at La Chapelle (hereafter ENCS) was situated on the grounds of a vast forest domain, including two chateaux, a farm, and various outbuildings. AN, F 17 13367, report concerning the history of the ENCS, January 1943, 4 pp.

18. On Lavastine's role at La Chapelle, see AN, F 17 13367, course syllabus, 17 June 1942; F 17 13353, letter from Vandal to Bousquet, 13 July 1942. On his sympathy for closer cultural ties with Germany, see Philippe Burrin, *La France à l'heure allemande, 1940–1944* (Paris, 1995), 357.

19. Burrin, *La France à l'heure allemande,* 332, 354; AN, AJ 40 1005, dossier 7 (Gerhard Heller), and Heller's own memoir, *Un Allemand à Paris, 1940–1944* (Paris, 1981). Heller's course syllabus for the six-month internship may be found in AN, F 17 13367, program announcement for the six-month session at the ENCS, 17 June 1942.

20. Ariès, *Historien du dimanche,* 80. One of these was André Chastel (later a well-known art historian), whom Bousquet cashiered in April for being insufficiently sympathetic to his pro-German policy. AN, 2 AG 440 CC3, memorandum, June 1942; 2 AG 496 CC 78, dossier "Education nationale, divers," report 12 August 1942; 2 AG 570 CC 175, dossier "Questions diverses," report June 1942.

21. AN, F 17 13367, program of the ENCS de la Chapelle for the six-month internship (April–October 1942), 17 June 1942.

22. AN F 17 13367, memorandum, Bousquet's statement of purpose for the first six-month internship, 5 January–26 June 1942 at the ENCS.

23. This project quickly became a favorite theme of Vichy educators. AN, F 17 13341 (Instruction publique), dossier "Cycle de conférences à l'ENCS, juillet–août 1942," document no. 64.

24. Ibid., document no. 76.

25. AN, F 17 13367, dossier "Ecole des cadres," report on the history of the Ecole des Cadres Supérieurs de la Chapelle-en-Serval, undated (circa January 1943), 4 pp.

26. AN F 17 13339 (Activités personnelles du ministre [Abel Bonnard], 1942–43), dossier "Enseignement de l'histoire-géographie."

27. AN, 2 AG 497 CC 79, dossier "Jeunesse," report June 1942. The extent of Ariès's participation in the Jeunes du Maréchal is unclear. Particularly intriguing is an empty folder labeled "Propagande Ariès," in 2AG 457 CC 32 (propagande).

28. AN, F 17 13366, brochure "Jeunes du Maréchal," 15 June 1942, p. 76.

29. AN, F 17 13367, program announcement for the ENCS, 17 June 1942 (Ariès's course syllabus for the six month session, April–October 1942).

30. For his lecture on the history of history, Ariès chose three historians as his reference points: Titus Livy (classicism) from antiquity; Bossuet (Christian theology) from the ancien régime; and Hippolyte Taine (biological determinism) from the modern era. All three were innovators in the framing of history. See his preface to François Leger, *La Jeunesse d'Hippolyte Taine* (Paris, 1980), 11.

31. Philippe Ariès, *Le Temps de l'Histoire* (Monaco, 1954). See his interview "Confessions d'un anarchiste de droite," *Contrepoint* no. 16 (1974): 90–95.

32. Ariès, *Le Temps de l'Histoire,* 43–44.

33. See his articles on the subject, published shortly before the war, in *L'Etudiant*

français: "Le Problème national en Autriche," 8 June 1936; "Les Nations romantiques," May 1939.

34. Maurice-Henry Lenormand, *Vers le régime corporatif* (Paris, 1943).

35. Ariès identifies his views on this subject with those of his friend Raoul Girardet, for whom it was the principal interest. *Historien du dimanche,* 144.

36. Ibid., 82. On the Center itself, see Stanislas Reizler, René van den Berg, Philippe Ariès, and Mathieu Le Minor, *Fonctionnement d'un centre de documentation* (Paris, 1946).

37. André Burguière, "La Singulière Histoire de Philippe Ariès," *Le Nouvel Observateur,* 20 February 1978, 80.

38. AN, F 17 13356 (Correspondances), dossier "généralités," lecture by Philippe Renaudin at the Sorbonne, 17 July 1943; 2 AG 459 CC 34 (Transmission no. 2), dossier "Famille, société"; 2 AG 497 CC 79, dossier "Famille"; Fernand Boverat, *Fécondité ou servitude; Comment relever la natalité française* (Lyon, 1941).

39. Ariès, *Histoire du dimanche,* 80.

40. AN, F17 14178, report 15 June 1942.

41. Bousquet had connections in high places. In June 1942, he was named chief of cabinet to Abel Bonnard, the new minister of education, who became his protector. Bousquet maintained close connections with the school and continued to teach a course in its long-term internship.

42. Philippe Ariès, "La Réforme de l'enseignement historique," *L'Etudiant français,* December 1938.

43. Philippe Ariès, "Fustel de Coulanges, 1889–1939," *L'Etudiant français,* April 1939, 1, 3; idem, "Daniel Halévy," *La Nation française,* 7 February 1962; Françine Muel-Dreyfus, "Cercle Fustel-de-Coulanges," in *Dictionnaire des intellectuels français,* ed. Jacques Julliard and Michel Winock (Paris, 1996), 239–40.

44. Interview with Marie-Rose Ariès (in Le Chesnay, Yvelines), 3 January 1996.

45. Interview with Gilbert Picard (in Versailles), 28 February 1996; interview with François Leger (in Paris), 23 February 1996. See also François Leger, "Philippe Ariès: L'histoire d'un historien," *Revue universelle des faits et des idées* 65 (1986): 65.

46. Ariès, *Historien du dimanche,* 78–79; Burguière, "La Singulière Histoire de Philippe Ariès," 81.

47. See the article by François Leger, "Les Fidélités de Philippe Ariès," *Aspects de la France,* 2 October 1980.

48. Leger mentions Ariès's appreciation of the courses of Emmanuel de Martonne, a specialist in the geography of regional France, and of Jerôme Carcopino, a respected historian of ancient Rome, later to become Vichy's minister of education. "Philippe Ariès: L'histoire d'un historien," 65.

49. Ariès, *Le Temps de l'Histoire,* 9–24.

50. Philippe Ariès, "Les Commissaires-Examinateurs au Châtelet de Paris au XVIe siècle," diplôme d'études supérieures, Sorbonne, 1936. See also his article in *L'Etudiant français,* summarizing his argument, "Le Roi arbitre et les libertés," 10 May 1937.

51. Ariès, "Les Commissaires-Examinateurs," 198–203.

52. Ariès took up this theme after the war in some of his articles in the newspaper *La Nation française:* "Notre Administration est-elle en décadence?" 1 January 1958; "La Classe sociale dans la vie moderne," 10 September 1958; and "Le Refus des différences dans la société d'aujourd'hui," 1 October 1958.

53. Ariès likened his community to that of the Jansenists in the seventeenth century. "If one were to write a history of the Action Française," he explained, "one would do well to reread all that has been written about Port Royal, one would find an astonishing resemblance." *Historien du dimanche*, 45, 63–67, 69, 71.

54. François Leger, *Les Influences occidentales dans la révolution de l'Orient*, 2 vols. (Paris, 1955).

55. François Leger, *La Jeunesse d'Hippolyte Taine* (Paris, 1980), and idem, *Monsieur Taine* (Paris, 1993).

56. Raoul Girardet, *Singulièrement libre* (Paris, 1990), 41.

57. Robert Brasillach, *Notre Avant-guerre* (Paris, 1992), 445–46.

58. François Brigneau, *Mon Après-guerre* (Paris, 1966), 14.

59. Ibid., 48–49. On the Group of Five, see William Hoisington, *A Businessman in Politics in France* (Ann Arbor, Mich., 1968), 222–54.

60. Brigneau, *Mon Après-guerre*, 58–63.

61. On Boutang's career, see Alain-Gérard Slama, "Boutang (Pierre)," in *Dictionnaire des intellectuels français*, 180–81.

62. Ariès wrote an article on the Picard family at the time of the father's death, "Charles Picard," *La Nation française*, 30 December 1965.

63. François Leger, *Une Jeunesse réactionnaire* (Paris, 1993), 101–5, 113–23; Girardet, *Singulièrement libre*, 37–43, 125; interview with Philippe Brissaud (in Paris), 19 April 1996.

64. These ties were put to the test during the Algerian crisis of the early 1960s, when his circle of friends divided bitterly over policy. Later they were reconciled. As Leger later remarked, "Philippe Ariès remains a man of attachments, one who does not break profound ties, one who knows their importance and holds fast to them." "Les Fidélités de Philippe Ariès," *Aspects de la France*, 2 October 1980.

65. While Maurras's writings are not much read anymore, there has been renewed interest of late in his intellectual role in the Action Française. See the review essay by Christophe Prochasson, "Sur le cas Maurras: Biographie et histoire des idées politiques," *Annales HSS* 50 (1995): 579–87.

66. Philippe Ariès, "A Propos de Balzac," in *Trois Socialistes français: Quatre Etudes*, ed. Paul Chanson (Paris, 1945), 149–65. There is also an unpublished manuscript of a long essay by Ariès on George Sand, preserved among his personal papers in the Archives Ariès at the Ecole des Hautes Etudes (hereafter Arch. Ariès).

67. See Victor Nguyen, *Aux origines de l'Action Française* (Paris, 1991).

68. For "men of letters" as right-wing counterparts to "public intellectuals" on the left, see Michel Winock, *Le Siècle des intellectuels* (Paris, 1999), 247–58.

69. Ariès's articles in *L'Etudiant français* concerning Maurras include: "Un Aspect de la pensée de Charles Maurras," 25 November 1936; "L'Enseignement de Maurras," 10 December 1936; "Pascal et Maurras," 10 January 1937; "Avec Maurras: Sceptique ou dogmatique?" 10 March 1937; "L'Anschluss et ses répercussions sur la politique anglaise et italienne," 25 March 1938; and "Charles Maurras et la tradition littéraire," 10 June 1938.

70. "Entretien avec Philippe Ariès," *La Nouvelle Action Française* no. 144 (30 January 1974): 6.

71. Philippe Ariès, "Le Thème de la mort dans 'le Chemin de Paradis' de Maurras," (1972), in *Essais sur l'histoire de la mort en Occident du Moyen Age à nos jours* (Paris, 1975), 115–22.

72. Ariès, *Historien du dimanche*, 87 n. 1.

73. Philippe Ariès, "Inconscient collectif et idées claires," *Anthinéa* no. 8 (August–September 1975): 3–4; "Table ronde sur la communication de Roger Chartier," in *La Mort aujourd'hui*, ed. Roger Chartier (Marseille, 1982), 127–30.

74. Ariès in *L'Etudiant français*: "Réflexions sur la Contre-Révolution," 25 January, 10 and 25 February 1938, and "La Terreur," March 1939. At the time, Ariès admitted an intellectual debt to Augustin Cochin, and late in life he was struck by the degree to which his critique of Jacobinism anticipated the thesis of François Furet in his *Penser la Révolution française* (Paris, 1978). Ariès, *Historien du dimanche*, 54–55, esp. n.1. See also Ariès's preface to *La Jeunesse d'Hippolyte Taine*, by Leger, 7–11.

75. In his essay "La Ressemblance," (1983) in *Essais de mémoire*, 59–67, Ariès reflects on the historical attitudes of the right in the years before the Second World War, and notes his reasons for rejecting them.

76. Philippe Ariès, "La Terre promise," *L'Etudiant français*, 10 January 1938.

77. Ariès in *L'Etudiant français*: "L'Anschluss et ses répercussions sur la politique anglaise et italienne," 25 March 1938, and "L'Italie après l'Anschluss," 10 May 1938. See also Jeannine Verdès-Leroux, *Refus et violences* (Paris, 1996), 116–41.

78. Ariès in *L'Etudiant français*: "Le Problème national en Autriche," 8 June 1936; "Le Pouvoir politique," January 1939; and "Les Nations romantiques," May 1939 (text of a lecture he delivered at the Institut de l'Action Française, 30 April 1939).

79. Something of Ariès's disillusionment with the teachings at the ENCS may be gleaned from the book he published shortly after leaving, *Les Traditions sociales dans les pays de France* (Paris, 1943). Avoiding direct discussion of current political issues, he presents a cool, matter-of-fact analysis of the evolution of local customs in the ancient provinces of France during the modern era. Indirectly, he reveals his idealized vision of what Vichy might have been. See Roger Chartier's preface to *Essais de mémoire*, 16–19.

80. Alison Browning, "Une Conversation avec Philippe Ariès," *Cadmos* no. 12 (Winter 1980), 14–15; Ariès, *Historien du dimanche*, 84–85.

81. See Ariès's reflection on this notion of History in his essay "Le Temps de l'Histoire," (1983) in *Essais de mémoire*, 46–49.

82. *Le Temps de l'Histoire*, 61–78. Ariès's commentary on the uprooted intellectuals of the mid-twentieth century invites comparison with that of Maurice Barrès on their counterparts in the late nineteenth century in *Les Déracinés* (1897; Paris, 1967).

83. Arch. Ariès, Note of invitation to the dinner cruise in honor of Ariès, 14 October 1981,

84. Interview with Jean Bruel (on board a bateau mouche, Paris), 21 August 1997.

85. Letters from Gilbert Picard (15 December 1978; 24 May 1980) and Philippe Brissaud (15 November 1975), Archives Ariès.

86. Philippe Ariès, "Réflexions sur l'histoire de l'homosexualité," *Communications* 35 (1982): 56–67, quote 62.

87. Ariès, "Le Secret," 33–34.

88. Ariès, "Le Temps de l'Histoire," 47–49.

89. Ariès, *Historien du dimanche*, 79. The key article illuminating Ariès's move from demography to mentalities is his "Interpretation pour une histoire des mentalités," in *La Prévention des naissances dans la famille*, ed. Hélène Bergues (Paris, 1960), 311–27.

90. Ernest Labrousse, "Introduction," *L'Histoire sociale: Sources et méthodes*, ed. anon. (Paris, 1967), 4–5; Michel Vovelle, "L'Histoire et la longue durée," in *La Nouvelle Histoire*, ed. Jacques Le Goff (Paris, 1988), 79.

91. Philippe Ariès, "La Nostalgie du roi," *H-Histoire* no. 5 (1980): 48.

Chapter 4

1. Ariès was introduced to Halévy by Henri Boegner, founder of the Cercle. Ariès, "Daniel Halévy," *La Nation française* (hereafter cited as *NF*) 7 February 1962, 1.

2. Philippe Ariès, *Un Historien du dimanche*, ed. Michel Winock (Paris, 1980), 87; "Le Secret" (1978), in *Essais de mémoire, 1943–1983*, ed. Roger Chartier (Paris, 1993), 29–30. A dossier of Halévy's letters to Ariès, most dating from the 1950s, is found among Ariès's personal papers in the Archives Ariès at the Archives de l'Ecole des Hautes Etudes (hereafter Arch. Ariès).

3. Daniel Halévy, *La Fin des notables*, 2 vols. (Paris, 1930–37).

4. Philippe Ariès, "Daniel Halévy," *NF*, 7 February 1962, 1, 11. For his obituary on Halévy the same year, he chose as his theme Halévy's essay *Histoire d'une histoire* (1939), a meditation on the limits of the revolutionary tradition. Philippe Ariès, "*Histoire d'une histoire*: Laissez l'ordre rentrer en vous," *NF*, 21 February 1962, 20–23.

5. Philippe Ariès, "Le Temps de l'Histoire" (1983), in *Essais de mémoire*, 46.

6. See the portraits of Boutang by Raoul Girardet, *Singulièrement libre: Entretiens*, ed. Pierre Assouline (Paris 1990), 41, and François Brigneau, *Mon Après-guerre* (Paris, 1985), 14. On Boutang's career, see Alain-Gérard Slama, "Boutang (Pierre)," in *Dictionnaire des intellectuals français*, ed. Jacques Julliard and Michel Winock (Paris, 1996), 180–81.

7. Boutang wrote appreciative reviews of Ariès's *Histoire des populations françaises* in *Aspects de la France*, 3 and 10 March 1949.

8. Ariès, *Historien du dimanche*, 99. Boutang also wrote sympathetic reviews of Ariès's book on demography, *Histoire des populations françaises et de leurs attitudes devant la vie depuis le XVIIIe siècle* (Paris, 1948) in *Aspects de la France*, 3 and 10 March 1949.

9. On Ariès's reaction to the purge, see Ariès, *Historien du dimanche*, 98–101, and *Le Temps de l'Histoire* (Monaco, 1954), 63–64.

10. Ariès noted their similarities to the "déracinés" identified by Maurice Barrès two generations before at the time of the Dreyfus Affair. Barrès likewise had been critical of intellectuals without roots in particular traditions. Ariès, *Le Temps de l'Histoire*, 67–78. This image of the "intellectual" may explain his own preference for the term "man of letters" to characterize the role he aspired to play. Philippe Ariès, "L'Intellectuel ès-qualité," *NF*, 5 October 1960, 1–2.

11. On the composition of the staff at *Les Paroles française*, see Brigneau, *Mon Après-guerre*, 31–32, 48–51. On the exposé of the massacre at Katyn, see Ariès, "Sagesse de J. Czapski," *NF*, 1 March 1961, 1, 13.

12. Ariès, *Historien du dimanche*, 151.

13. Ariès wrote only three articles during his tenure at *Les Paroles françaises*: "Ce que pense l'Amérique," dealing with public opinion polling, 2 March 1946; "Le Pro-

testantisme français," 9 March 1946; and "L'Evolution sociale d'après le referendum," which dealt with the political geography of French elections, 18 May 1946. For the context in which this paper operated, see esp. Jeannine Verdès-Leroux, *Refus et violences* (Paris, 1996), 423–26.

14. See Brigneau, *Mon Après-guerre*, 31–32, 70–73, and Verdès-Leroux, *Refus et violence*, 442.

15. The complete collection of these essays has been edited by Jeannine Verdès-Leroux, *Le Présent quotidien (1955–1966)* (Paris, 1997). In her insightful prefatory essay, "La 'Fidélité inventive' de Philippe Ariès," 7–38, she describes Ariès's journalistic accomplishment as an eclectic and spontaneous response to the issues of the day. I agree, but would also insist on the way they evoke the deeper themes that he was simultaneously developing as a historian of mentalities. My point is that Ariès's journalism helps us to contextualize his development as a historian.

16. Ariès, *Le Temps de l'Histoire*, 299–304; "La Ressemblance" (1980), in *Essais de mémoire*, 64–66; Ariès, *NF*: "Histoire et tradition," 18 January 1956, 4; "Excès et limites de la publicité," 6 May 1959, 7.

17. See their manifesto, "Préface," to *Ecrits pour une renaissance*, ed. Pierre Andreu et al. (Paris, 1958), i–viii. For the larger context of this journalism, see Raoul Girardet, "L'Héritage de l'Action française," (1957), in *Révoltes de l'esprit: Les revues des années trente*, ed. Pierre Andreu (Paris, 1991), 149–74; and Pierre Nora, "Les Deux Apogées de l'Action française," *Annales ESC* 19 (January–February 1964), 127–41. Also of interest is Ariès's late reflection on the launching of the newspaper, "Le Devoir des royalistes," *NF*, 2 April 1964, 1–2.

18. Philippe Ariès, "Une Civilisation à construire," in *Ecrits pour une renaissance*, 211–12.

19. Cf. Verdès-Leroux, "La 'Fidélité inventive' de Philippe Ariès," 14–16.

20. Ariès, "Une Civilisation à construire," 203–22, and "Le 'Politique d'abord,' est-il passé à gauche?" *NF*, 10 January 1962, 1, 8.

21. Philippe Ariès, "Non, nous n'allons pas vers une civilisation des loisirs," *NF*, 9 December 1959, 1, 5.

22. Thus the Fondation Française pour l'Etude des Problèmes Humains (Fondation Carrel) was transformed into the Institut National d'Etudes Démographiques. Philippe Ariès, "Pourquoi la démographie française n'est pas restée malthusienne," *NF*, 16 December 1959, 9.

23. Philippe Ariès, "Suicides paysans," *NF*, 12 February 1958, 7.

24. Philippe Ariès, "A propos de Balzac," in *Trois Socialistes français*, ed. Paul Chanson (Paris, 1945), 149–65.

25. Ariès, *NF*: "Les Aspects biologiques de l'histoire de Paris," 5 November 1958, 5; "Quelle société?" 11 March 1959, 1, 5. Ariès was involved in a scholarly exchange with Chevalier as early as 1949, when Chevalier was a researcher at the Institut National d'Etudes Démographique. They corresponded regularly in later years. Arch. Ariès: Chevalier to Ariès, 12 February 1949, 12 April 1966, 20 April 1971, 20 November 1973, 9 December 1977, and 20 May 1983. See also Daniel Halévy's comments about Chevalier in his letter to Ariès, 13 July 1956.

26. Ariès, "La Condition ouvrière," *NF*, 21 December 1955.

27. It is interesting to note that Ariès gave a public lecture at the Fondation Nationale des Sciences Politiques in November 1949 entitled "Quelques Types d'évolution

des populations ouvrières sous la Troisième République." Arch. Ariès, invitation to the lecture, sponsored by the Société d'Histoire de la Troisième République.

28. Ariès, *NF*: "Le Déclin du syndicalisme," 27 August 1958, 1–2; "Le Retour à la vie privée," 10 April 1963, 1, 15.

29. Ariès, "Technocrats et techniciens," *NF*, 21 March 1956, 4.

30. Ariès, *NF*: "Le Poujadisme," 8 February 1956, 4–5; "Le Socialisme vu par les députés travaillistes," 29 February 1956, 4–5; "L'Indépendance des 'cadres'," 15 August 1962, 1, 10.

31. Ariès, "Une Civilsation à construire," 213–15; idem, *NF*: "La Spécialisation de la culture," 4 April 1956, 4; "La Morale 'bourgeoise'," 3 August 1960, 6–7.

32. Philippe Ariès, "Les Commissaires-Examinateurs au Châtelet de Paris au XVIe siècle," diplôme d'études supérieures, Sorbonne, 1936.

33. Ariès, "Une Civilisation à construire," 215; idem, *NF*: "Technocrats et techniciens," 21 March 1956, 4; "La Classe sociale dans la vie moderne," 10 September 1958, 4–5.

34. Ariès, *NF*: "Le Refus des différences dans les sociétés d'aujourd'hui," 1 October 1958, 1–2; "Le Racisme dans notre société," 25 October 1961, 8–9.

35. Ariès, *NF*: "Déplacements dans le budget familial," 2 November 1955, 4; "La Répartition de la culture est aujourd'hui inversement proportionnelle à celle des richesses," 30 November 1955, 4–5; "Dans le journal du peintre Jean Colin," 21 June 1961, 10–11, 14; "La Valeur du refus," 19 July 1961, 1, 12.

36. Ariès, "Une Civilisation à construire," 212.

37. Ariès, "L'Intellectuel ès-qualité," *NF*, 5 October 1960, 1–2.

38. Ariès, "Litanies bêtes," *NF*, 29 May 1957, 1–2.

39. Ariès, *NF*: "Démobilsation de la démocratie," 25 June 1958, 1, 4; "Réalités sociales sous le phénomène électoral," 8–9.

40. Ariès, "Les Réprouvés," *NF*, 3 May 1961, 9. On the decline of the public intellectual in France, see esp. Pascal Ory and Jean-François Sirinelli, *Les Intellectuels en France de l'affaire Dreyfus à nos jours* (Paris, 1992), and Michel Winock, *Le Siècle des intellectuels* (Paris, 1999).

41. Ariès, *NF*: "Démobilisation de la démocratie," 25 June 1958, 1, 4; "Une Ville 'ennemie'," 10 May 1961, 1, 11; "Le Retour à la vie privée," 10 April 1963, 1, 15.

42. Ariès, *NF*: "La Droite, cette inconnue," 15 January 1964, 1, 11; "Fonctions profondes sous 'la gauche' et 'la droite'," 22 January 1964, 10.

43. Ariès, *NF*: "Réalités sociales sous le phénomène électoral," 24 December 1958, 8–9; "Le Retour à la vie privée," 10 April 1963, 1, 15.

44. Ariès, "Sociologie pour tous," *NF*, 6 May 1959, 1–2.

45. Ariès, "Une Civilisation à construire," 219.

46. After the publication of *L'Enfant et la vie familiale sous l'Ancien Régime*, Ariès continued to write articles on the subject, but put far more emphasis on the problems of the contemporary age. Ariès, *NF*: "Remarques sur la conception traditionaliste de la famille," 7 August 1957, 6–7; "Pour une meilleure intelligence entre catholiques," 7 November 1962, 14, 15; "Le Retour à la vie privée," 10 April 1963, 1, 15. See also his overview, "La Famille hier et aujourd'hui," *Contrepoint* no. 11 (July 1973), 94–96.

47. Ariès, *NF*: "La Mobilité sociale en France et en Allemagne," 28 March 1956, 4; "Démobilisation de la démocratie," 25 June 1958, 1, 4; "Non, nous n'allons pas vers une civilisation des loisirs," 9 December 1959, 1, 5.

48. Ariès, *NF:* "Une Jeunesse conformiste et réfractaire," 16 October 1957, 1–2; "L'Ecole ne remplace pas la famille," 5 August 1959, 7; "Naives Hirondelles," 25 November 1964, 1, 14; "Moderne Violence," 17 February 1965, 1, 3. See also his overview, "Problèmes de l'éducation," in *La France et les français,* ed. Michel François (1972; Paris, 1981), 954–60.

49. Ariès, *NF:* "Notre Administration est-elle en décadence?" 1 January 1958, 1–2; "L'Ecole dans notre civilisation," 8 July 1959, 1, 5.

50. Ariès, *NF:* "La Présence des princes," 3 July 1957, 11; "La Mort violente," 13 March 1963, 1, 15; "La Droite, cette inconnue," 15 January 1964, 1, 11.

51. Ariès, *NF:* "L'Echec des 'organisateurs' devant les troubles de notre temps," 10 February 1960, 8–9; "Deux nationalismes," 7 December 1960, 1, 15; "Le Devoir des royalistes," 2 April 1964, 1–2.

52. Ariès, *Le Temps de l'Histoire,* esp. 9–12, 22–23, 36–39. In one of his last essays, Ariès alluded to the similarities between his youthful association of History and destiny with that of Malraux. Philippe Ariès, "Le Temps de l'Histoire" (1983), in *Essais de mémoire,* 49.

53. Ariès, "La Vraie Décolonisation," *NF,* 19 April 1961, 1, 10.

54. Ariès did not like the term decolonization, for he understood the conflict in terms of opposing, violent nationalisms. Ariès, "Une Echarde dans la chair," *NF,* 24 May 1961, 1, 15.

55. Ariès, *NF:* "Les Méthodes du pouvoir et la plainte des paysans," 23 March 1960, 8–9; "La Cinquième République et la représentation nationale," 6 April 1960, 8; "'Non,' contre le manque de coeur, nullement contre l'Etat," 4 January 1961, 10; "De la haine civile," 18 January 1961, 1–2; "Les Réprouvés," 3 May 1961, 9.

56. Ariès, *NF:* "A l'heure où les camps se retranchent," 20 December 1961, 1, 8; "Détournement d'un sacrifice," 7 March 1962, 1, 14.

57. Ariès, *NF:* "M. Martinez, rapatrié," 22 March 1961, 8–9; "Une Ville 'ennemie'," 10 May 1961, 1, 11; "Détournement d'un sacrifice," 7 March 1962, 1, 14; "Les Nouveaux 'Versailles'," 28 March 1962, 1, 14; "Ces Citoyens perdus, nos frères," 4 April 1962, 1, 15; "Une Fidélité plus forte que le bonheur," 16 May 1962, 1, 10; "Le Mauvais Chirurgien," 4 July 1962, 1, 11; "Les Enfants des autres," 11 July 1962, 1, 14; "La Mort violente," 13 March 1963, 1, 15.

58. Ariès, *NF:* "Celui qui n'a jamais le temps de faire grâce," 25 July 1962, 1, 14; "Piété envers un mort," 12 September 1962, 1, 11; "Examen d'un régime," 2 January 1963, 1, 15.

59. Ariès, *NF:* "A Michel Debré," 27 September 1961, 1; "Le Devoir du parlement," 4 October 1961, 1; "Raison d'Etat? Non, règlements de comptes," 18 October 1961, 1, 14.

60. Ariès, *Historien du dimanche,* 159.

61. "Libres Débats," *L'Esprit public* no. 22 (July–August 1961), 21; Archives Ariès: letter from François Leger to Philippe Ariès, [28 May 1961]; Ariès, *NF:* "De la haine civile," 18 January 1961, 1–2; "Lui et nous . . . ," 7 August 1963, 1, 6–7. See also Verdès-Leroux, "La 'Fidélité inventive' de Philippe Ariès," 17.

62. Ariès, *NF:* "Punitions d'un magistrat," 25 September 1963, 1, 5; "Après Chartres: tout commence," 2 October 1963, 1, 4; "La 'Justice' de Brueghel," 11 December 1963, 1–2; "La Justice et le pouvoir," 23 June 1965, 1, 3.

63. Henry Rousso, *Le Syndrome de Vichy: De 1944 à nos jours,* 2d ed. (Paris, 1990), 95–100.

64. François Regel, "La Question juive," *L'Etudiant français*, 10 January 1938, 2–4.

65. Claude Singer, *Vichy, l'université et les juifs* (Paris, 1992), 71–78.

66. Jews were also denied admission to Jacques Bousquet's Jeunes du Maréchal. Archives Nationales, F17 14178 (Jeunes du Maréchal), dossier "Mouvements de jeunesse, 'Jeunes du Maréchal,'" memo on requirements of admission, 20 July 1942.

67. Brigneau, *Mon Après-guerre*, 31–32.

68. Pierre Birnbaum, *Anti-Semitism in France* (Oxford, 1992), 247–50, 287.

69. Pierre Boutang, *La République de Joinovici* (Paris, 1949); Brigneau, *Mon Après-guerre*, 70–73.

70. Michael R. Marrus and Robert O. Paxton, *Vichy France and the Jews* (New York, 1981). On the return of the repressed memory of the Holocaust, see Rousso, *Le Syndrome de Vichy*, 155–94.

71. Arch. Ariès, Joseph Czapski to Ariès (undated). Ariès quotes extensive passages from this letter in his *Historien du dimanche*, 157 n.1.

72. Ariès, *Historien du dimanche*, 87–88.

73. Arch. Ariès, Dominique Schnapper to Philippe Ariès, 8 June 1980.

74. Ariès, "Nos Impatiences et nos fidélités," *NF*, 7 October 1964, 1–2.

75. Philippe Ariès, "Une Interprétation tendancieuse de l'histoire des mentalités," *Anthinéa* 3/2 (February 1973): 7–10.

76. Philippe Ariès, "Confessions d'un anarchiste de droite," *Contrepoint* no. 16 (1974): 92; Alison Browning, "Une Conversation avec Philippe Ariès," *Cadmos* no. 12 (Winter 1980): 11–13; "Entretien avec Philippe Ariès," *La Nouvelle Action Française* no. 144 (30 January 1974): 6–7.

77. Ariès, *Le Temps de l'Histoire*, 23, 35–39, 321–25; "Le Temps de l'Histoire," in *Essais de mémoire*, 49.

78. Ariès, *NF*: "Une Fraternité secrète," 18 September 1963, 1, 11; "La Droite, cette inconnue," 15 January 1964, 1, 11; "Fonctions profondes sous 'la gauche' et 'la droite'," 22 January 1964, 10; "La Langue, héritage vivant," 18 March 1964, 1, 11; "Le Fond des temps," 21 October 1964, 1, 3; "Les Retours de l'histoire," 7 July 1965, 1, 15.

79. Ariès: "Confessions d'un anarchiste de droite," 96, "Une Interprétation tendancieuse de l'histoire des mentalités," 7–10, "L'Histoire des mentalités," in *La Nouvelle Histoire*, ed. Jacques Le Goff et al. (Paris, 1978), 423.

80. The most important of these Annalistes was Roger Chartier, who edited many of Ariès's writings. See especially his prefatory essay "L'Amitié de l'histoire," to his 1986 edition of Ariès's *Le Temps de l'Histoire*, 9–31.

81. Arch. Ariès, cartons "Correspondance," among them Maurice Agulon, J. P. Aron, Fernand Braudel, Pierre Chaunu, Robert Darnton, Georges Duby, Michel Foucault, François Furet, Carlo Ginzburg, Peter Laslett, Jacques Le Goff, Emmanuel Le Roy Ladurie, Philippe Levillain, Robert Mandrou, Jean-Claude Margolin, Jean-Marie Mayeur, Roland Mousnier, Pierre Nora, Le Comte Panat de d'Adhémar, Jean-Pierre Poussou, René Rémond, Yves Renouard, Pierre Renouvin, Jacques Revel, Michel Rocard, Daniel Roche, Edward Shorter, André Siegfried, and Paul Veyne.

82. Arch. Ariès, letters to Ariès from Jean-Louis Flandrin, 23 May 1971; Lawrence Stone, 6 June 1980; François Crouzet, 27 June 1980; Marie-Elizabeth d'Harcourt, 9 January 1981; and Antoine Prost (undated).

83. Hervé Coutau-Bégarie, *Le Phénomène nouvelle histoire* (Paris, 1989), 350–53; François Dosse, *L'Histoire en miettes* (Paris, 1987), 201–4.

84. Philippe Ariès, "Le Secret" (1978), in *Essais de mémoire*, 34–41.

85. See for example Peter Gay, "Annales of Childhood," *Saturday Review*, 23 March 1963, 73–74. Ariès, *Historien du dimanche*, 177–82. In addition to Orest Ranum, Ariès became acquainted with Natalie Davis and Edward Shorter. Arch. Ariès, Natalie Davis to Ariès (undated), Edward Shorter to Ariès, 10 January 1978.

86. Jean-François Sirinelli, "Les Intellectuels," in *Pour une histoire politique*, ed. René Rémond (Paris, 1988), 199–231; Ory and Sirinelli, *Les Intellectuels en France* 225–41; Tony Judt, *Past Imperfect: French Intellectuals, 1944–1956* (Berkeley, Calif.,1992); Winock, *Le Siècle des intellectuels*. See the discussion of the issue by David Schalk, *War and the Ivory Tower* (New York, 1991), 162–71.

87. See the memoirs by Emmanuel Le Roy Ladurie, *Paris/Montpellier: P.C.-P.S.U., 1945–1963* (Paris, 1982), and François Furet, *Histoire de la Révolution et la révolution dans l'histoire* (Paris, 1994).

Chapter 5

1. Philippe Ariès, *Un Historien du dimanche*, ed. Michel Winock (Paris, 1980), 81.

2. To his unhappiness over the fate of royalism was later added his grief over the death of his brother Jacques in a military campaign of the French army in the last days of the war. He afterward confided in a friend that this loss brought home all the others, and inspired him to launch his historical inquiry into the collapse of the culture of old France. Interview with Philippe Brissaud (in Paris), 19 April 1996.

3. For his references to his conversations with students in the youth camps, see Philippe Ariès, *Le Temps de l'Histoire* (Monaco, 1954), 43–45.

4. In *Un Historien du dimanche*, 89–90, Ariès remembers only the general ignorance of his students about their family history. But in his postwar memoir, *Le Temps de l'Histoire*, 44–45, he made distinctions among regions, noting that family memories were longer in places where traditions remained more fully intact. In this respect, Ariès's observation at the time was closer to the thinking of Vichy educators, who argued that young adults lacked a sense of community and needed to have it built into their education. AN F17 13353 (papiers de Jacques Bousquet), dossier "Neidinger et Bousquet, jeunesse, avril-mai 1942," memorandum "Les Cellules Françaises," 4 pp.

5. Ariès, *Historien du dimanche*, 90.

6. Ariès, *Le Temps de l'Histoire*, 26–33. For Ariès's critique of Bainville, see William R. Keylor, *Jacques Bainville and the Renaissance of Royalist History in Twentieth-Century France* (Baton Rouge, 1979), 214–18.

7. Ariès, *Historien du dimanche*, 91.

8. Archives Ariès, Archives of the Ecole des Hautes Etudes en Sciences Sociales, Paris (hereafter Arch. Ariès), "Entretien avec Philippe Ariès," *Je Suis Français* (1982) (typescript).

9. On the politics of the natalist/Malthusian debate in relationship to the eugenics movement in France, see William H. Schneider, *Quantity vs. Quality* (Cambridge, U.K., 1990), 33–45, 272–80.

10. Philippe Ariès, "Contribution à l'histoire des pratiques contraceptives: Chaucer et Mme de Sévigné" (1954), in *Essais de mémoire*, ed. Roger Chartier (Paris, 1993), 323–27.

11. Some may have tacitly recognized the widening practice of contraceptive tech-

niques among married couples, even among the most traditional elements of the rural population, but it was not a subject to which they alluded. In official memoranda on family life, the issue of contraception is not mentioned. AN, 2 AG 459 CC 34 (transmission, no. 2), dossier "Famille, société." For the Vichyite position, see Fernand Boverat, *Fécondité ou servitude* (Lyon, 1941).

12. AN, F17 13356 (Correspondances et autres documents relatifs à l'enseignement), dossier "Généralités," report of Philippe Renaudin, 16 June 1943, 15 pp.

13. AN, F17 13339 (Activités personnelles du ministre [Abel Bonnard], 1942–43), dossier "Enseignement de l'histoire-géographie"; F17 13367, dossier "Ecole des cadres," memorandum about the program at the ENCS.

14. AN, 2AG 440 CC3 (Archives du cabinet civil), dossier "Reformes de la jeunesse," memorandum "Programme pour la jeunesse," 2 April 1942, 2 AG 496 CC 78, dossier "Education nationale, divers," confidential report "note sur le ministre de l'éducation nationale à Vichy," 2 August 1942; 2 AG 570 CC 175 (Education nationale et jeunesse), dossier "Jeunesse," note from R. Courtot to G. Lamirand, 18 July 1942. See also Philippe Burrin, *La France à l'heure allemande, 1940–1944* (Paris, 1995), 357.

15. Alexis Carrel, *L'Homme, cet inconnu* (Paris, 1935), trans. as *Man, the Unknown* (New York, 1938), esp. 272–322. See also Alain Drouard, *Une Inconnue des sciences sociales: La Fondation Alexis Carrel, 1941–45* (Paris, 1992) 271–78, and idem, *Alexis Carrel (1873–1944): De la mémoire à l'histoire* (Paris, 1995), 165–98.

16. Drouard, *Une Inconnue des sciences sociales*, 271–78. See also Andrés Horacio Reggiani, "Alexis Carrel, the Unknown: Eugenics and Population Research under Vichy," *French Historical Studies* 25 (2002): 331–56.

17. Ariès's early essays on demography, originally published in *Population*—"Attitudes devant la vie et devant la mort du XVIIe au XIXe siècle" (1949), "Sur les origines de la contraception en France" (1953), and "Contribution à l'histoire des pratiques contraceptives: Chaucer et Mme de Sévigné" (1954),—are reproduced in Ariès, *Essais de mémoire*, 309–28. On Ariès's gratitude to Sauvy for his support of his scholarship, see his preface to the 1979 edition of *Histoire des populations françaises*, 3, and his "Pourquoi la démographie française n'est pas restée malthusienne," *La Nation française*, 16 December 1959, 9.

18. Philippe Ariès, "Le Secret" (1978), in *Essais de mémoire*, 46–49.

19. In his article "Attitudes devant la vie et la mort du XVIIIe au XIXe siècle," 463, Ariès credits Adolphe Landry's *Traité de démographie* (Paris, 1945) for uncovering the "demographic revolution." On his debt to Landry, see also Ariès, *Histoire des populations françaises*, 2, 15, 358; and idem, "Pourquoi la démographie n'est pas restée malthusienne," 9.

20. Ariès, *Histoire des populations françaises*, 344–412.

21. Arch. Ariès, dossier "My Work," lecture (ca. 1976) on his path into history (manuscript).

22. Ariès, "Le Secret," 33–34, "Attitudes devant la vie et la mort du XVIIIe au XIXe siècle," *Population* 4 (1949), 463–70, "Sur les origines de la contraception en France," *Population* 7 (1953), 465–72, and "Le XIXe Siècle et la révolution des moeurs familiales," in *Renouveau des idées sur la famille*, ed. Robert Pringent (Paris, 1954), 111–18.

23. Ariès, *Historien du dimanche*, 90.

24. See Ariès, "Pourquoi la démographie française n'est pas restée malthusienne," 9, in which he cites the persistence of Vichyite attitudes in postwar France. He notes

the more enlightened attitudes of Sauvy and Landry, who helped transform the Fondation Alexis Carrel into a major center for demographic studies after the war. But also in *La Nation française* at about the same time, one sees the Vichyite natalist position reaffirmed by Lucien Gachon, "Les Français reviendraient-ils malthusiens?" 6 July 1960, 8–9.

25. Ariès, *Histoire des populations françaises*, 312–21, 344–72.

26. Ariès, "Le Secret," 34.

27. Ariès, *Histoire des populations françaises*, 343, 364, 366, 383. 411.

28. In 1954, Ariès refers to the "new mentality" attending family life, though not yet in the broad historiographical sense. See his "Familles du démi-siècle," in *Renouveau des ideés sur la famille*, ed. Pringent, 169.

29. Georges Duby dates the philosophical usage of the term to a reference by Emile Littré in 1877, and its historical conceptualization to Lucien Febvre in 1922: "Histoire des mentalités," in *L'Histoire et ses méthodes*, ed. Charles Samaran (Paris, 1961), 940–41. In his published writings, Ariès first used the term in a prewar newspaper article, "Le Nationalisme de Ronsard," *L'Etudiant français*, 10 February 1937, 2. His historiographical use of the term to define a field of history, however, dates from the postwar era.

30. See, for example, Gaston Bouthoul, *Les Mentalités* (Paris, 1952).

31. Robert Mandrou, *Introduction à la France moderne, 1500–1640* (Paris, 1961), 12–13, 321–50; idem, *La France aux XVIIe et XVIIIe siècles* (Paris, 1967), 270–90.

32. Philippe Ariès, "Interprétation pour une histoire des mentalités," in *La Prévention des naissances dans la famille*, ed. Hélène Bergues (Paris, 1960), 311–27.

33. See also Philippe Ariès, "La Famille d'Ancien Régime," *Revue des travaux de l'académie des sciences morales et politiques* 109 (4th series) (1956), 52–53.

34. Ariès, "Interprétation pour une histoire des mentalités," 325–26.

35. Philippe Ariès, *L'Enfant et la vie familiale sous l'Ancien Régime* (1960; Paris, 1971), 66.

36. Ariès, "Interprétation pour une histoire des mentalités," 323–25.

37. Ibid., 321–23. Only the first edition of *L'Enfant et la vie familiale sous l'Ancien Régime* contained the illustrations that are among his most important sources. Oddly, these were deleted from subsequent editions, including the English translation, *Centuries of Childhood* (New York, 1962).

38. Georges Duby, "La Rencontre avec Robert Mandrou et l'élaboration de la notion d'histoire des mentalités," in *Histoire sociale, sensibilités collectives et mentalités: Mélanges Robert Mandrou*, ed. anon (Paris, 1985), 33–35.

39. Duby, "Histoire des mentalités," in *L'Histoire et ses méthodes*, 937–66.

40. Ariès nonetheless notes that there was a "subterranean interest" in his work, esp. that on populations. *Historien du dimanche*, 118–19.

41. *L'Histoire sociale: Sources et méthodes* (Colloque de l'Ecole Normale Supérieure de Saint-Cloud [15–16 mai 1965]), ed. Ecole Normale Supérieure de Saint-Cloud (Paris, 1967): Albert Soboul, "Description et mesure en histoire sociale," 21–23; Ernest Labrousse, "Introduction," 4–5. The "third level" of research argument was reiterated by Pierre Chaunu, "Un Nouveau Champ pour l'histoire sérielle: Le quantitatif au troisième niveau," in *Méthodologie de l'histoire et des sciences humaines*, ed. anon (Toulouse, 1972), 1: 105–25, and passed thenceforth as the standard account of the integration of mentalities into academic historiography.

42. Typical of this historiography is Georges Lefebvre, *La Naissance de l'historio-graphic moderne* (Paris, 1971). This is not to imply that Annales historians openly endorsed the scheme of history affirmed by the academic historians of the revolutionary tradition, with its mildly Marxist leanings and expectations about the future of history. But they did not openly oppose them and tended to be noncommittal about the issue of progress. In effect, Annales historians undermined the grand narrative, but did not speak to the issue directly.

43. Michel Vovelle, "Histoire des mentalités, histoire des résistances, ou les prisons de longue durée," (1980), in his *Idéologie et mentalités* (Paris, 1985), 236–61.

44. For the proceedings of the debate between Ariès and Vovelle, see esp. the *Archives de sciences sociales des réligions* 39 (1975), 7–29, and *La Mort aujourd'hui* (Les Cahiers de Saint-Maximin), ed. Roger Chartier (Marseille, 1982).

45. Philippe Ariès, "Une Interpretation tendancieuse de l'histoire des mentalités," *Anthinéa* 3/2 (February 1973): 7–10.

46. Philippe Ariès, "Confessions d'un anarchiste de droite," *Contrepoint* no. 16 (1974): 97. Peter Laslett's *The World We Have Lost* (New York, 1965) is a prosaic empirical study that conveys little of the nostalgia its title suggests. Laslett and Ariès were in scholarly contact. See Laslett's forward to Philippe Ariès and André Begin, eds., *Western Sexuality: Practice and Precept in Past and Present Times* (Oxford, 1985), vii–ix. Ariès and Laslett first met at Yale University when they were both visiting the United States. In 1977, Laslett invited Ariès to lecture at Cambridge University. Arch. Ariès, Laslett to Ariès, 22 April 1971 and 2 December 1977.

47. Ariès, "Une Interprétation tendancieuse," 7–10. See also Philippe Ariès, "Le Régionalisme, perspective historique," *Critère* no. 24 (Winter 1979), 41–50.

48. Ariès, "Une Interprétation tendancieuse," 9, 8.

49. Ariès, "Confessions d'un anarchiste de droite," 87–99.

50. Philippe Ariès, "Le Secret," 29–43.

51. Ariès may have been encouraged in this formulation of the problem by his reading of recent "microhistories" by Natalie Davis, Carlo Ginzburg, and Emmanuel Le Roy Ladurie, who used judicial documents to extrapolate about the mentalities of the oral cultures they described. For his commentary on their work, see his "Culture orale et culture écrite," in *Le Christianisme populaire: Les dossiers de l'histoire*, ed. Bernard Plongeron and Robert Pannet (Paris, 1976), 227–40.

52. This was the approach of Frances Yates, who studied largely forgotten sixteenth-century intellectual movements with an eye to their diversity. She shows how many intellectuals in that era were still caught up in an older, Aristotelian science that looked for correspondences between the signs of nature and the secrets of the universe. She is best known for her study of mnemonic schemes in the hermetic science of the Renaissance, *The Art of Memory* (Chicago, 1966).

53. Despite the obvious correspondences, Ariès does not mention the similarities between his conception of mentalities and Sigmund Freud's conception of the psyche. Indeed, Ariès's conception of the "secret" might be construed as analogous to the Freudian "ego," which limits the filtration of the unconscious into conscious life. Trained in the classicism of the Action Française, he had long professed to be suspicious of psychoanalytic theory. Only in a few late-life articles did he acknowledge Freud, and then to contextualize his theory within the intellectual life of the late nineteenth century. Ariès questioned whether Freud's conceptions were applicable to an earlier age.

See Jacques Mousseau, "The Family, Prison of Love: A Conversation with Philippe Ariès," *Psychology Today* (August 1975), 56.

54. Ariès's interest in secret societies dates from his days as a student at the Sorbonne, when he took a course on the French Revolution with Georges Lefebvre and challenged his view of the Terror with references to Augustin Cochin, who wrote about the role of secret societies during the Revolution. Philippe Ariès, "Réflexions sur la Contre-Révolution (III), La Fronde Vendéenne," *L'Etudiant français*, 25 February 1938, 1–2; cf. Ariès, *Historien du dimanche*, 54–55.

55. Ariès, "Le Secret," 33–34. It is worth noting that Ariès delivered this lecture on secrecy not long after the passage of legislation liberalizing sexual practices; the law legalizing contraception was enacted in 1967 (Neuwirth law) and that on abortion in 1974 (Veil law).

56. Philippe Ariès, "Histoire des mentalités," in *La Nouvelle Histoire*, ed. Jacques Le Goff, Roger Chartier, and Jacques Revel (Paris, 1978), 402–23. His pilot study for this article, "L'Histoire des mentalités," typescript of a lecture for the symposium "Blueprint for Interdisciplinary Regional History, 7–10 September 1977, at the University of Western Ontario, London, may be found among his papers in the Arch. Aries.

57. Ariès, "Histoire des mentalités," 416–17, 420–22.

58. Ibid., 403–6.

59. Ibid., 409–10.

60. Ibid., 410–11, 419–20.

61. Georges Duby, *L'Histoire Continue* (Paris, 1991), 120–24.

62. Herman Lebovics, *True France* (Ithaca, N.Y., 1992), 6, 162, 189.

63. Ariès, "Histoire des mentalités," 423.

64. Roger Chartier, "L'Histoire culturelle," in *Une Ecole pour les sciences sociales*, ed. Jacques Revel and Nathan Wachtel (Paris, 1996), 73–92.

65. Jacques Le Goff, "Les Mentalités: Une histoire ambiguë," in *Faire de l'histoire*, ed. Jacques Le Goff and Pierre Nora (Paris, 1974), 3: 76–94.

66. Philippe Ariès, "Pour une histoire de la vie privée," in *Histoire de la vie privée*, ed. Roger Chartier (Paris, 1986), 3: 1–11.

67. Philippe Ariès and Georges Duby, eds., *Histoire de la vie privée*, 5 vols. (Paris, 1985–87). For Ariès's influence on the project, see especially Gérard Vincent, "Secrets de l'histoire et histoire du secret," 5: 157–99. I am struck by how faithfully Vincent follows up on Ariès's ideas, notably his use of the concept of secrecy as the essential organizational principle of his study.

68. Cf. Jean Bouvier and Dominique Julia, "A quoi pensent les historiens?" in *Passés recomposés: Champs et chantiers de l'histoire*, ed. Bouvier and Julia (Paris, 1995), 44–45.

69. Philippe Ariès, "Le Temps de l'Histoire" (1983), in *Essais de mémoire*, 57.

70. Philippe Ariès, "Les Ages de la vie," *Contrepoint* 1 (May 1970): 273.

Chapter 6

1. The first edition, by Plon, included illustrations. Subsequent editions, including the American one by Random House in 1962 and the now standard one by Seuil in 1973, excised them, and abridged the text as well.

2. Ariès expanded on this discussion a few years later with a long essay titled "Problèmes de l'éducation," in *La France et les français*, ed. Michel François (Paris,

1972), 871–961. See also his "L'Education familiale," in *Histoire mondiale de l'éducation*, ed. Gaston Mialaret and Jean Vial (Paris, 1981), 2: 233–45.

3. Philippe Ariès, "Remarques sur la conception traditionaliste de la famille," *La Nation française*, 7 August 1957, 6–7(hereafter cited as *NF*). The America historian Christopher Lasch later popularized the expression by making it the title of a book, *Haven in a Heartless World: The Family Besieged* (New York, 1977).

4. Michelle Perrot, "The Family Triumphant," in *A History of Private Life*, ed. Michelle Perrot (Cambridge, Mass.,1990), 4: 107–8.

5. Frédéric Le Play, *L'Organisation de la famille selon le vrai modèle signalé par l'histoire* (Paris, 1871). For Ariès on Le Play, see his "Remarques sur la conception traditionaliste de la famille," *NF*, 7 August 1957, 6–7.

6. Jean-Louis Flandrin, "Enfance et société," *Annales ESC* 19 (1964): 322–29. Ariès notes the significance of Jan Hendrik van den Berg's *Metabletica* (1961) in "Naïves Hirondelles" *NF*, 25 November 1964, 1, 14. On the Ariès/van den Berg comparison, see Judith Hokke, "Philippe Ariès en de gezinsgeschiedenis," *Volkscultuur* 5 (1988): 50–63.

7. Sterling Fishman, "Changing the History of Childhood: A Modest Proposal," *Journal of Psychohistory* 13 (1985): 69–70.

8. John R. Gillis, *Youth and History* (New York, 1981); Alan B. Spitzer, *The French Generation of 1820* (Princeton, 1987).

9. Erik H. Erikson, *Childhood and Society*, 2d ed. (1950; New York, 1963), 247–74.

10. Philippe Ariès, *NF*: "Une Jeunesse conformiste et réfractaire," 16 October 1957, 1–2; "Démobilisation de la démocratie," 5 August 1959, 7; "L'Ecole ne remplace pas la famille," 20 January 1960, 1, 3; and "Naïve Hirondelles," 25 November 1964, 1, 14.

11. Philippe Ariès, "Confessions d'un anarchiste de droite," *Contrepoint* no. 16 (1974): 87–99; idem, "At the Point of Origin," *Yale French Studies* 43 (1969): 15–23.

12. Lawrence Stone, "The Massacre of the Innocents," *New York Review of Books*, 14 November 1974, 25–31.

13. Lawrence Stone, *The Family, Sex, and Marriage in England, 1500–1800* (New York, 1977), 149–80.

14. In a letter written in 1980, Stone was more conciliatory, noting that he now understood Ariès's interpretation better. Archives de l'Ecole des Hautes Etudes, Archives Ariès (hereafter Arch. Ariès), Stone to Ariès, 6 June 1980, also Stone to Ariès, 15 November 1983, in which he invited him to give a lecture at Princeton.

15. Adrian Wilson, "The Infancy of the History of Childhood: An Appraisal of Philippe Ariès," *History and Theory* 19 (1980): 132–53.

16. See the discussion of pragmatism vs. objectivity in Peter Novick, *That Noble Dream* (Cambridge, U.K., 1986), 273–74, 374–75; also David Harlan, *The Degradation of American History* (Chicago, 1997), 15–31.

17. Richard T. Vann, "The Youth of *Centuries of Childhood*," *History and Theory* 21 (1982): 279–97, provides a useful analysis of scholarly reviews of this work across two decades.

18. Ibid., 296.

19. Linda A. Pollock, "Parent-Child Relations," in *The History of the European Family: Family Life in Early Modern Times, 1500–1789*, ed. David I. Kertzer and Marzio Barbagli (New Haven, Conn., 2001), 1: 218.

20. Steven Ozment, *Ancestors: The Loving Family in Old Europe* (Cambridge, Mass., 2001), 21.

21. Steven Ozment, *When Fathers Ruled: Family Life in Reformation Europe* (Cambridge, Mass., 1983), and *Flesh and Spirit: A Study of Private Life in Early Modern Germany* (New York, 1999).

22. Ozment, *Ancestors*, 104–12.

23. Ariès, *Centuries of Childhood*, 375.

24. Nicholas Orme, *Medieval Children* (New Haven, Conn., 2001), 9.

25. Pollock, "Parent-Child Relations," 219.

26. Emily Eakin, "Did Cradles Always Rock?" *New York Times,* 30 June 2001, A15, 17; Eamon Duffy, "The Cradle Will Rock," *New York Review of Books,* 19 December 2002, 61.

27. Duffy, "The Cradle Will Rock," 61.

28. Ariès addressed the issue of permanence vs. change in human nature in a late-life essay, "La Sensibilité au changement dans la problématique de l'historiographie contemporaine," in *Y a-t-il une nouvelle histoire?,* ed. Emmanuel Le Roy Ladurie and Gilbert Gadoffre (Loches-en-Touraine, 1980), 17–18. He acknowledged a deep genetic structure to human nature, but insisted on the reality of changing mores and sensibilities. As a historian, he saw his task as one of exposing these differences as they develop over time.

29. Eakin, "Did Cradles Always Rock?" A15, 17.

30. In his *The Disappearance of Childhood* (New York, 1982), 155 n. 2, Neil Postman quotes Lawrence Stone's assertion that between 1971 and 1976 more than nine hundred books and articles were published on the topic of childhood and family, in comparison with only ten or fifteen a year during the 1930s.

31. Emmanuel Le Roy Ladurie, "Philippe Ariès: Un historien en réaction," newspaper article, 1997. Arch. Ariès. About the same time, Le Roy Ladurie published a critical edition of the Platter memoir on which Ariès's insight into changing attitudes toward the education of children in the early modern era had been based. Le Roy Ladurie, ed., *Le Voyage de Thomas Platter, 1595–1599,* vol. 2 of *Le Siècle des Platter* (Paris, 1995).

32. Philippe Ariès, *Un Historien du dimanche,* ed. Michel Winock (Paris, 1980), 134–35.

33. Ibid., 133–34. Ariès reviewed Braudel's work in *La Table ronde* no. 26 (February 1950): 147–52.

34. Philippe Ariès, "Interprétation pour une histoire des mentalités," in *La Prévention des naissances dans la famille,* ed. Hélène Bergues (Paris, 1960), 311–27.

35. Ariès, *Historien du dimanche,* 136.

36. Philippe Ariès, *Histoire des populations françaises* (1948; Paris, 1971), 344–72.

37. Philippe Ariès, "La Famille et ses âges," *Cahiers de pastorale familiale* (January–March 1956): 11–18, and "La Famille d'Ancien Régime," *Revue des travaux de l'académie des sciences morales et politiques* 109 (1956): 46–55.

38. William L. Langer, "The Next Assignment," *America Historical Review* 63 (1958): 283–304.

39. See Peter Loewenberg, "Psychohistory," in *The Past before Us,* ed. Michael Kammen (Ithaca, N.Y., 1980), 408–32; Bruce Mazlish, "Reflections on the State of Psychohistory," *Psychohistory Review* 5 (1977): 3–11; Richard L. Schoenwald, "Using Psychohistory in History: A Review Essay," *Historical Methods Newsletter* 7 (1973): 9–24.

40. David E. Stannard, *Shrinking History: On Freud and the Failure of Psychohistory* (Oxford, 1980).

41. Erik H. Erikson, *Young Man Luther: A Study in Psychoanalysis and History* (New York, 1958).

42. David Hunt, *Parents and Children in History: The Psychology of Family Life in Early Modern France* (New York, 1970), 11–51.

43. Patrick H. Hutton, "The Psychohistory of Erik Erikson from the Perspective of Collective Mentalities," *Psychohistory Review* 12 (1983): 18–25.

44. Peter Gay, "Annales of Childhood," *Saturday Review,* 23 March 1963, 73–74.

45. Saul Friedländer, *History and Psychoanalysis,* trans. Susan Suleiman (New York, 1978), 100–119.

46. Edward Shorter, *The Making of the Modern Family* (New York, 1975); Lasch, *Haven in a Heartless World.*

47. The third was the *Psychohistory Review.*

48. Postman, *The Disappearance of Childhood,* xii–xiii, 3–5, 71, 98, 120, 126, 134.

49. Ibid., 143–44.

50. Ibid., 155 n. 2.

51. Roger Chartier, "L'Amitié de l'histoire," preface to *Le Temps de l'Histoire,* by Philippe Ariès, rev. ed. (Paris, 1986), 9–31, and "Avant-propos," in *Essais de mémoire,* by Philippe Ariès (Paris, 1993), 7–24.

52. Roger Chartier, *On the Edge of the Cliff: History, Language, and Practices,* trans. Lydia G. Cochrane (Baltimore, 1997), 107–23.

53. Michel Foucault, "Le Souci de la vérité," *Le Nouvel Observateur,* 2 February 1984, 56–57.

54. Hayden White, *Metahistory* (Baltimore, 1973), 26, 33, 433–34.

55. On historical writing as a form of moral reflection, see Harlan, *The Degradation of American History,* 105–26.

Chapter 7

1. Philippe Ariès, *Histoire des populations françaises et de leurs attitudes devant la vie depuis le XVIIIe siècle* (1948; Paris, 1971), 344–98.

2. Interview with Philippe Brissaud, 19 April 1996 (Paris).

3. Ariès, *Histoire des populations françaises,* 374–98.

4. Daniel Halévy, *Trois Epreuves: 1814, 1871, 1940* (Paris, 1941), 127–73.

5. Philippe Ariès, *Un Historien du dimanche,* ed. Michel Winock (Paris, 1980), 74–76.

6. Ariès, *Histoire des populations,* 322–43; *L'Enfant et la vie familiale sous l'Ancien Régime* (1960; Paris, 1973), 176–86, 306–16.

7. Philippe Ariès, "A l'heure où les camps se retranchent," *La Nation française,* 20 December 1961, 1, 8.

8. This was the article for which Ariès was arrested. He used Vidal-Naquet's article on the same topic in the journal *L'Esprit* to persuade the judge to dismiss the charge. Ariès, *Historien du dimanche,* 159.

9. Archives de l'Ecole des Hautes Etudes, Archives Ariès, Pierre Vidal-Naquet to Ariès, 22 July 1964, 14 November 1973, 2 December 1977, 13 May 1980.

10. Baltimore, 1974. A French version, augmented with related essays, was published as *Essais sur l'histoire de la mort en Occident du Moyen Age à nos jours* (Paris, 1975).

11. Ariès was fascinated with this conception of tamed death early on. In one of his newspaper articles while a student at the Sorbonne before the war, he cited the tableau of such an edifying deathbed scene from Fyodor Dostoyevski, *The Brothers Karamazov*. Philippe Ariès, "La Terre promise," *L'Etudiant français*, 10 January 1938, 3. His interest at the time may have been piqued by his witness of the ceremonies attending the death of his grandparents in the 1930s. See his reference in his *L'Homme devant la mort* (Paris, 1977), 2: 282.

12. One wonders how Ariès would have interpreted the renewed compassion for the dying shown in the hospice movement together with the growing sympathy for euthanasia, phenomena that have become prominent since his own death.

13. On Ariès's critique of the illusion of progress in contemporary culture, see esp. his "Une Interprétation tendancieuse de l'histoire des mentalités," *Anthinéa* 3/2 (February 1973): 7–10; and "Confessions d'un anarchiste de droite," *Contrepoint* no. 16 (1974): 87–99.

14. Henry Rousso, *Le Syndrome de Vichy: De 1944 à nos jours* (Paris, 1990).

15. Michel Vovelle, *Les Aventures de la raison: Entretiens avec Richard Figuier* (Paris, 1989), 11–12; Georg Lichtheim, *Marxism and the French Left* (New York, 1966), 69–111.

16. Vovelle, *Les Aventures*, 11–14. For Vovelle's appreciation of Labrousse's role, see his article "La Mémoire d'Ernest Labrousse," in a special issue devoted to him in *Annales historiques de la Révolution française* (hereafter *AHRF*) no. 276 (April–June 1989): 99–107. See also Labrousse's interesting personal commentary in an interview with Christophe Charle, "Entretiens avec Ernest Labrousse," *Actes de la recherche en sciences sociales* no. 32–33 (April–June 1980): 111–25.

17. Michel Vovelle, "Pourquoi nous sommes encore Robespierristes," *AHRF* no. 274 (October–December 1988): 498–506; idem, "La Galerie des ancêtres" (1988), in his *Combats pour la Révolution française* (Paris, 1993), 13–23.

18. Vovelle, *Les Aventures*, 19–22; idem, "Histoire des mentalités, histoire des résistances, ou les prisons de longue durée" (1980), in his *Idéologies et mentalités* (Paris, 1985), 236–61.

19. Vovelle is thus a good example of the way intellectuals who remained loyal to the Marxist vision redirected their work from social and economic to cultural and religious topics. His intellectual progress thus parallels that of the philosopher Henri Lefebvre as well as that of Goldmann, and Althusser. Vovelle, *Les Aventures*, 14–15, 18–22, 27.

20. Two such prominent historians were Emmanuel Le Roy Ladurie, author of the best-selling *Montaillou* (1976), and François Furet, acclaimed for his revisionist history of the French Revolution. See Le Roy Ladurie, *Paris-Montpellier* (Paris, 1982), and Furet, *Histoire de la Révolution et la révolution dans l'histoire* (Paris, 1994), personal accounts of their repudiation of their youthful Marxism.

21. Michel Vovelle, "L'Historiographie de la Révolution française à la veille du bicentenaire," *AHRF* no. 272 (April–June 1988): 113–26, and no. 273 (July–September 1988): 307–15.

22. Michel Vovelle, *L'Irrésistible Ascension de Joseph Sec, bourgeois d'Aix* (Aix-en-Provence, 1975).

23. Vovelle, *Les Aventures*, 40.

24. Michel Vovelle, "Idéologies et mentalités: Une clarification nécessaire" (1980), in *Idéologies et mentalités*, 5–17; idem, "Jalons pour une histoire des mentalités sous la Révolution," in his *La Mentalité révolutionnaire* (Paris, 1985), 9–16.

25. Michel Vovelle, *Piété baroque et déchristianisation en Provence au XVIIIe siècle* (1973; Paris, 1978); and with Gaby Vovelle, *Vision de la mort et de l'au-delà en Provence* (Paris, 1970).

26. Michel Vovelle, *Mourir autrefois: Attitudes collectives devant la mort aux XVIIe et XVIIIe siècles* (Paris, 1974).

27. Michel Vovelle, *La Mort et l'Occident de 1300 à nos jours* (Paris, 1983), 7–12. See also his essay on method, "L'Histoire et la longue durée," in *La Nouvelle Histoire*, ed. Jacques Le Goff (1978; Paris, 1988), 96–104.

28. Vovelle, *Mourir autrefois*, 81–137.

29. Ibid., 183–204.

30. Ibid., 39–53, 141–48, 231–32.

31. Ibid., 233–34; *La Mort et l'Occident*, 33, 651–70.

32. See Michel Vovelle, "Albert Soboul, Historien de la société," *AHRF* no. 250 (October–December 1982): 547–53.

33. The proceedings of the debate between Ariès and Vovelle at Strasbourg are found in the *Archives de sciences sociales des réligions* 39 (1975): 7–29; those for the conference at Saint-Maximin in *La Mort aujourd'hui* (Les Cahiers de Saint-Maximin), ed. Roger Chartier (Marseille, 1982).

34. In comparing the scholarship of Ariès and Vovelle on attitudes toward death, see also Robert Darnton, *The Kiss of Lamourette* (New York, 1990), 268–90.

35. Michel Vovelle, "Les Attitudes devant la mort, front actuel de l'histoire des mentalités," *Archives de sciences sociales des réligions* 39 (1975): 23–24.

36. Ariès, *L'Homme devant la mort*, 2: 9–26.

37. Michel Vovelle, "Y a-t-il un inconscient collectif?" *Pensée* no. 205 (May–June 1979): 125–36.

38. Philippe Ariès, "Inconscient collectif et idées claires," *Anthinéa* no.8 (August–September 1975): 3–4; idem, "Table ronde sur la communication de Roger Chartier," in *La Mort aujourd'hui*, 127–30.

39. Philippe Ariès, "Du livre (à paraître) de Michel Vovelle: 'La mort en Occident'," in *La Mort aujourd'hui*, 159–68.

40. Vovelle, *La Mort et l'Occident*, 25–26. See also his historiographical reflection, "Sur la mort" (1978), in *Idéologies et mentalités*, 101–19.

41. Philippe Ariès, "Vie et mort des civilisations," in *La Mort, un terme ou un commencement?*, ed. Christian Chabanis (Paris, 1982), 103–18; idem, "La Sensibilité au changement dans la problématique de l'historiographie contemporaine," in *Certitudes et incertitudes de l'histoire*, ed. Gilbert Gadoffre (Paris, 1987), 169–75.

42. François Hartog, "Temps et histoire, 'Comment écrire l'histoire de France?'," *Annales HSS* no. 6 (November–December 1995): 1219–36; Lutz Niethammer, *Posthistoire* (London, 1992), 17–19.

43. On the Ariès/Vovelle debate, see also Pierre Chaunu, *L'Historien en cet instant* (Paris, 1985), 224–42.

44. On Vovelle's role on the bicentennial committee, see the detailed account by Steven Laurence Kaplan, *Farewell, Revolution: The Historians' Feud, France, 1789–1989* (Ithaca, N.Y., 1995), 144–92.

45. On the centennial, see Pascal Ory, "La Preuve par 89," in *Les Lieux de mémoire*, ed. Pierre Nora (Paris, 1984–92), 1: 523–60; and Steven D. Kale, "The Countercentenary of 1889," *Historical Reflections* 23 (1997): 1–28.

46. François Furet, *Penser la Révolution française* (Paris, 1976).

47. François Furet, "Faut-il célébrer le bicentenaire de la Révolution française?" *Histoire* 52 (1983): 71–77.

48. Kaplan, *Farewell, Revolution*, 12–24. See also Vovelle's reply to Furet, "La Révolution est-elle terminée?" (1979), in *Combats pour la Révolution française*, 87–94.

49. Ariès, "Confessions d'un anarchiste de droite," 87–99; idem, "La Ressemblance" (1980), in *Essais de mémoire*, ed. Roger Chartier (Paris, 1993), 59–67. See also Hartog, "Temps et histoire, 'Comment écrire l'histoire de France?'," 1219–36.

50. Michel Vovelle, "Réflexions sur l'interprétation révisionniste de la Révolution française" (1990), in *Combats pour la Révolution française*, 99–100.

51. Nora has since been criticized for having adopted a mournful approach to French history. See Steven Englund, "The Ghost of Nation Past," *Journal of Modern History* 64 (1992): 299–320. But one might argue that Nora was studying why the French past was no longer mourned as it had been in the rivalry of royalists and republicans over the fate of the revolutionary tradition. If anything is to be mourned, he suggests, it is the ways of modern historiography, marked by the death of the grand narrative. Pierre Nora, "Comment écrire l'histoire de France," in *Lieux de mémoire*, 3: 11–32.

52. The legend was dramatized by Maurice Maeterlinck in a play (1892) and by Claude Debussy in an opera (1902).

53. A copy of the death certificate (dated 29 April 1964) for Yvonne Ariès, who died on 27 April 1964, was kindly given to me by James Friguglietti.

54. Ariès, *L'Homme devant la mort*, 2: 282. Ariès borrowed the image from Vladimir Jankélévitch, *La Mort* (Paris, 1966), 246, 282. On Ariès's use of the image of the death of Mélisande, cf. Albert van der Zeijden, "Geschiedschrijver van de dood," *Volkscultuur* 5 (1988): 64–82.

55. Ariès, "Les Attitudes devant la mort," 73, 75.

56. Ariès, *L'Homme devant la mort*, 2: 324.

Chapter 8

1. Raoul Girardet, *Singulièrement libre: Entretiens* (Paris, 1990), 41–42.

2. Philippe Ariès, *Un Historien du dimanche*, ed. Michel Winock (Paris, 1980), 187–219.

3. Ibid., 191–93.

4. Ibid., 194–96.

5. Ibid., 197.

6. Philippe Ariès, *La Nation française*: "Les Poids d'ombre," 23 October 1963, 1, 12; "Le Sentiment religieux dans la jeunesse," 11 February 1958, 6–7.

7. Ariès, *Historien du dimanche*, 190, 199; idem, *La Nation française*: "Un Regard sur le monde," 16 January 1957, 4–5; "Quelle Société?" 11 March 1959, 1, 5; "Pour une meilleure intelligence entre catholiques," 17 October 1962, 1, 14;

8. *Historien du dimanche*, 200–201.

9. Philippe Ariès, "La Politique," in *Cinquante Ans de pensée Catholique*, ed. Emile Blanchet (Paris, 1955), 116–27. On Ariès's views on Dupront, see also "Le Fond des temps," *La Nation française*, 21 October 1964, 1, 3.

10. Philippe Ariès, "Religion populaire et réformes religieuses," in *Religion populaire et réforme liturgique*, ed. Jean-Yves Hameline (Paris, 1975), 84.

11. On Ariès's interest in Ginzburg's work, see his "Culture orale et culture écrite," in *Le Christianisme populaire*, ed. Bernard Plongeron and Robert Pannet (Paris, 1976), 231–32.

12. Philippe Ariès, "Le Monde moderne sans le Christ," *La Nation française*, 14 October 1959, 6–7.

13. Ariès, "Religion populaire," 97.

14. Philippe Ariès, *Le Temps de l'Histoire* (Monaco, 1954), 11, 16, 22.

15. Ibid., 20–23; Ariès, *Historien du dimanche*, 51–57.

16. Ariès, *Le Temps de l'Histoire*, 10–11.

17. Ibid., quote, 23, also 36–39, 315–16.

18. Ibid., 61–87.

19. Ibid., 22–24.

20. Ariès, *Historien du dimanche*, 219.

21. Ibid., 202–3, 211.

22. Ibid., 219.

23. Ibid., 218.

24. Philippe Ariès, "Une Interprétation tendancieuse de l'histoire des mentalités," *Anthinéa* 3/2 (February 1973): 7–10.

25. On Mounier's life, intellectual formation, and philosophy of personalism, see esp. John Hellman, *Emmanuel Mounier and the New Catholic Left, 1930–1950* (Toronto, 1981).

26. On Mounier and the politics of personalism, see David Schalk, *The Spectrum of Political Engagement* (Princeton, 1979), 17–25; Zeev Sternhell, *Neither Left nor Right* (Princeton, 1996), 215–21; and Seth D. Armus, "The Eternal Enemy: Emmanuel Mounier's *Esprit* and French Anti-Americanism," *French Historical Studies* 24 (2001): 271–80.

27. Emmanuel Mounier, *Personalism* (Notre Dame, Ind., 1952), xx–xxii.

28. Emmanuel Mounier, *Communisme, anarchie et personnalisme* (Paris, 1966), 171–72.

29. One wonders what Ariès was doing there at a time of such crisis in central Europe. In his autobiography, he alludes cryptically to his trip as a shared journey with historians and geographers "with views similar to our own, without being a doctrinaire group." *Historien du dimanche*, 69. See also Philippe Ariès, *L'Etudiant français*, "Le Problème national en Autriche," 8 June 1936, 2–4; "L'Anschluss et ses répercussions sur la politique anglaise et italienne," 25 March 1938, 1–2.

30. Philippe Ariès, *L'Etudiant français*: "Le Roi arbitre et les libertés," public lecture delivered at the Institut de l'Action Française and published 10 May 1937, 2–4; "Le Pouvoir politique," January 1939, 1; "La Doctrine: L'Hérédité," February 1939, 1.

31. Philippe Ariès, "Un Aspect de la pensée de Charles Maurras," *L'Etudiant français*, 25 November 1936, 1.

32. Ariès, *Historien du dimanche*, 41–42, 63–71.

33. Ibid., 60–61.

34. Ariès, *Le Temps de l'Histoire*, 9–16; Alison Browning, "Une Conversation avec Philippe Ariès," *Cadmos* no. 12 (Winter 1980): 14–15.

35. François Leger, "Philippe Ariès: L'Histoire d'un historien," *Revue universelle des faits et des idées* 65 (1986): 65.

36. Ariès, *Le Temps de l'Histoire*, 47.

37. Philippe Ariès, "Journal de l'Estoile: Pour le règne de Henri III," in *La Fin de la Ligue (1589–1593)*, ed. François Leger (Paris, 1944), 159–75.

38. Philippe Ariès, *Les Traditions sociales dans les pays de France* (Paris, 1943), 13–15, 38, 155–59.

39. Regional geography was then much in vogue, and for his book Ariès drew upon studies by Georges Lizerand, Pierre Deffontaines, Marc Bloch, André Sigfried, and Yann Morvan Goblet. Goblet's *La Formation des régions: Introduction à une géographie régionale de France* (Paris, 1942) is the source for Ariès's discussion of "new industrial zones."

40. Ariès, *Les Traditions sociales*, 109–23.

41. Ibid., 155–59.

42. Ariès, "Journal de l'Estoile," 159–62.

43. Ibid., 162–72.

44. Ibid., 172. Here we see Ariès's intuition about a method that historians of mentalities would come to employ successfully a generation later. In an article of the mid-1970s, he notes the skill with which Natalie Davis, Carlo Ginzburg, and Emmanuel Le Roy Ladurie defined the field through their capacity to interpolate judicial documents written by highly educated jurists as a means of seeing into the culture of ordinary people who conceptualized their understanding of the world in a different idiom. See Ariès, "Culture orale et culture écrite," 230–31.

45. Ariès, "Journal de l'Estoile," 159–60, 172–75.

46. See Peter Novick, *The Resistance versus Vichy:The Purge of Collaborators in Liberated France* (New York, 1968), 68–72, 126–30, 158–64, 186–88.

47. Ariès, *Historien du dimanche*, 100–102; François Brigneau, *Mon Après-guerre* (1966; Paris, 1985), 31–32, 48–51.

48. Ariès, *Le Temps de l'Histoire*, 40, 46, 61–64.

49. Philippe Ariès, "Le Régionalisme, perspective historique," *Critère* no. 24 (Winter 1979): 45.

50. From the outset, Ariès's love of history was closely tied to his love of provincial French culture. Ariès, *Historien du dimanche*, 46–48.

51. Ibid., 47; Ariès, "Culture orale et culture écrite," 238.

52. Ariès, "Le Régionalisme," 47; "Culture orale et culture écrite," 239–40.

53. Philippe Ariès, "La Nostalgie du roi" (1980), in *Essais de mémoire*, ed. Roger Chartier (Paris, 1993), 194–96. At the time of François Mitterrand's inauguration as president of the Fifth Republic, Ariès reaffirmed his royalist political convictions in an anonymous interview, "Entretien avec Philippe Ariès," *Je Suis Français* (1982), typescript, Archives Ariès, Archives de l'Ecole des Hautes Etudes en Sciences Sociales.

54. See Lynn Hunt, *The Family Romance of the French Revolution* (Berkeley, Calif., 1992), 151–91.

55. Philippe Ariès, "Une Fraternité secrète," *La Nation française*, 18 September 1963, 1, 11.

56. Philippe Ariès, "Réflexions sur l'histoire de l'homosexualité," *Communications* 35 (1982): 63.

Chapter 9

1. The name Primerose was a diminutive for Marie Rose Lascazas de Saint Martin. The Ariès were married 10 April 1947 in Toulouse. Curriculum vitae of Philippe Ariès,

1978, Archives Ariès, Archives de l'Ecole des Hautes Etudes en Sciences Sociales (hereafter Arch. Ariès).

2. Philippe Ariès, *Un Historien du dimanche*, ed. Michel Winock (Paris, 1980), 121–23, 132–33.

3. It was meant to illustrate Philippe's *L'Homme devant la mort* (Paris, 1977), the major work of his later years.

4. Philippe Ariès, *Images de l'homme devant la mort* (Paris, 1983), dedication.

5. François Leger, "Deux livres d'histoire sociale," *Présent*, 3 July 1993.

6. Raoul Girardet, *Singulièrement libre* (Paris, 1990), 42.

7. François Leger, "La Mort de l'historien de la mort," *Aspects de la France*, 16 February 1984, 13.

8. Philippe Ariès, "La Famille hier et aujourd'hui," *Contrepoint* no. 11 (July 1973): 96–97, "D'hier à aujourd'hui, d'une civilisation à l'autre," in *Couples et familles dans la société d'aujourd'hui*, ed. Semaine Sociale de France (Lyon, 1973), 124–26.

9. Paris: Plon, 1960, republished in an abridged edition by Seuil in 1973; translated by Robert Baldick as *Centuries of Childhood* (New York: Random House, 1962).

10. Philippe Ariès, "Confessions d'un anarchiste de droite," *Contrepoint* no. 16 (1974): 97.

11. François Dosse, *L'Histoire en miettes: Des Annales à la Nouvelle Histoire* (Paris, 1987), 97, 201, 218–19, Hervé Coutau-Bégarie, *Le Phénomène nouvelle histoire* (Paris, 1989), 11, 160–62, 350–52; Gérard Noiriel, *Sur la "crise" de l'histoire* (Paris, 1996), 298–99. Also of interest is a press clipping of a review by Emmanuel Le Roy Ladurie, "Philippe Ariès: Un Historien en réaction," 1997, Arch. Ariès, which characterizes him as an eccentric genius.

12. Documents relating to Ariès's election to the EHESS may be found in dossier "Ariès Philippe, directeur d'études cumulant," Arch. Ariès. These include correspondence between Ariès and François Furet (then president of the EHESS), 1978–82, a report on Ariès's candidacy by Pierre Nora, 1978, and Ariès's curriculum vitae, 1978. Under the terms of his appointment to the EHESS, Ariès proposed a plan for his seminar centered on three themes: attitudes toward death, the relationship between the family and the city, and the family and sexuality. Dossier "Ariès Philippe," supporting documents to the official recommendation of his appointment by François Furet, 14 June 1978, Arch. Ariès.

13. In 1987, the Centre d'Information et de Documentation en Agronomie des Régions Chaudes (CIDARC) that Ariès had directed was relocated in Montpellier. In September 1994, it was renamed the Centre d'Information et de Documentation Philippe Ariès. See the information brochure, "Philippe Ariès, un documentaliste pas comme les autres," for the Centre de Coopération Internationale en Recherche Agronomique pour le Développement, 1994, Arch. Ariès.

14. See the bibliography compiled by Bruno Somalvico, appended to Philippe Ariès, *Essais de mémoire*, ed. Roger Chartier (Paris, 1993), 363–72.

15. Originally published as Philippe Ariès and Georges Duby, eds., *Histoire de la vie privée*, 5 vols. (Paris, 1985–87), subsequently translated by Arthur Goldhammer as *A History of Private Life*, 5 vols. (Cambridge, Mass., 1987–91).

16. Esp. insightful is David Hunt, *Parents and Children in History* (New York, 1970), 27–51, who draws a comparison between Ariès and Erik Erikson.

17. Ariès, *Historien du dimanche*, 138; Elizabeth Hall, "A Sketch of Philippe Ariès, Man on Hobby Horseback," *Psychology Today*, August 1975, 55.

18. Philippe Ariès, *Western Attitudes toward Death*, trans. Patricia Ranum (Baltimore: Johns Hopkins University Press, 1974), provides his first synthesis of his research on this subject. An augmented French edition was subsequently published as *Essais sur l'histoire de la mort en Occident du Moyen Age à nos jours* (Paris, 1975).

19. Ariès, *Historien du dimanche*, 177–79.

20. See Edward Shorter, *The Making of the Modern Family* (New York, 1975), 169–70, 192. There was some correspondence between them, Arch. Ariès, Shorter to Ariès, 10 January 1978. Ariès discussed Shorter's work in his new preface to his 1979 edition of *Histoire des populations françaises*, 7–8, noting Shorter's distinction between middle-class and popular sexual revolutions, whereas he had identified only one.

21. In a late-life observation on the reviews of *L'Enfant et la vie familiale*, Ariès notes that most critics neglected or were unable to see the balance between continuity and change that he presented. *Historien du dimanche*, 136–37.

22. For Ariès's late-life reflection on *Centuries of Childhood*, see Michel Winock, "L'Enfant à travers les siècles: Entretien avec Philippe Ariès," *L'Histoire* no. 19 (January 1980): 85–87.

23. Philippe Ariès, "Sur l'enfant," unpublished lecture prepared for a UNESCO colloquium at Paris, 17–19 February 1981, 23 pp., Arch. Ariès.

24. For his first thoughts on the contemporary family, see Ariès, "La Famille hier et aujourd'hui," 93–96. Also, Jacques Mousseau, "The Family, Prison of Love: A Conversation with Philippe Ariès," *Psychology Today*, August 1975, 53–58.

25. Philippe Ariès, "The Family and the City," *Daedalus* 106 (1977): 232–35; *Historien du dimanche*, 116. Ariès had earlier addressed this theme in his newspaper articles for *La Nation française*: "Déplacements dans le budget familiale," 2 November 1955, 4; "La Répartition de la culture est aujourd'hui inversement proportionnelle à celle des richesses," 30 November 1955, 4–5; "La Valeur du refus," 19 July 1961, 1, 12.

26. Ariès recapitulates that thesis well in "L'Evolution des rôles parentaux," in *Familles d'aujourd'hui*, ed. anon.(Brussels, 1968), 35–55.

27. Philippe Ariès, "L'Enfant: La fin d'un règne," *Autrement* no. 3 (Autumn 1975): 171; "L'Enfance écartée," *Autrement* no. 22 (November 1979): 24–25; "Sur l'enfant," UNESCO colloquium, 15–23; "Deux Motivations successives du déclin de la fécondité en Occident," in the proceedings of a seminar, "Les Déterminants de la fécondité: Théories principales et nouvelles directions de recherche," Bad Homburg, Germany, 14–17 April 1980, 6–7.

28. Philippe Ariès, "Les Ages de la vie," *Contrepoint* no. 1 (May 1970): 23–30, "La Famille hier et aujourd'hui," 96.

29. Ariès, *Centuries of Childhood*, 261–62, 268, 285, 329; "Problèmes de l'éducation," in *La France et les français*, ed. Michel François (Paris, 1972), 958–60. In light of his reading of Natalie Davis's study of adolescents in the sixteenth century in her *Society and Culture in Early Modern France* (Stanford, 1975), Ariès conceded that adolescence had been recognized as a stage of life since the Middle Ages. But he continued to maintain that "modern" adolescence was a new conception closely tied to a lengthening process of developmental education. Ariès, "Sur l'enfant," UNESCO colloquium, 3–6.

30. Philippe Ariès, "Les Grands-Parents dans notre société," in *Les Grands-Parents dans la dynamique psychique de l'enfant*, ed. Michel Soulé (Paris, 1979), 20; "Les Ages de la vie," 29–30; "D'hier à aujourd'hui," 124.

31. Ariès became interested in comparing the socialization of yesterday's orphaned

children with today's mainstream adolescents. The former were exposed to the public sphere from too early an age; the latter had too little exposure to it, at least in a constructive way. He may have been drawn to this topic by the work of Arlette Farge, his colleague at the EHESS, to whom he makes several references. See Arlette Farge, *Vivre dans la rue à Paris au XVIIIe siècle* (Paris, 1979).

32. Philippe Ariès, "Le Régionalisme, perspective historique," *Critère* no. 24 (Winter 1979): 41; *Historien du dimanche*, 159–60.

33. Ariès, "The Family and the City," 229; "Le Travail des enfants et la famille populaire," *Critère* no. 25 (Spring 1979): 251–55.

34. Ariès, *Historien du dimanche*, 149–50.

35. In distinguishing his approach from the thesis of Jacques Donzelot and Michel Foucault about the "policing" of society, Ariès noted that he was more interested in the "secrets of mentalities than in the mechanisms of power." Philippe Ariès, "A Propos de *La Volonté de Savoir*," *L'Arc* no. 70 (1977): 32.

36. Ariès, "Les Grands-Parents dans notre société," 21–22, "D'hier à aujourd'hui," 126.

37. Ariès's line of inquiry accords closely with that of the American cultural historian Christopher Lasch. Two decades before Lasch wrote *Haven in a Heartless World* (New York, 1977), Ariès had formulated the notion of "un lieu d'asile contre la société." Philippe Ariès, "Remarques sur la conception traditionaliste de la famille," *La Nation française*, 7 August 1957, 7.

38. Mousseau, "The Family, Prison of Love," 57–58; Ariès, L'Enfant à travers les siècles," 86.

39. Ariès, "D'hier à aujourd'hui," 117.

40. Philippe Ariès, "L'Amour dans le mariage et en dehors," *La Maison-Dieu* no. 127 (1976): 144–45, "La Naissance du mariage occidental," *La Maison-Dieu* no. 149 (1982): 107–12, "Indissoluble Marriage," *Proceedings of the Ninth Annual Meeting of the Western Society for French History* (October 1981), ed. John F. Sweets (Lawrence, Kans., 1982), 1–14.

41. Philippe Ariès, "L'Amour dans le mariage," *Communications* 35 (1982): 121–22.

42. Class lists of the Ariès seminar at the EHESS, 1979–80, Arch. Ariès. Among those attending were André Béjin, who would coedit the proceedings with him, Jean-Louis Flandrin, a well-known historian of the family, and David Troyansky, an American historian of French social history.

43. *Communications* 35 (1982); Philippe Ariès and André Béjin, eds., *Sexualités occidentales* (Paris, 1982), subsequently trans. by Anthony Forster as *Western Sexuality: Practice and Precept in Past and Present Times* (Oxford, 1985).

44. Here I follow Ariès's pilot study, *Western Attitudes toward Death*. In his culminating study, *L'Homme devant la Mort*, trans. by Helen Weaver as *The Hour of our Death* (New York, 1981), he modified his scheme by adding a fifth stage (Baroque age).

45. Ariès makes specific reference to the parallel between medieval attitudes toward marriage and death rituals in "The Indissoluble Marriage," *Western Sexuality*, 143. See also his "Les Rituels de mariage," *La Maison-Dieu* no 121 (1975): 145–46, and "Marriage," *London Review of Books*, 16 October 1980, 8.

46. Ariès, "Les Rituels de mariage," 147–48.

47. For Ariès, the church's attempt to regularize matrimonial rites signaled the rising ecclesiastical absolutism of the Baroque age. Ibid., 149.

48. This distinction worked both ways. As the church intervened to define the public terms of marriage, the betrothed retreated into a private understanding of their own marriage. Ariès, "La Naissance du mariage occidental," 112; "The Indissoluble Marriage," in *Western Sexuality*, 146–53.

49. Ariès, "Love in Married Life," in *Western Sexuality*, 137–38.

50. Romantic love as a foundation of marriage, however, was problematized by the birth of a child, which reinforced a more conventional conception of marital responsibility. Ariès, "D'hier à aujourd'hui," 125.

51. Ariès, "Love in Married Life," in *Western Sexuality*, 135.

52. Ariès, "The Indissoluble Marriage," 156–57; Mousseau, "The Family, Prison of Love," 58.

53. Ariès, *Histoire des populations françaises*, 344–412.

54. Philippe Ariès, "La Contraception autrefois," *L'Histoire* no. 1 (May 1978): 36–44; "L'Amour dans le mariage et en dehors," 139–45; "A Propos de 'La Volonté de savoir'," 31.

55. Some of the research by participants in Ariès's seminar at the EHESS was directed to this topic, among them that of Paul Veyne. For his own seminar project, Ariès wrote an essay about the decline of same-sex friendship in the modern age. Here he showed how contemporary social pressures to define same-sex friendship in explicitly sexual terms narrowed the complex meaning such friendship had traditionally held. Ariès, "Thoughts on the History of Homosexuality," in *Western Sexuality*, 62–75.

56. More frequently in his late-life writings, Ariès makes reference to Foucault's importance as a historian of mentalities. See esp. Ariès, "Le Travail des enfants et la famille populaire," 251–53, and *Historien du dimanche*, 145.

57. Michel Foucault, "The Battle for Chastity," in *Western Sexuality*, 14–35; Philippe Ariès, "St. Paul and the Flesh," ibid., 36.

58. Their relationship dated from the early 1960s. As an editor at Plon, Ariès had recommended Foucault's history of madness for publication after others had turned it down. André Burguière, "La Singulière Histoire de Philippe Ariès," *Le Nouvel Observateur*, 20 February 1978, 82, 88.

59. Foucault, *The History of Sexuality: An Introduction*, trans. Robert Hurley (New York, 1978), 1: 53–73.

60. Ariès, *Historien du dimanche*, 136, 149.

61. Ibid., 117.

62. Ariès's turn from "mentalities" to "private vs. public life" as the focus of his evolving interpretation of popular culture is signaled in his essay "L'Enfant et la rue, de la ville à l'anti-ville," *URBI* 2 (1979), 3–14 (based on a lecture he gave in Montreal in 1979), and in a presentation he made at a colloquium on "Sociabilités urbaines," sponsored by the Université de Lyon II, 5–10 March 1979, typescript 15 pp., Arch. Ariès. In both, he draws on the ideas of his colleague Arlette Farge on popular social life in Paris, as well as those of the French historian Maurice Agulhon on Mediterranean sociability and the American sociologist Richard Sennett on the decline of the public sphere.

63. Arch. Ariès, letter of invitation from Heinz-Dieter Kittsteiner. During his sojourn in Berlin, Ariès received invitations to speak at other institutions of higher education there as well. Dietmar Görlitz to Ariès, 1 March and 29 May 1983.

64. Among featured participants were Maurice Aymard, Hennerk Bruhns, Yves and

Nicole Castan, Roger Chartier, Norbert Elias, Arlette Farge, Madeleine Foisil, Karen Hausen, Ivan Illich, Heinz-Dieter Kittsteiner, Christine Meier, Michelle Perrot, and Orest Ranum. Arch. Ariès, memorandum, "Séminaire Philippe Ariès, à propos de l'histoire de l'espace privé," dossier "Séminaire Ariès à Berlin, 11 mai 1983." Because of his role as conference organizer, Ariès attended, even though Primerose was then in the throes of her terminal illness.

65. The French edition was published as *La Civilisation des moeurs* in the Livre de poche paperback series in 1973. See the sketch of Elias's life by Roger Chartier, *On the Edge of the Cliff: History, Language, Practices,* trans. Lydia G. Cochrane (Baltimore, 1997), 132–35.

66. There is much recent interest in Elias's work among British and American scholars. Recent editions of his writings in English translation include: Norbert Elias, *On Civilization, Power, and Knowledge: Selected Writings,* ed. Stephen Mennell and Johan Goudsblom (Chicago, 1998), and Johan Goudsblom and Stephen Mennell, eds., *The Norbert Elias Reader* (Oxford, 1998).

67. Patrick Hutton, "The History of Mentalities: The New Map of Cultural History," *History and Theory* 20 (1981): 250–51.

68. Norbert Elias, "Discussion of Ariès's presentation at the Berlin conference," typescript, 11 May 1983, dossier "Séminaire à Berlin," Arch. Ariès. Elias's critique of Ariès for offering too little theory ironically contrasts with that of the new historians of family, who today contend that he offers too much.

69. Elias, "The Civilizing of Parents" (1980), in *The Norbert Elias Reader,* 189–203.

70. Norbert Elias, *La Civilisation des moeurs* (1939; Paris, 1973), 191.

71. Philippe Ariès, "Pour une histoire de la vie privée," in *Histoire de la vie privée,* ed. Roger Chartier, 3: 2–4. See also Philippe Ariès, "La Sensibilité au changement dans la problématique de l'historiographie contemporaine," in *Y a-t-il une nouvelle histoire?,* ed. Emmanuel Le Roy Ladurie and Gilbert Gadoffre (Loches-en-Touraine, 1980), 17–20.

72. Ariès lays out these stages in a lecture for a colloquium on urban sociability at the Université de Lyon II, 5–10 March 1979, typescript, Arch. Ariès.

73. Ariès, *Historien du dimanche,* 163.

74. Ariès hoped to treat the subject one day, but did not have a chance to do so. *Historien du dimanche,* 163. He alludes to the personal significance he invested in this topic in his inaugural lecture at the EHESS, "Le Secret," in *Essais de mémoire,* 29–43. See also Roger Chartier, "L'Histoire culturelle," in *Une Ecole pour les sciences sociales,* ed. Jacques Revel and Nathan Wachtel (Paris, 1996), 84–85.

75. Philippe Ariès, "La Famille et la ville" (1979), in *Essais de mémoire,* 259–69; "The Family and the City in the Old World and the New," in *Changing Images of the Family,* ed. Virginia Tufte and Barbara Myerhoff (New Haven, Conn.,1979), 29–41; "L'Enfant et la rue, de la ville à l'anti-ville," *URBI* 2 (1979): 3–14; *Historien du dimanche,* 182; "D'hier à aujourd'hui," 120–24.

76. Ariès, "Pour une histoire de la vie privée," in *Histoire de la vie privée,* 3: 1–11.

77. See the interesting dialogue concerning the significance of Ariès's scholarship between Michel Foucault and Arlette Farge a few days after his death, "Le Style de l'histoire," *Le Matin des livres,* 21 February 1984, 20–21. Foucault emphasized Ariès's insight into "styles of existence," by which he meant the behaviors and sentiments associated with humankind's responses to its most fundamental problems of life and

death. Farge noted the appeal of Ariès's psychological approach to history in the 1960s, a time when French intellectuals were tiring of Marxist pieties.

78. See the listing of obituaries in the bibliography. Longer commemorative essays on the meaning of his life work include: Pierre Chaunu, "Avec Philippe Ariès, un regard en arrière," *L'Histoire en cet instant* (Paris, 1985), 224–42; François Leger, "Philippe Ariès: L'histoire d'un historien," *Revue universelle des faits et des idées* 65 (1986): 63–73; Roger Chartier, "L'Amitié de l'histoire," preface to *Le Temps de l'Histoire*, by Philippe Ariès (Paris, 1986), 9–30; and Jeannine Verdès-Leroux, "La 'Fidélité inventive' de Philippe Ariès," preface to *Le Présent quotidien*, by Philippe Ariès (Paris, 1997), 7–38.

79. Their dedication to volume 3 of the *L'Histoire de la vie privée* reads: "This book was inspired, conceptualized, and prepared by Philippe Ariès. Death prevented him from seeing it through to completion. We [his contributors] have done so in loyalty to him, and in remembrance of his friendship."

80. Philippe Ariès, "Histoire et nature humaine," mss., dossier "Textes, articles et manuscrits de Philippe Ariès," Arch. Ariès; *Historien du dimanche*, 129; "L'Enfant à travers les siècles," 87.

81. Michel Foucault, "Le Souci de la vérité," *Le Nouvel Observateur*, 12 February 1984, 56–57.

Chapter 10

1. Philippe Ariès, *Un Historien du dimanche*, ed. Michel Winock (Paris, 1980), 123.

2. Philippe Ariès, *Le Temps de l'Histoire* (Monaco, 1954), 202–11.

3. Roger Chartier, "Avant-propos," in *Essais de mémoire*, by Philippe Ariès (Paris, 1993), 7–24, 45 n.

4. Philippe Ariès, "Le Temps de l'Histoire" (1983), in *Essais de mémoire*, 45–67.

5. The term is that of François Hartog, and my formulation of this material on privileged moments of time owes much to what I learned in his seminar at the Ecole des Hautes Etudes en Sciences Sociales in 1995–96. See his "Temps et Histoire: 'Comment écrire l'histoire de France?'," *Annales HSS* no. 6 (November–December 1995): 1235, and idem, "Time, History and the Writing of History: The *Order* of Time," *KVHAA Konferenser* 37 (1996): 96–97.

6. Ariès, *Le Temps de l'Histoire*, 89–93.

7. Ariès, "Le Temps de l'Histoire," 49.

8. Jean-Paul Sartre, *Search for a Method*, trans. Hazel E. Barnes (1960; New York, 1968), 30. Ariès does not cite Sartre. But he does use the term "existential history" to characterize subject matter he would later label "mentalities." Ariès, *Le Temps de l'Histoire*, 291–311.

9. Ariès, "Le Temps de l'Histoire," 52.

10. Ibid., 53.

11. See Lucien Febvre, *Combats pour l'Histoire* (Paris, 1992).

12. Among critical studies of the evolution of Annales historiography, see Krzysztof Pomian, "L'"Heure des *Annales*," in *Les Lieux de mémoire*, ed. Pierre Nora (Paris, 1986), 2 (part 1): 377–429; François Dosse, *L'Histoire en miettes: Des Annales à la nouvelle histoire* (Paris, 1987); Hervé Coutau-Bégarie, *Le Phénomène nouvelle histoire*, 2d ed. (Paris, 1989).

13. See esp. Jacques Le Goff and Pierre Nora, eds., *Faire de l'histoire*, 3 vols. (Paris,

1974), and Jacques Le Goff, Roger Chartier, and Jacques Revel, eds., *La Nouvelle Histoire* (Paris, 1978).

14. Traian Stoianovich, *French Historical Method: The Annales Paradigm* (Ithaca, N.Y., 1976); Peter Burke, *The French Historical Revolution; The Annales School, 1929–89* (Stanford, 1990).

15. François Dufay, Olivier Dumoulin, and Jacques Revel, "Faut-il brûler Fernand Braudel," *L'Histoire* no. 192 (October 1995): 78–84. See also the essay by Jean Boutier and Dominique Julia, "A quoi pensent les historiens?" in *Passés recomposés*, ed. Jean Boutier and Dominique Julia (Paris, 1995), 23–28.

16. Pierre Chaunu, "Un Nouveau Champ pour l'histoire sérielle: Le quantitatif au troisième niveau," in *Méthodologie de l'histoire et des sciences humaines*, ed. anon. (Toulouse, 1972), 108–12, 116.

17. Jacques Le Goff, "Les Mentalités: Une histoire ambiguë," in *Faire de l'histoire*, 3: 86. On the problems and limits of mentalities as an approach to history, see also Georges Duby, *L'Histoire continue* (Paris, 1991), 115–25.

18. On the decline of civic involvement in the late twentieth century, see Benjamin R. Barber, *Jihad vs. McWorld* (New York, 1996), 281–88, and Robert D. Putnam, *Bowling Alone* (New York, 2000), 48–64.

19. Henry Rousso, *Le Syndrome de Vichy: De 1944 à nos jours*, 2d ed. (Paris, 1990), 29–76.

20. Ibid., 77–117, 132–67.

21. Michael R. Marrus and Robert O. Paxton, *Vichy France and the Jews* (New York, 1981).

22. Rousso, *Syndrome de Vichy*, 155–94.

23. Ibid., 118–54, 251–308, 335–45. See the reappraisal of the Vichy syndrome by Eric Conan and Henry Rousso, *Vichy, un passé qui ne passe pas* (Paris, 1994); also Richard J. Golsan, *Vichy's Afterlife* (Lincoln, Neb., 2000), 1–2, 9–10.

24. Philippe Ariès, "Inconscient collectif et idées claires," *Athinéa* no. 8 (August–September 1975): 3–4.

25. This is a large topic that cannot be pursued here, but see the essay by Guy Bois, "Marxisme et histoire nouvelle," in *La Nouvelle Histoire*, ed. Jacques Le Goff (Paris, 1988), 255–75.

26. See François Furet, "Le Quantitatif en histoire," in *Faire de l'histoire*, 1: 42–61.

27. For the nature of the appeal of communism to idealistic youth in the years after the war, see Edgar Morin, *Autocritique*, 3d ed. (Paris, 1975), 76–107.

28. See Tony Judt, *Marxism and the French Left* (Oxford, 1986), 169–98, and idem, *Past Imperfect* (Berkeley, Calif., 1992), 288–92. See also the older but still useful studies by Georg Lichtheim, *Marxism in Modern France* (New York, 1966), 69–111, and by Annie Kriegel, *Les Communistes français: Essai d'ethnographie politique*, 2d ed. (Paris, 1970), 227–60.

29. Emmanuel Le Roy Ladurie, *Paris-Montpellier; P.C.-P.S.U., 1945–1963* (Paris, 1982).

30. See Michel Vovelle, "La Galerie des ancêtres," *Combats pour la Révolution française* (Paris, 1993), 13–23.

31. For an appreciation of Labrousse's role, see the special issue "A la mémoire d'Ernest Labrousse," *Annales historiques de la Révolution française* no. 276 (April–June 1989). See also Labrousse's interesting personal commentary in an interview with Chris-

tophe Charle, "Entretiens avec Ernest Labrousse," *Actes de la recherche en sciences sociales* no. 32–33 (April–June 1980): 111–25.

32. For his self-assessment see the interview with François Furet, *Histoire de la Révolution et la révolution dans l'histoire*, ed. Mona Ozouf, Jacques Revel, and Pierre Rosanvallon (Paris, 1994). See also the commentary on Furet's career by Steven Laurence Kaplan, *Farewell Revolution; The Historians' Feud, 1789–1989* (Ithaca, N.Y., 1995), 50–143.

33. François Furet, *Penser la Révolution française* (Paris, 1978). See also the essay by Michael Scott Christofferson, "An Antitotalitarian History of the French Revolution: François Furet's *Penser la Révolution française* in the Intellectual Politics of the Late 1970s," *French Historical Studies* 22 (1999): 557–611.

34. François Furet, "Faut-il célébrer le bicentenaire de la Révolution française?" *L'Histoire* 52 (1983): 71–77; idem, "La Révolution dans l'imaginaire politique français," *Le Débat* 26 (1983): 173–81.

35. François Furet, *The Passing of an Illusion*, trans. Deborah Furet (Chicago, 1999), vii–xi, 487–503. See also his interview with Michel Schifres, "Les Vérités de François Furet," *Le Figaro*, 2 January 1996, 11.

36. Michel Vovelle, *La Mentalité révolutionnaire: Société et mentalités sous la révolution française* (Paris, 1985). On Vovelle, see Bois, "Marxisme et histoire nouvelle," 261–62.

37. Michel Vovelle, *Les Aventures de la raison*, ed. Richard Figuier (Paris, 1989), 18–19.

38. Cf. the commentary on the debate by Pierre Chaunu, *L'Histoire en cet instant* (Paris, 1985), 234–35.

39. Pierre Nora, ed., *Les Lieux de mémoire*, 3 vols. (Paris, 1984–92).

40. Ariès, *Le Temps de l'Histoire*, 313–25; idem, "L'Histoire des mentalités," in *La Nouvelle Histoire*, ed. Le Goff, Chartier, and Revel., 423.

41. On the unpredictable past, see Hartog, "Time, History, and the Writing of History," 110–11.

42. See esp. Pierre Nora, ed., *Essais d'égo-histoire* (Paris, 1987).

43. On the historiographical context, cf. Jeremy D. Popkin, "*Ego-histoire* and Beyond: Contemporary French Historian-Autobiographers," *French Historical Studies* 19 (1996): 1139–67, and idem, "Historians on the Autobiographical Frontier," *American Historical Review* 104 (1999): 725–48.

44. See "Autour de l'égo-histoire," *Le Débat* no. 49 (March–April 1988): 122–40, which includes reviews of the project by François Dosse, Arlette Farge, François Hartog, Jacques Revel, and Henry Rousso.

45. Philippe Ariès, "Pourquoi écrit-on des Mémoires?" (1978), in *Essais de mémoire*, 345–54.

46. Raoul Girardet, "L'Ombre de la guerre," in *Essais d'égo-histoire*, 164.

47. See also his "La Ressemblance," (1980) in *Essais de mémoire*, 59–67.

48. Philippe Ariès, "Vie et mort des civilisations," in *La Mort, un terme ou un commencement?*, ed. Christian Chabanis (Paris, 1982), 103–18.

49. Pierre Nora, "Conclusion," in *Essais d'égo-histoire*, 358.

BIBLIOGRAPHY

Bibliographies of the Writings of Philippe Ariès

Somalvico, Bruno, and Roger Chartier, eds. "Bibliographie de Philippe Ariès." In *Essais de mémoire*, ed. Roger Chartier. Paris: Seuil, 1993, 363–72. A comprehensive inventory of Ariès's books and scholarly articles, indexed by year of publication.

Verdès-Leroux, Jeannine, ed. *Le Présent quotidien, 1955–1966*, by Philippe Ariès. Paris: Seuil, 1997, 545–49. An anthology of the articles by Ariès published in *La Nation française*.

Books, Anthologies, and Thesis by Philippe Ariès

La Commerce de la banane dans le monde en France et dans les colonies françaises. With Roger Cadillat. Paris: Institut des Fruits et Agrumes Coloniaux, 1944.

"Les Commissaires-Examinateurs au Châtelet de Paris au XVIe siècle." Diplôme d'études supérieures, Université de Paris (Sorbonne), 1936.

L'Enfant et la vie familiale sous l'Ancien Régime. Paris: Plon, 1960. Rev. ed. Paris: Seuil, 1973. Trans. by Robert Baldick as *Centuries of Childhood*. New York: Random House, 1962.

Essais de mémoire. Ed. Roger Chartier. Paris: Seuil, 1993.

Fonctionment d'un centre de documentation. With Stanislas Reizler, René van den Berg, and Mathieu Le Minor. Paris, 1946.

Histoire de la vie privée. Ed. Philippe Ariès and Georges Duby. 5 vols. Paris: Seuil, 1985–87. Trans. by Arthur Goldhammer as *A History of Private Life*. Cambridge: Harvard University Press, 1987–91.

Histoire des populations françaises et de leurs attitudes devant la vie depuis le XVIIIe siècle. Paris: Editions Self, 1948. Rev. ed. Paris: Seuil, 1979.

Un Historien du dimanche. Ed. Michel Winock. Paris: Seuil, 1980.

L'Homme devant la mort. Paris: Seuil, 1977. Trans. by Helen Weaver as *The Hour of Our Death*. Oxford: Oxford University Press, 1981.

Images de l'homme devant la mort. Paris: Seuil, 1983.

Les Jeux à la Renaissance. Ed. Philippe Ariès and Jean-Claude Margolin. Paris: J. Vrin, 1982.

Le Présent quotidien, 1955–1966. Ed. Jeannine Verdès-Leroux. Paris: Seuil, 1997.

Sexualités Occidentales. Ed. Philippe Ariès and André Béjin. Paris: Seuil, 1982. Trans. by Anthony Forster as *Western Sexuality: Practice and Precept in Past and Present Times*. Oxford: Basil Blackwell, 1985.

Le Temps de l'Histoire. Monaco: Rocher, 1954. Rev. ed. by Roger Chartier. Paris: Seuil, 1986.

Les Traditions sociales dans les pays de France. Paris: Les Editions de la Nouvelle France, 1943.

Western Attitudes toward Death. Trans. Patricia Ranum. Baltimore: Johns Hopkins University Press, 1974. Rev. and augmented ed. as *Essais sur l'histoire de la mort en Occident du Moyen Age à nos jours*. Paris: Seuil, 1975.

Articles, Essays, and Reviews by Philippe Ariès

"Les Ages de la vie." *Contrepoint* 1 (May 1970): 23–30.

"L'Amour dans le mariage." *Communications* 35 (1982): 116–22.

"L'Amour dans le mariage et en dehors." *La Maison-Dieu* no. 127 (1976): 139–45.

"A Propos de Balzac." In *Trois Socialistes français: Quatre Etudes*, ed. Paul Chanson. Paris: La Nouvelle France, 1945, 149–65.

"A Propos de *La Volonté de savoir*." *L'Arc* no. 70 (1977): 27–32.

"At the Point of Origin," *Yale French Studies* no. 43 (1969): 15–23.

"Attitudes devant la vie et la mort du XVIIIe au XIXe siècle." *Population* 4 (1949): 463–70.

"La Contraception autrefois." *L'Histoire* no. 1 (May 1978): 36–44.

"Culture orale et culture écrite." In *Le Christianisme populaire:: Les dossiers de l'histoire*, ed. Bernard Plongeron and Robert Pannet. Paris: Le Centurion, 1976, 227–40.

"Deux Contributions à l'histoire des pratiques contraceptives: Chaucer et Mme. de Sévigné." *Population* 9 (1954): 692–98.

"D'hier à aujourd'hui, d'une civilisation à l'autre." In *Couples et familles dans la société d'aujourd'hui*, ed. Semaine Sociale de France. Lyon: Chronique sociale de France, 1973, 117–27.

"Le XIXe Siècle et la révolution des moeurs familiales." In *Renouveau des idées sur la famille*, ed. Robert Pringent. Paris: Presses Universitaires de France, 1954, 111–18.

"Du Livre (à paraître) de Michel Vovelle: 'La mort en Occident'." In *La Mort aujourd'hui*, ed. Roger Chartier. Marseille: Rivages, 1982, 159–68.

"L'Education familiale." In *Histoire mondiale de l'éducation*, ed. Gaston Mialaret and Jean Vial. Paris: Presses Universitaires de France, 1981, 2: 233–45.

"L'Enfance écartée." *Autrement* no. 22 (November 1979): 23–26.

"L'Enfant et la rue, de la ville à l'anti-ville." URBI 2 (1979): 3–14.

"L'Enfant: La fin d'un règne." *Autrement* no. 3 (Autumn 1975): 169–71.

"L'Evolution des rôles parentaux." In *Familles d'aujourd'hui*, ed. anon. Brussels: Editions de l'Institut de Sociologie, Université Libre de Bruxelles, 1968), 35–55.

"La Famille d'Ancien Régime." *Revue des travaux de l'académie des sciences morales et politiques* 109 (4th series)(1956): 46–55.

"La Famille et la ville" (1978). In *Essais de mémoire*, 257–70.

"La Famille et ses âges." Cahiers de pastorale familiale (January–March 1956): 11–18.

"La Famille hier et aujourd'hui." *Contrepoint* no. 11 (July 1973): 89–97.

"Familles du démi-siècle." In *Renouveau des idées sur la famille*, ed. Robert Pringent. Paris: Presses Universitaires de France, 1954, 162–70.

"The Family and the City." *Daedalus* 106 (1977): 227–37.

"The Family and the City in the Old World and the New." In *Changing Images of the Family*, ed. Virginia Tufte and Barbara Myerhoff. New Haven: Yale University Press, 1979, 29–41.

"Les Grandes Etapes et le sens de l'évolution de nos attitudes devant la mort." *Archives de sciences sociales des réligions* 39 (1975): 7–15.

"Les Grands-Parents dans notre société." In *Les Grands-Parents dans la dynamique psychique de l'enfant*, ed. Michel Soulé. Paris: Editions ESF, 1979, 13–26.

"L"Histoire des mentalités." In *La Nouvelle Histoire*, ed. Jacques Le Goff, Roger Chartier, and Jacques Revel. Paris: Retz, 1978, 402–23.

"Inconscient collectif et idées claires." In *Anthinéa* no. 8 (August–September 1975): 3–4.

"Indissoluble Marriage." *Proceedings of the Ninth Annual Meeting of the Western Society for French History*, ed. John F. Sweets. Lawrence: University of Kansas Press, 1982, 1–14.

"Interprétation pour une histoire des mentalités." In *La Prévention des naissances dans la famille*, ed. Hélène Bergues. Paris: Presses Universitaires de France, 1960, 311–27.

"Une Interprétation tendancieuse de l'histoire des mentalités." *Anthinéa* 3/2 (February 1973): 7–10.

"Journal de l'Estoile: Pour le règne de Henri III." In *La Fin de la Ligue (1589–1593): Trois ètudes sur le seizième siècle*, ed. François Leger. Paris: La Nouvelle France, 1944, 159–75.

"Le Mariage indissoluble." *Communications* 35 (1982): 123–37.

"Marriage" *London Review of Books* 16 October 1980, 8.

"La Naissance du mariage occidental." *La Maison-Dieu* no. 149 (1982): 107–12.

"La Nostalgie du roi." *H-Histoire* no. 5 (1980): 37–48.

"La Politique." In *Cinquante Ans de pensée Catholique*, ed. Emile Blanchet. Paris: Fayard, 1955, 116–27.

"Pour une histoire de la vie privée." In *Histoire de la vie privée*, ed. Roger Chartier. Paris: Seuil, 1986), 3: 1–11.

"Pourquoi écrit-on des Mémoires?" (1978). In *Essais de mémoire*, 345–54.

"Problèmes de l'éducation." In *La France et les français*, ed. Michel François. 1972; Paris: Gallimard, 1981, 871–961.

"Réflexions sur l'histoire de l'homosexualité." *Communications* 35 (1982): 56–67.

"Le Régionalisme, perspective historique." *Critère* no. 24 (Winter 1979): 41–50

"Religion populaire et réformes religieuses." In *Religion populaire et réforme liturgique*, ed. Jean-Yves Hameline. Paris: Cerf, 1975, 84–97.

"La Ressemblance" (1980). In *Essais de mémoire*, 59–67.

"Les Rituels de mariage." *La Maison-Dieu* no. 121 (1975): 143–50.

"Saint-Pierre ou la douceur de vivre?" In *Catastrophe à la Martinique*, ed. Philippe Ariès, Charles Daney, and Emile Berlé. Paris: Hercher, 1981, 11–24.

"Le Secret" (1978). In *Essais de mémoire*, 29–43.

"La Sensibilité au changement dans la problématique de l'historiographie contemporaine." In *Y a-t-il une nouvelle histoire?* ed. Emmanuel Le Roy Ladurie and Gilbert Gadoffre. Loches-en-Touraine: Institut Collégial Européen, 1980, 17–20. Rpt. in *Certitudes et incertitudes de l'histoire*, ed. Gilbert Gadoffre. Paris: Presses Universitaires de France, 1987, 169–75.

"Sur les origines de la contraception en France." *Population* 7 (1953): 465–72.
"Table ronde sur la communication de Roger Chartier." In *La Mort aujourd'hui*, ed. Roger Chartier. Marseille: Rivages, 1982, 127–30.
"Le Temps de l'Histoire" (1983). In *Essais de mémoire*, 45–67.
"Le Travail des enfants et la famille populaire." *Critère* no. 25 (1979): 251–55.
"Vie et mort des civilisations." In *La Mort, un terme ou un commencement?* ed. Christian Chabanis. Paris: Fayard, 1982, 103–18.

Newspapers to Which Philippe Ariès Contributed

L'Etudiant français 1934–39.
La Nation française 1955–66.
Paroles françaises 1946.

Published Interviews with Philippe Ariès

Anon. "Confessions d'un anarchiste de droite." *Contrepoint* no. 16 (1974): 87–99. Rpt. in *La Droite aujourd'hui*, ed. Jean-Pierre Apparu. Paris: Albin Michel, 1979, 107–14.
Anon. "Entretien avec Philippe Ariès." *La Nouvelle Action Française* no. 144 (30 January 1974): 6–7.
Benoit-Lapierre, Nicole. "Une Histoire de la vieillesse? Entretien avec Philippe Ariès." *Communications* 37 (1983): 47–54.
Browning, Alison. "Une Conversation avec Philippe Ariès." *Cadmos* no. 12 (Winter 1980): 4–16.
Builly, Pierre. "Entretien avec Philippe Ariès." *Je Suis Français* 1982. Typescript, Arch. Ariès.
Burguière, André. "La Singulière Histoire de Philippe Ariès." *Le Nouvel Observateur*, 20 February 1978.
Fabvre, Armand. "Il y a une infinité d'amériques. . . ." *Royaliste* no. 330 (22 January–4 February 1981): 6–7.
Mousseau, Jacques. "The Family, Prison of Love." *Psychology Today*, August 1975, 53–58.
Winock, Michel. "L'Enfant à travers les siècles." *Histoire* no. 19 (January 1980): 85–87.

Obituaries of Philippe Ariès

Chamboredon, Jean-Claude. "Philippe Ariès, 1914–1984." *Revue française de sociologie* 26 (1985): 150–52.
Chartier, Roger. "La Mort de Philippe Ariès, historien du dimanche." *Libération*, 10 February 1984, 21–22.
Chaunu, Pierre. "Le Parcours solitaire." *Histoire, économie et société* 3 (1984): 3–5.
———. Philippe Ariès, l'historien solitaire." *L'Express*, 17–23 February 1984, 107–8.
Farge, Arlette. "Un Regard attentif et passionné." *Le Matin*, 10 February 1984, 32.
Foucault, Michel. "Le Souci de la vérité." *Le Nouvel Observateur*, 12 February 1984, 56–57.
———, and Arlette Farge. "Le Style de l'histoire." *Le Matin des livres*, 21 February 1984, 20–21.

Friguglietti, James. "Philippe Ariès, 1914–1984." *French Historical Studies* 13 (1984): 573–75.

Girardet, Raoul. "Sur l'Historien disparu: Philippe Ariès ou l'esprit de la Liberté." *Le Quotidien de Paris*, 15 February 1984, 12.

Leclerc, Gérard. "La Mort de Philippe Ariès, un amateur prestigieux." *Le Quotidien de Paris*, 10 February 1984.

Leger, François. "La Mort de l'historien de la mort." *Aspects de la France*, 16 February 1984, 13.

———. "Philippe Ariès: L'Histoire d'un historien." *La Revue universelle des faits et des idées* 65 (1986): 63–73.

Poussou, Jean-Pierre. "Philippe Ariès, In Memoriam," *Annales de démographie historique* (1984).

Vovelle, Michel. "Explorateur des mentalités." *Le Matin*, 10 February 1984, 32.

Winock, Michel. "Un Rire extraordinaire. . . ." *Libération*, 10 February 1984, 21.

Archives Ariès, Archives de l'Ecole des Hautes Etudes en Sciences Sociales

Extant since 2000, the Archives Ariès contain documents from four principal sources:

Dossier "Ariès Philippe, directeur d'études cumulant." Curriculum vitae, reports, papers, and correspondence relating to his appointment as a director of studies at the Ecole des Hautes Etudes en Sciences Sociales.

Fond "Marie-Rose Ariès." Correspondence and manuscripts of Philippe Ariès given by his sister to the Archives.

Fond Seuil. A valise of offprints of articles, and some manuscript writings of Philippe Ariès, originally held by the Seuil publishing house.

Fond St. Martin. Papers of Philippe Ariès until recently held by his wife's family.

These collections have been amalgamated by Brigitte Mazon and inventoried by Guillaume Gros as "Inventaire des archives Philippe Ariès," annex to his doctoral thesis, Institut d'Etudes Politiques de Paris, 2002.

Files from the Archives Nationales, Paris, Germane to Ariès's Teaching Assignments during Vichy

F17 (Instruction publique):

13339 Activités personnelles du ministre [Abel Bonnard], 1942–43
13341 Instruction publique
13353 Correspondance divers
13356 Correspondances
13366 Jeunesse et sports
13367 Jeunesse et sports, 1942–44
13377 Etablissements d'enseignement, 1941–43
14178 Affaires disciplinaire, les Jeunes du Maréchal

2 AG Papiers des chefs de l'Etat (1940–44)

440 CC3 Archives du cabinet civil
457 CC32 Propagande

459 CC34 Transmission no. 2
496 CC78 Education nationale
497 CC79 Jeunesse, famille, santé
570 CC175 Education nationale et jeunesse
654 Archives, documents

AJ40 Archives allemandes de la seconde guerre mondiale (1940–45)
1005, dossier 7 Gerhard Heller

Personal Interviews Conducted by the Author
Ariès, Marie-Rose: February 1996, August 1997 (Le Chenay)
Brissaud, Philippe: 19 April 1996 (Paris)
Bruel, Jean: 21 August 1997 (Paris)
Castan, Yves and Nicole: 30 May 2001 (Toulouse)
Chartier, Roger: 9 May 1996 (Paris)
Chaunu, Pierre: 28 June 1999 (Paris)
Darnton, Robert: 8 June 1998 (Princeton)
Farge, Arlette: 5 June 2001 (Paris)
Flandrin, Jean-Louis: 4 June 2001 (Paris)
Girardet, Raoul: 1 April 1996 (Paris)
Leger, François: 23 February 1996, 26 June 1999, 2 June 2001 (Paris)
Picard, Gilbert: 22 February 1996 (Versailles)
Ranum, Orest: 28–29 May 2001 (Le Panat, Aveyron)
Revel, Jacques: January 1996 (Paris)
Verdès-Leroux, Jeannine: 1 April 1996 (Paris)

Graduate Theses concerning Philippe Ariès

Gros, Guillaume. "Philippe Ariès: Un Réactionnaire authentique: itinéraire d'un maur-rassien non-conformiste de l'Etudiant français à la Nation française." D.E.A., histoire contemporaine. Institut d'Etudes Politiques de Paris (under the direction of Alain-Gérard Slama), 1994.
———. "Philippe Ariès (1914–1984): Un Traditionaliste non-conformiste: de l'Action française à l'Ecole des hautes études en sciences sociales." Thèse de doctorat, Institut d'Etudes Politiques de Paris (under the direction of Serge Berstein), 2002.
Veneu, Marcos Guedes. "Temps, tradition, et conscience historique chez Philippe Ariès." D.E.A., histoire et civilisations. Ecole des Hautes Etudes en Sciences Sociales (under the direction of François Hartog), 1994.

Secondary and Related Works

Agulhon, Maurice. Histoire vagabonde. 2 vols. Paris: Gallimard, 1998.
Andreu, Pierre, ed. Révoltes de l'esprit: Les Revues des années trente. Paris: Kimé, 1991.
———, et al., eds. Ecrits pour une renaissance. Paris: Plon, 1958.
Armus, Seth D. "The Eternal Enemy: Emmanuel Mounier's Esprit and French Anti-Americanism." French Historical Studies 24 (2001): 271–304.

Aron, Robert. *The Vichy Regime, 1940–44*. Trans. Humphrey Hare. 1955; Boston: Beacon Press, 1969.

Azéma, Jean-Pierre, and François Bédarida, eds. *La France des années noires*. 2 vols. Paris: Seuil, 1993.

——, eds. *Le Régime de Vichy et les français*. Paris: Fayard, 1992.

Bainville, Jacques. *Histoire de deux peuples, continuée jusqu'à Hitler*. 85th ed. Paris: A. Fayard, 1933.

Barber, Benjamin R. *Jihad vs. McWorld*. New York: Random House, 1996.

Bell, Daniel. *The End of Ideology*. Cambridge: Harvard University Press, 1988.

Birnbaum, Pierre. *Anti-Semitism in France: A Political History from Léon Blum to the Present*. Trans. Miriam Kochan. Oxford: Blackwell, 1992.

Bloch, Marc. *Apologie pour l'histoire, ou métier d'historien*. 5th ed. 1941; Paris: Colin, 1964.

Bodart, M. G. *Philippe Ariès, un documentaliste pas comme les autres*. Montpellier: Centre de Coopération Internationale en Recherche Agronomique pour le Développement, 1994.

Bois, Guy. "Marxisme et histoire nouvelle." In *La Nouvelle Histoire*, ed. Jacques Le Goff. Paris: Complexe, 1988, 255–75.

Bonnard, Abel. *Des Jeunes Gens ou une jeunesse?* Paris: Ecole Estienne, 1943.

Bonnet, Serge. *Prières secrètes des français d'aujourd'hui*. Paris: Cerf, 1976.

Bourdé, Guy, and Hervé Martin. *Les Ecoles historiques*. Paris: Seuil, 1983.

Boutang, Pierre. *La Politique: La politique considérée comme souci*. Paris: Jean Froissart, 1948.

——. *La République de Joinovici*. Paris: Amiot-Dumont, 1949.

——. *Maurras, la destinée et l'oeuvre*. Paris: Plon, 1984.

Boutang, Pierre, and Henri Dubreuil. *Les Amis du Maréchal*. Paris: Anon, 1941.

Bouthoul, Gaston. *Les Mentalités*. Paris: Presses Universitaires de France, 1952.

Boutier, Jean, and Dominique Julia, eds. *Passés recomposés: Champs et chantiers de l'histoire*. Paris: Autrement, 1995.

Boverat, Fernand. *Fécondité ou servitude: Comment relever la natalité française*. Lyon: Editions de l'Alliance Nationale contre la Dépopulation, 1941.

Boyd, Kelly, ed. *Encyclopedia of Historians and Historical Writing*. London: Fitzroy Dearborn, 1999.

Brassillach, Robert. *Notre Avant-guerre*. 1941; Paris: Le Livre de poche, 1992.

Brigneau, François. *Mon Après-guerre*. 1966; Paris: Editions du présent, 1985.

Burguière, André. "The Fate of the History of *Mentalités* in the *Annales*." *Comparative Studies in Society and History* 4 (1982): 424–37.

——. "La Monarchie selon Ariès." *Le Nouvel Observateur*, 5 July 1980, 70–71.

——, ed. *Dictionnaire des sciences historiques*. Paris: Presses Universitaires de France, 1986.

Burke, Peter. *The French Historical Revolution: The "Annales" School, 1929–89*. Stanford: Stanford University Press, 1990.

Burrin, Philippe. *La France à l'heure allemande, 1940–1944*. Paris: Seuil, 1995.

Cantor, Norman. *The American Century*. New York: Harper/Collins, 1997.

Carcopino, Jérôme. *Souvenirs de sept ans, 1937–1944*. Paris: Flammarion, 1953.

Carrel, Alexis. *Man, the Unknown*. 1935; New York: Halcyon House, 1938.

Charle, Christophe. "Entretiens avec Ernest Labrousse." *Actes de la recherche en sciences sociales* no. 32–33 (April–June 1980): 111–25.

Chartier, Roger. "L'Amitié de l'histoire." Preface to *Le Temps de l'Histoire*, by Philippe Ariès. Paris: Seuil, 1986, 9–30.

———. *Cultural History: Between Practices and Representations*. Ithaca: Cornell University Press, 1988.

———. *On the Edge of the Cliff: History, Language, and Practices*. Trans. Lydia G. Cochrane. Baltimore: Johns Hopkins University Press, 1997.

———, ed. *La Mort aujourd'hui* (Cahiers de Saint-Maximin). Marseille: Rivages, 1982.

Chaunu, Pierre. *Colère contre colère*. Paris: Seghers, 1991.

———. *L'Historien en cet instant*. Paris: Hachette, 1985.

———. "Un Nouveau Champ pour l'histoire sérielle: Le quantitatif au troisième niveau." In *Méthodologie de l'histoire et des sciences humaines*, ed. anon. Toulouse: Privat, 1972, 105–25.

———. "Sur le chemin de Philippe Ariès, historien de la mort." *Histoire, économie et société* 3 (1984): 651–63.

Chiroux, René. *L'Extrême Droite sous la Ve République*. Paris: Librairie Générale de Droit et de Jurisprudence, 1974.

Christofferson, Michael Scott. "An Antitotalitarian History of the French Revolution: François Furet's *Penser la Révolution française* in the Intellectual Politics of the Late 1970s." *French Historical Studies* 22 (1999): 557–611.

Cointet-Labrousse, Michèle. "Le Gouvernement de Vichy et les réformes de l'enseignement de l'histoire (1940–1944)." *Revue d'histoire moderne et contemporaine* (1984): 41–48.

Comte, Bernard. *Une Utopie combattante: L'Ecole des cadres d'Uriage, 1940–1942*. Paris: Fayard, 1991.

Conan, Eric, and Henry Rousso. *Vichy, un passé qui ne passe pas*. Paris: Fayard, 1994.

Coutau-Bégarie, Hervé. *Le Phénomène nouvelle histoire*. 2d ed. Paris: Economica, 1989.

Daix, Pierre. *Braudel*. Paris: Flammarion, 1995.

Darnton, Robert. "Death's Checkered Past." *New York Review of Books*, 13 June 1974.

———. *The Great Cat Massacre and Other Episodes in French Cultural History*. New York: Random House, 1984.

———. *The Kiss of Lamourette: Reflections in Cultural History*. New York: Norton, 1990.

Davis, Natalie. *Society and Culture in Early Modern France*. Stanford: Stanford University Press, 1975.

Delestre, Antoine. *Uriage, une communauté et une école dans la tourmente, 1940–1945*. Nancy: Presses Universitaires de Nancy, 1989.

Dioudonnat, Pierre-Marie. "Les Trois Ages du fascisme français." *Contrepoint* no. 11 (July 1973): 149–69.

Dosse, François. *L'Histoire en miettes: Des Annales à la Nouvelle Histoire*. Paris: La Découverte, 1987.

———, et al. "Autour de l'égo-histoire." *Le Débat* no. 49 (March–April 1988): 122–40.

Drouard, Alain. *Alexis Carrel (1873–1944): De la mémoire à l'histoire*. Paris: L'Harmattan, 1995.

———. *Une Inconnue des sciences sociales: La Fondation Alexis Carrel, 1941–45*. Paris: La Maison des Sciences de l'Homme, 1992.

Duby, Georges, ed. "Braudel, le patron de la nouvelle histoire." *L'Histoire* no. 212 (November 1984): 16–39.

———. *L'Histoire continue.* Paris: Odile Jacob, 1991.

———. "Histoire des mentalités." In *Histoire et ses méthodes,* ed. Charles Samaran. Paris: Gallimard, 1961, 937–66.

———. "La Rencontre avec Robert Mandrou et l'élaboration de la notion d'histoire des mentalités." In *Histoire sociale, sensibilités collectives et mentalités: Mélanges Robert Mandrou,* ed. anon. Paris: Presses Universitaires de France, 1985, 33–35.

Dufay, François, Olivier Dumoulin, and Jacques Revel. "Faut-il brûler Fernand Braudel?" *L'Histoire* no. 192 (October 1995): 78–84.

Duffy, Eamon. "The Cradle Will Rock." *New York Review of Books,* 19 December 2002, 61–63.

Duprat, François. *Les Mouvements d'extrême droite en France depuis 1945.* Paris: Albatros, 1972.

Eakin, Emily. "Did Cradles Always Rock?" *New York Times,* 30 June 2001.

Ecole Normale Supérieure de Saint-Cloud, ed. *L'Histoire sociale: Sources et méthodes.* Colloque de l'Ecole Normale Supérieure de Saint-Cloud (15–16 mai 1965). Paris: Presses Universitaires de France, 1967.

Elias, Norbert. *La Civilisation des moeurs.* 1939; Paris: Calmann-Lévy, 1973.

———. *On Civilization, Power, and Knowledge: Selected Writings,* ed. Stephen Mennell and Johan Goudsblom. Chicago: University of Chicago Press, 1998.

Englund, Steven. "The Ghost of Nation Past." *Journal of Modern History* 64 (1992): 299–320.

Erikson, Erik H. *Childhood and Society.* 2d ed. 1950; New York: Norton, 1963.

———. *Young Man Luther: A Study in Psychoanalysis and History.* New York: Norton, 1958.

Farge, Arlette. *Vivre dans la rue à Paris au XVIIIe siècle.* Paris: Gallimard, 1979.

Faure, Christian. *Le Projet culturel de Vichy: Folklore et révolution nationale, 1940–1944.* Lyon: Presses Universitaires de Lyon, 1989.

Faure, Edgar. *L'Ame du combat.* Paris: Fayard, 1970.

Febvre, Lucien. *Combats pour l'Histoire.* Paris: Colin, 1992.

———. "La Sensibilité et l'Histoire: Comment reconstituer la vie affective d'autrefois." *Annales d'histoire sociale* 3 (1941): 5–20.

Fishman, Sterling. "Changing the History of Childhood: A Modest Proposal." *Journal of Psychohistory* 13 (1985): 65–78.

Flandrin, Jean-Louis. "Enfance et société." *Annales ESC* 19 (1964): 322–29.

Foucault, Michel. "The Battle for Chastity." In *Western Sexuality,* ed. Philippe Ariès and André Béjin. Paris: Seuil, 1984, 14–35.

———. *The History of Sexuality: An Introduction.* Trans. Robert Hurley. New York: Pantheon, 1978.

Fouché, Pascal. *L'Edition française sous l'Occupation, 1940–1944.* 2 vols. Paris: Bibliothèque de Littérature Française Contemporaine de l'Université de Paris VII, 1987.

Friedländer, Saul. *History and Psychoanalysis.* Trans. Susan Suleiman. New York: Holmes & Meier, 1978.

Funck Brentano, Frantz. *The Old Regime in France.* 1929; New York: Fertig, 1970.

Furet, François. "Faut-il célébrer le bicentenaire de la Révolution française?" *Histoire* 52 (1983): 71–77.

———. *Histoire de la Révolution et la révolution dans l'histoire.* Ed. Mona Ozouf, Jacques Revel, and Pierre Rosanvallon. Paris: AREHSS, 1994.

———. *The Passing of an Illusion.* Trans. Deborah Furet. Chicago: University of Chicago Press, 1999.

———. *Penser la Révolution française.* Paris: Gallimard, 1978.

———. "La Révolution dans l'imaginaire politique français." *Le Débat* 26 (1983): 173–81.

Gaxotte, Pierre. *Histoire des français.* 2 vols. Paris: Flammarion, 1951.

Gay, Peter. "Annales of Childhood." *Saturday Review,* 23 March 1963, 73–74.

Gillis, John R. *A World of Their Own Making: Myth, Ritual, and the Quest for Family Values.* New York: Basic Books, 1996.

———. *Youth and History.* New York: Academic Press, 1981.

Girardet, Raoul. "L'Héritage de l'Action française." *Revue française de science politique* 7 (1957): 765–92. Rpt. in *Révoltes de l'esprit: Les Revues des années trente,* ed. Pierre Andreu. Paris: Kimé, 1991: 149–74.

———. *Singulièrement libre: Entretiens.* Ed. Pierre Assouline. Paris: Perrin, 1990.

———. "Le Temps de l'Histoire." *La Table ronde* no. 86 (February 1955): 105–7.

Goblet, Yann Morvran. *La Formation des régions: Introduction à une géographie régionale de France.* Paris: Librairie Générale de Droit et de Jurisprudence, 1942.

Golsan, Richard J. *Vichy's Afterlife.* Lincoln: University of Nebraska Press, 2000.

Goubert, Pierre. *La France d'Ancien Régime.* Toulouse: Privat, 1984.

Goudsblom, Johan, and Stephen Mennell, eds. *The Norbert Elias Reader.* Oxford: Blackwell, 1998.

Gross, David. *The Past in Ruins: Tradition and the Critique of Modernity.* Amherst: University of Massachusetts Press, 1992.

Halévy, Daniel. *Essai sur l'accéleration de l'histoire.* Paris: Editions Self, 1948.

———. *La Fin des notables.* 2 vols. Paris: Grasset, 1930–37.

———. *Histoire d'une histoire.* Paris: Grasset, 1939.

———. *Trois Epreuves: 1814, 1871, 1940.* Paris: Plon, 1941.

———. *Visites aux paysans du centre (1907–1934).* Paris: Grasset, 1935.

Hall, Elizabeth. "A Sketch of Philippe Ariès, Man on Hobby Horseback." *Psychology Today,* August 1975.

Halls, Wilfred D. *Les Jeunes et la politique de Vichy.* Trans. Jean Sénémaud. Paris: Syros Alternatives, 1988.

Harlan, David. *The Degradation of American History.* Chicago: University of Chicago Press, 1997.

———. "Intellectual History and the Return of Literature." *American Historical Review* 94 (1989): 581–609.

Hartman, Geneviève. "Philippe Ariès, le documentaliste." *Fruits* 39/3 (1984): 211–14.

Hartog, François. "Temps et histoire, 'Comment écrire l'histoire de France?'" *Annales HSS* no. 6 (November–December 1995): 1219–36.

———. "Time, History, and the Writing of History: The *Order* of Time." *KVHAA Konferenser* (Stockholm) 37 (1996): 95–113.

Heller, Gerhard. *Un Allemand à Paris, 1940–1944.* Paris: Seuil, 1981.

Hellman, John. *Emmanuel Mounier and the New Catholic Left, 1930–1950.* Toronto: University of Toronto Press, 1981.

——. *The Knight-Monks of Vichy France: Uriage, 1940–45*. Montreal: McGill-Queen's University Press, 1993.

Heywood, Colin. *A History of Childhood*. Cambridge, U.K.: Polity, 2001.

Hobsbawm, Eric, and Terence Ranger, eds. *The Invention of Tradition*. Cambridge: Cambridge University Press, 1983.

Hoisington, William A., Jr. *A Businessman in Politics in France, 1935–55: The Career of Jacques Lemaigre Dubreuil*. Ann Arbor, Mich.: University Microfilms, 1969.

Hokke, Judith. "Philippe Ariès en de gezinsgeschiedenis." *Volkscultuur* 5 (1988): 50–63.

Homans, Peter, ed. *Symbolic Loss: The Ambiguity of Mourning and Memory at Century's End*. Charlottesville: University Press of Virginia, 2000.

Hunt, David. *Parents and Children in History: The Psychology of Family Life in Early Modern France*. New York: Harper & Row, 1970.

Hunt, Lynn. *The Family Romance of the French Revolution*. Berkeley: University of California Press, 1992.

——, ed. *The New Cultural History*. Berkeley: University of California Press, 1989.

Hutton, Patrick. "The History of Mentalities: The New Map of Cultural History." *History and Theory* 20 (1981): 237–59.

——. "The Psychohistory of Erik Erikson from the Perspective of Collective Mentalities." *Psychohistory Review* 12 (1983): 18–25.

Jankélévitch, Vladimir. *La Mort*. Paris: Flammarion, 1966.

Judt, Tony. *Marxism and the French Left*. Oxford: Oxford University Press, 1986.

——. *Past Imperfect: French Intellectuals, 1944–1956*. Berkeley: University of California Press, 1992.

Julliard, Jacques, and Michel Winock, eds. *Dictionnaire des intellectuels français*. Paris: Seuil, 1996.

Kale, Steven D. "The Countercentenary of 1889." *Historical Reflections* 23 (1997): 1–28.

Kammen, Michael. *In the Past Lane*. New York: Oxford University Press, 1997.

Kaplan, Steven Laurence. *Farewell, Revolution: The Historians' Feud, France, 1789–1989*. Ithaca: Cornell University Press, 1995.

Keylor, William R. *Jacques Bainville and the Renaissance of Royalist History in Twentieth-Century France*. Baton Rouge: Louisiana State University Press, 1979.

Kriegel, Annie. *Les Communistes français: Essai d'ethnographie politique*. 2d ed. Paris: Seuil, 1970.

Landry, Adolphe. *La Révolution démographique: Etudes et essais sur les problèmes de la population*. Paris: Librairie du Recueil Sirey, 1934.

——. *Traité de démographie*. 1945; Paris: Payot, 1949.

Langer, William L. "The Next Assignment." *American Historical Review* 63 (1958): 283–304.

Lasch, Christopher. *Haven in a Heartless World: The Family Besieged*. New York: Basic Books, 1977.

Laslett, Peter. *The World We Have Lost*. New York: Scribner, 1965.

Lebovics, Herman. *True France: The Wars over Cultural Identity, 1900–1945*. Ithaca: Cornell University Press, 1992.

Lefebvre, Georges. *La Naissance de l'historiographie moderne*. Paris: Flammarion, 1971.

Leger, François. "Deux livres d'histoire sociale." *Présent*, 3 July 1993.

——. "Les Fidélités de Philippe Ariès." *Aspects de la France*, 2 October 1980.

―――. *Les Influences occidentales dans la révolution de l'Orient (Inde, Malaisie, Chine).* 2 vols. Paris: Plon, 1955.

―――. *La Jeunesse d'Hippolyte Taine.* Paris: Albatros, 1980.

―――. *Une Jeunesse réactionnaire.* Paris: Publications F.B., 1993.

―――. *Monsieur Taine.* Paris: Critérion, 1993.

Le Goff, Jacques. *Une Vie pour l'histoire.* Ed. Marc Heurgon. Paris: La Découverte, 1996.

LeGoff, Jacques, Roger Chartier, and Jacques Revel, eds. *La Nouvelle Histoire.* Paris: Retz-CEPL, 1978. Abridged edition ed. Jacques Le Goff. Paris: Editions Complex, 1988.

Le Goff, Jacques, and Pierre Nora, eds. *Faire de l'histoire.* 3 vols. Paris: Gallimard, 1974.

Lenormand, Maurice-Henry. *Vers le régime corporatif.* Paris: Editions de la Nouvelle France, 1943.

Le Play, Frédéric. *L'Organisation de la famille selon le vrai modèle signlé par l'histoire.* Paris, 1871.

Le Roy Ladurie, Emmanuel. *Paris-Montpellier: P.C.-P.S.U., 1945–1963.* Paris: Gallimard, 1982.

―――. *Le Siècle des Platter.* 2 vols. Paris: Fayard, 1995.

Lichtheim, Georg. *Marxism in Modern France.* New York: Columbia University Press, 1966.

Lizerand, Georges. *Le Régime rural de l'ancienne France.* Paris: Presses Universitaires de France, 1942.

Loewenberg, Peter. "Psychohistory." In *The Past before Us,* ed. Michael Kammen. Ithaca: Cornell University Press, 1980, 408–32.

Loubet del Bayle, Jean-Louis. *Les Non-Conformistes des années 30: Une tentative de renouvellement de la pensée politique française.* Paris: Seuil, 1969.

McManners, John. "Death and the French Historian." In *Mirrors of Mortality,* ed. Joachim Whaley. New York: St. Martin's Press, 1981, 106–30.

Mandrou, Robert. *La France aux XVIIe et XVIIIe siècles.* Paris: Presses Universitaires de France, 1967.

―――. *Introduction à la France moderne, 1500–1640.* Paris: A. Michel, 1961.

Marrus, Michael R., and Robert O. Paxton. *Vichy France and the Jews.* New York: Basic Books, 1981.

Maurras, Charles. *Mes Idées politiques.* Paris: Albatros, 1937.

Mazlish, Bruce. "Reflections on the State of Psychohistory." *Psychohistory Review* 5 (1977): 3–11.

Morin, Edgar. *Autocritique.* 3d ed. Paris: Seuil, 1975.

Mounier, Emmanuel. *Communisme, anarchie et personnalisme.* Paris: Seuil, 1966.

―――. *Personalism.* Trans. Philip Mairet. Notre Dame: Notre Dame University Press, 1952.

Nguyen, Victor. *Aux Origines de l'Action française: Intelligence et politique vers 1900.* Paris: Fayard, 1991.

Niethammer, Lutz. *Posthistoire: Has History Come to an End?* Trans. Patrick Camiller. London: Verso, 1992.

Noiriel, Gérard. *Sur la "crise" de l'histoire.* Paris: Belin, 1996.

Nora, Pierre. "Les Deux Apogées de l'Action française." *Annales ESC* 19 (1964): 127–41.

―――, ed.. *Essais d'égo-histoire.* Paris: Gallimard, 1987.

―――, ed. *Les Lieux de mémoire.* 3 vols. Paris: Gallimard, 1984–92.

Novick, Peter. *That Noble Dream*. Cambridge: Cambridge University Press, 1986.

———. *The Resistance versus Vichy: The Purge of Collaborators in Liberated France*. New York: Columbia University Press, 1968.

Orme, Nicholas. *Medieval Children*. New Haven: Yale University Press, 2001.

Ory, Pascal. *L'Anarchisme de droite*. Paris: Grasset, 1985.

———, and Jean-François Sirinelli. *Les Intellectuels en France de l'affaire Dreyfus à nos jours*. Paris: Colin, 1992.

Ozment, Steven. *Ancestors: The Loving Family in Old Europe*. Cambridge: Harvard University Press, 2001.

———. *Flesh and Spirit: Private Life in Early Modern Germany*. New York: Viking, 1999.

———. *When Fathers Ruled: Family Life in Reformation Europe*. Cambridge: Harvard University Press, 1983.

Paxton, Robert. *Parades and Politics at Vichy*. Princeton: Princeton University Press, 1966.

———. *Vichy France: Old Guard and New Order, 1940–1944*. New York: Norton, 1975.

Pollock, Linda A. *Forgotten Children: Parent-Child Relations from 1500 to 1900*. Cambridge: Cambridge University Press, 1983.

———. "Parent-Child Relations." In *The History of the European Family: Family Life in Early Modern Times*, ed. David I. Kertzer and Marzio Barbagli. 3 vols. New Haven: Yale University Press, 2001, 1: 191–220.

Pomian, Krzysztof. "L'Heure des *Annales*." In *Les Lieux de mémoire*, ed. Pierre Nora. Paris: Gallimard, 1986, 2: 377–429.

———. *L'Ordre du temps*. Paris: Gallimard, 1984.

Popkin, Jeremy D. "Ego-histoire and Beyond: Contemporary French Historian-Autobiographers." *French Historical Studies* 19 (1996): 1139–67.

———. "Historians on the Autobiographical Frontier." *American Historical Review* 104 (1999): 725–48.

Postman, Neil. *The Disappearance of Childhood*. New York: Delacorte Press, 1982.

Prochasson, Christophe. "Sur le cas Maurras: Biographie et histoire des idées politiques." *Annales HSS* 50 (1995): 579–87.

Putnam, Robert D. *Bowling Alone*. New York: Simon & Schuster, 2000.

Reggiani, Andrés Horatio. "Alexis Carrel, the Unknown: Eugenics and Population Research under Vichy," *French Historical Studies* 25 (2002): 331–56.

Rémond, René. *Les Droites en France*. Paris: Aubier, 1982.

———, ed. *Pour une histoire politique*. Paris: Seuil, 1988.

Revel, Jacques. "Histoire et sciences sociales: Les Paradigmes des *Annales*." *Annales ESC* 34 (1979): 1360–76.

———, and Nathan Wachtel, eds. *Une Ecole pour les sciences sociales*. Paris: Editions de l'EHESS, 1996.

Rousso, Henry. *Le Syndrome de Vichy: De 1944 à nos jours*. 2d ed. Paris: Seuil, 1990.

———. "Vichy, Le Grand Fossé." *Vingtième Siècle* no. 5 (January–March 1985): 55–79.

Sartre, Jean-Paul. *Search for a Method*. Trans. Hazel E. Barnes. 1960; New York: Vintage, 1968.

Schalk, David L. *The Spectrum of Political Engagement: Mounier, Benda, Nizan, Brasillach, Sartre*. Princeton: Princeton University Press, 1979.

———. *War and the Ivory Tower*. New York: Oxford University Press, 1991.

Schifres, Michel. "Les Vérités de François Furet." *Le Figaro*, 2 January 1996.

Schneider, William H. *Quality and Quantity: The Quest for Biological Regeneration in Twentieth-Century France.* New York: Cambridge University Press, 1990.

Schoenwald, Richard L. "Using Psychohistory in History: A Review Essay." *Historical Methods Newsletter* 7 (1973): 9–24.

Sennett, Richard. *The Fall of Public Man.* New York: Random House, 1976.

Shorter, Edward. *The Making of the Modern Family.* New York: Basic Books, 1975.

Singer, Claude. *Vichy, l'université et les juifs.* Paris: Belles Lettres, 1992.

Sirinelli, Jean-François. *Les Droites françaises: De la Révolution à nos jours.* Paris: Gallimard, 1995.

Spengler, Joseph J. *France Faces Depopulation.* 1938; New York: Greenwood Press, 1968.

Spitzer, Alan B. *The French Generation of 1820.* Princeton: Princeton University Press, 1987.

Stannard, David E. *Shrinking History: On Freud and the Failure of Psychohistory.* Oxford: Oxford University Press, 1980.

Sternhell, Zeev. *Neither Right nor Left: Fascist Ideology in France.* Trans. David Maisel. 1983; Princeton: Princeton University Press, 1996.

Stoianovich, Traian. *French Historical Method: The Annales Paradigm.* Ithaca: Cornell University Press, 1976.

Stone, Lawrence. *The Family, Sex, and Marriage in England, 1500–1800.* New York: Harper & Row, 1977.

———. "The Massacre of the Innocents." *New York Review of Books,* 14 November 1974, 25–31.

Van den Berg, Jan Hendrik. *The Changing Nature of Man: Introduction to a Historical Psychology.* New York: Norton, 1961.

Van der Zeijden, Albert. "Geschiedschrijver van de dood." *Volkscultuur* 5 (1988): 64–82.

———. "Philippe Ariès." *Historisch Nieuwsblad* (April 2001): 26–29.

Vann, Richard T. "The Youth of *Centuries of Childhood.*" *History and Theory* 21 (1982): 279–97.

Verdès-Leroux, Jeannine. "La 'Fidélité inventive' de Philippe Ariès." Preface to *Le Présent quotidien,* by Philippe Ariès, ed. Jeannine Verdès-Leroux. Paris: Seuil, 1997, 7–38.

———. *Réfus et violences.* Paris: Gallimard, 1996.

Vigne, Eric, ed. "Autour de l'égo-histoire." *Le Débat* no. 49 (March–April 1988): 122–40.

Vovelle, Michel. "Albert Soboul, historien de la société." *Annales historiques de la Révolution française* no. 250 (October–December 1982): 547–53.

———. "Les Attitudes devant la mort, front actuel de l'histoire des mentalités." *Archives de sciences sociales des réligions* 39 (1975): 17–29.

———. *Les Aventures de la raison: Entretiens avec Richard Figuier.* Paris: Belfond, 1989.

———. *Combats pour la Révolution française.* Paris: La Découverte, 1993.

———. "L'Historiographie de la Révolution française à la veille du bicentenaire." *Annales historiques de la Révolution française*: no. 272 (April–June 1988): 113–26; no. 273 (July–September 1988): 307–15.

———. *Idéologie et mentalités.* Paris: La Découverte, 1985.

———. *L'Irrésistible Ascension de Joseph Sec, bourgeois d'Aix.* Aix-en-Provence: Edisud, 1975.

———. "La Mémoire d'Ernest Labrousse." *Annales historiques de la Révolution française* no. 276 (April–June 1989): 99–107.

———. *La Mentalité révolutionnaire: Société et mentalités sous la révolution française.* Paris: Editions Sociales, 1985.

———. *La Mort et l'Occident de 1300 à nos jours.* Paris: Gallimard, 1983.

———. *Mourir autrefois: Attitudes collectives devant la mort aux XVIIe et XVIIIe siècles.* Paris: Gallimard/Julliard, 1974.

———. *Piété baroque et déchristianisation en Provence au XVIIIe siècle.* 1973; Paris: Seuil, 1978.

———. Pourquoi nous sommes encore Robespierristes." *Annales historiques de la Révolution française* no. 274 (October–December 1988): 498–506.

———. "Y a-t-il un inconscient collectif?" *Pensée* no. 205 (May–June 1979): 125–36.

———, and Gaby Vovelle. *Vision de la mort et de l'au-delà en Provence.* Paris: Colin, 1970.

White, Hayden V. *Metahistory: The Historical Imagination in Nineteenth-Century Europe.* Baltimore: Johns Hopkins University Press, 1973.

Wilson, Adrian. "The Infancy of the History of Childhood: An Appraisal of Phillippe Ariès." *History and Theory* 19 (1980): 132–53.

Winock, Michel. *Le Siècle des intellectuels.* Rev. ed. Paris: Seuil, 1999.

———, ed. *Histoire de l'extrême droite en France.* Paris: Seuil, 1993.

PATRICK HUTTON is professor emeritus of history at the University of Vermont. Born in Trenton, New Jersey, he was educated at Princeton University (A.B.) and the University of Wisconsin, Madison (M.A., Ph.D.). A recipient of university awards for his teaching and his scholarship, he has taught courses on French history, European intellectual history, and historiography. He is the author of *The Cult of the Revolutionary Tradition* (1981) and *History as an Art of Memory* (1993). He also served as editor in chief of *An Historical Dictionary of the Third French Republic* (1986), and as coeditor of *Technologies of the Self: A Seminar with Michel Foucault* (1988). *Philippe Ariès and the Politics of French Cultural History* is based on his research in France as a Senior Fulbright Research Scholar at the Ecole des Hautes Etudes en Sciences Sociales, Paris, in 1995–96.